Teaching Children To Read and Write

Geoffrey R. Roberts

Teaching Children To Read and Write

Geoffrey R. Roberts

Blackwell Education

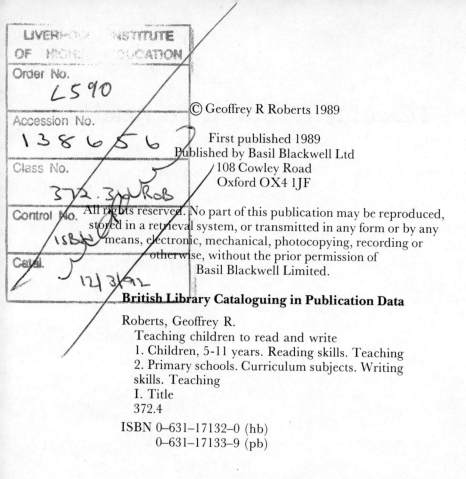
© Geoffrey R Roberts 1989

First published 1989
Published by Basil Blackwell Ltd
108 Cowley Road
Oxford OX4 1JF

British Library Cataloguing in Publication Data

Roberts, Geoffrey R.
Teaching children to read and write
1. Children, 5-11 years. Reading skills. Teaching
2. Primary schools. Curriculum subjects. Writing
skills. Teaching
I. Title
372.4
ISBN 0–631–17132–0 (hb)
      0–631–17133–9 (pb)

Typeset in 11/12½ pt Baskerville
by Opus, Oxford
Printed in Great Britain by T.J. Press, Padstow, Cornwall

Contents

activities to promote composition, and targets for the five
to seven year old

PART VI **Appendixes and bibliography**

Introduction

The purpose of this book is to introduce students and teachers to a study of the reading and writing process and to help them explore ways of teaching children to read, write and spell.

Many developments have taken place in recent years and a great deal of research has been done, especially on the problems posed in learning to read. All of these developments and researches are important, but no student can cope in the short time available for training with the mass of detail that has been generated. Hence those concerned with the training of teachers, and especially those involved in training people to teach in primary schools, have to ensure that these details are gathered into a manageable form, so that young people, whose experience of teaching is either limited or nonexistent, can formulate a basis for action when faced with the task of teaching children to read and write.

Many established teachers are horrified when students practising in their schools tell them that they do not know how to teach children to read because they have never been told how to teach by their lecturers. The first part of this assertion – that they do not know how to teach children to read – is usually true, but the second part – that they have never been told how – is rarely totally true these days. All initial courses for primary teachers contain instruction in the teaching of reading, ranging from lectures to workshops to individual guidance in tutorials. What the students are generally saying is that what they have been told is difficult to interpret in practical terms when face to face with children who are learning to read. Teaching children to write is seldom discussed in these terms, possibly because it is not so fashionable!

This lack of expertise in students is partly determined by the deep-seated difficulty of interpreting a mass of theoretical knowledge in relatively simple teaching terms. Learning to read is a highly complex process acquired with the help of numerous simple teaching ploys. If the teaching is not simple, direct, and uncomplicated the children will not be able to benefit from it. And, of course, the student teachers are afraid that simple reactions to complex problems will make them look foolish in the eyes of the experienced teacher. Only with experience are teachers sufficiently confident to simplify things for themselves and for the children; so what the students are really referring to is their lack of experience and the confidence that goes with it.

But there is a further explanation: the indigestability of the mass of detail concerning this and that aspect of the teaching of children to read, write and spell, which is frequently placed before students who, in all probability, are having problems unconnected with the teaching of specific aspects of the skill of reading. They are anxious about such matters as how to use their voice effectively, how and where to stand, what to do about the child who is about to spill the paint in the book corner, where to write on an already full blackboard, and about their relationship with the class teacher. Thus a whole mass of sensations and thoughts may be racing through the student's mind whilst the child she is helping is stuck on a word, and at the same time she is trying to remember whether the lecturer said that in such instances she should use a flash card, or use wooden letters to illustrate the parts of the word, or get the pupil to sound the letters of the word, or put the word in a different context or what else did the lecturer suggest? It is little wonder that some students retreat behind a plea of ignorance.

Unfortunately, there has been a tendency for many years now even for experienced teachers to rely upon an ad hoc reaction to the various elements that contribute to their approach to teaching. Some of them have forgotten that there has to be a pattern to learning; that learners have to be motivated and prepared for the task in hand because 'there can be no mental development without interest . . . the *sine qua non* for attention' (Whitehead, 1955); that this must be followed in most cases by precise learning of the details of the situation; and that the use of the new learning on numerous occasions must follow the actual learning of the elements of the task if they are to be remembered and incorporated into the general behaviour and skill of the learner. Many years ago Whitehead (1955) outlined a model of learning which was interpreted in terms of teaching children to write by Roberts (1972). Whitehead was worried by the notion that a pupil's progress was frequently thought of 'as a uniform steady advance undifferentiated by change of type or alteration of pace', and he was looking for a framework within which there would be scope for variations in the pace, intensity and form of learning that was taking place. The answer seemed to lie in rhythmic cycles covering various aspects of learning whilst allowing for a return at any point to those aspects not effectively accomplished. Hegel's three stages of progress – thesis, antithesis and synthesis – suggested to Whitehead three stages of intellectual progress: romance, precision and generalisation. These stages cover the sequence in the learning process mentioned above and, if they are regarded as a rhythmic or, more precisely, a cyclic process and not as a linear sequential progression, they remind teachers of the variety that exists in the learning process and of the opportunities for re-learning. At the stage of romance interest is aroused, excitement is fostered, thoughts are implanted and both learner and subject matter are prepared. This is followed by the stage of precision or precise learning where new knowledge or skills are acquired, but with the realisation that where learning falters a reversion to the stage of romance with further motivation or re-motivation will be necessary. Similarly with the stage of generalisation when the new learning or the new found skills are used in a wider setting, there may be a need to revert to a spell of more precise reinforcement of the learning and with it some further re-motivation. Operating on this model the teacher will be able to provide for variations in the pace and the nature of the children's development.

More recently Simon (1985) has questioned the wisdom of teaching without a clear pedagogy in mind and he suggests starting 'from what children have in common as members of the human species; to establish the general principles of teaching and, in the light of these, to determine what modifications of practice are necessary to meet specific individual needs.' Using evidence provided by the ORACLE researches (Galton, Simon and Croll, 1980) Simon argues that the Plowden Report (1967) with its insistence 'on the principle of the complete individualisation of the teaching/learning process as the ideal', distracted attention from the development of an effective pedagogy. Teachers' minds were turned to providing individually for almost every aspect of a child's development, intellectual, emotional and physical – a task not only daunting but impossible to perform with classes containing anything from fifteen to thirty five children. The result has been for the teacher to follow rather than lead a class, acting as an 'answering machine' to children's problems and seldom finding time to intervene positively to initiate learning by a group of children.

Later in this book the argument will be put for the adoption of small-group teaching, whereby the teacher identifies common needs amongst a group of children and, by matching presentation to ability, initiates a teaching and learning schedule. Obviously, on occasions children will need and sometimes demand individual attention. They may be experiencing a difficulty that is unique to them or they may have the emotional need for individual attention, but to proceed totally upon an individual basis would make progress for the majority slow, it would reduce the teacher to relative impotence, and it would ignore the advantages to be gained from group interaction within a progressively developing educational sequence. However, by adopting small grouping as the unit, the teacher will avoid the hidden pitfalls of class teaching, in which there is the inevitable mismatch of task or treatment and ability (one cannot teach effectively even a homogeneous class of children as a single unit, but the smaller the group, within certain limits, the greater the opportunity to match ability to task through interaction within the group whilst still leaving room for a planned pedagogy).

A reorientation in the initial training of teachers to meet the evidence of the ORACLE research carried out in Leicester and the arguments put forward in Simon's paper, and an acceptance of the challenge of Whitehead's cyclic process as a basis for teaching and learning, is long overdue. Such a move would encourage teacher trainers to present simplified models to their students, which subsequently, with the increasing efficiency of the student in practical terms, could be elaborated, refined and adjusted to meet the exigencies of any situation in which young teachers might find themselves. It would also give teachers a clear model for teaching and provide an effective basis for curriculum development. It would allay fears of teachers who self-critically wonder about the effectiveness of their teaching, and it would help to allay the fears of those parents who sometimes wonder if the school knows 'where it is going'.

It is the intention of this book to help students formulate pedagogical models and, at the same time, to enable them to begin the process of refinement and adjustment to the needs of children in differing circumstances. The model for this book will be to encourage students to consider first the complete skill that is to be taught, to arrange the learning and teaching activities within a pedagogical model, and then to begin to move towards a refinement of the teaching methods that emerge so that with mounting experience the young teacher will become increasingly efficient in the use of time and materials.

Further reading
Whitehead, A.N. (1955) *The Aims of Education.* London: Benn.

Roberts, G.R. (1972) *English in Primary Schools.* London: Routledge and Kegan Paul.

In the former book Whitehead outlines his cyclic model for learning, and in the latter that model is applied to the teaching of children to write.

Simon, B. (1985) Towards a revitalized pedagogy. In C. Richards with B. Lofthouse (eds) *The Study of Primary Education: A Source Book*, Volume 3. London: Falmer Press.

Whitehead's and Simon's theories should be kept in mind whilst reading the following chapters.

PART I
COMMUNICATION

1 The goal: communication through reading and writing

Whilst throughout the latter part of the nineteenth and the first half of the twentieth century there were some people who realised that reading was more than the summation of the sounds of letters of the alphabet, there was during this period an overemphasis by the majority of teachers upon the process of adding together the sounds of letters in the hope that meaning would emerge and that by adding together the meanings of discrete words a coherent message would be received. And, of course, by and large this did happen, eventually. The majority of children picked up enough information both directly from learning the sounds of letters and indirectly from incidental and hidden learning about the necessary behaviour required of them in handling the separate sounds and about the nature of written language to enable them to make sense of what they were reading. Hence, there tended to be two stages in the development of reading ability. The first was an ability to respond phonically to print, and the second stage was the emergence of an ability to understand the message contained in the written text.

This two stage development was reflected in the primers or reading schemes of the time. The content of introductory books to each scheme was comprised of discrete words, such as *cat, mat, sat*, followed by terse phrases such as *the cat, the mat*, and eventually arriving at the exciting news, *The cat sat on the mat*, and similar statements. Subsequent books in the scheme contained slightly longer but loosely connected sentences in the sense that they did not develop a train of thought and therefore had to be interpreted by the readers relying upon their ability to interpret phonically the separate parts of the text before them. They could not guess what might follow, and thus thinking about the emerging message was unhelpful to the stumbling reader. In the worst instances of the use of this approach teachers frequently assumed that so long as a child could say the words then it proved that the meaning was understood.

This is what happened in many schools – it happened to the writer – but what should be remembered, in fairness to the writers and publishers of reading primers, is that in many cases it was assumed that teachers would institute word-study programmes to precede and accompany the use of the primers. Dale (1898) outlined a clear programme of study connected with the sounds and formations of the words she used in her primers, and she hoped it would appeal to the child's 'love of fun'.

Later phonic schemes expanded the scope of their stories. Book One in the *Gay Way* series (1957) began:

> The big red lorry went up the hill. The pots and pans went up the hill in the lorry. Big pans, little pans, big pots and little pots. Red pans, tin pans, red pots and tin pots. Up and up to the top went the big red lorry. Up and up and up went the pots. Up went the pans . . .

It can be seen that the burden for the reader falls heavily upon word recognition – there being little in the form of a tightly-knit sequential story line – and although there is repetition, thus encouraging some degree of anticipation, it is anticipation of the wrong kind. It is anticipation of a repetition of words that have already been read previously. In this way anticipation is being encouraged merely to practise what is known rather than being used as a cue to help identify the unfamiliar, which would be a more useful device for the hesitant reader.

When 'Look-and-Say' (Gates, 1927; Schonell, 1945, amongst others) replaced the phonic method many teachers still looked askance at anything that smacked of guessing in relation to texts. The identification of unfamiliar words through their context was not considered in any way a substitute for the recognition of that word through its graphemic structure. There might not be the emphasis on the phonic analysis of words that existed when a phonic method of teaching children to read was used, but it was still expected that the child would learn to recognise the word per se, and the interpretation of the message by using semantic cues was mainly ignored for the purposes of teaching because it was assumed to follow automatically from the recognition of each word in the first place. The identification of those words which were not immediately recognisable, once the child had progressed from the sight recognition of whole words to a programme of phonic analysis, was expected to emerge from a phonic analysis of that word rather than from trying to think what the word could be in terms of the text.

Many writers have inveighed against the inadequacy of these approaches: Plaisted (1909) and Goddard (1958) mainly because the phonic method as generally used tended to take the fun out of learning to read, and Huey (1908) and Smith (1971), amongst others, who felt that such restricted approaches ignored the composite nature of print and in doing so misrepresented print to children during the early stages of learning to read. Both these points of view are valid, but the latter is the more telling. Lack of fun or a sense of purpose could be partially compensated for in other ways, such as by the teacher's enthusiastic responses to the children's efforts, but there is something very worrying about a methodology that gives an inaccurate idea of the nature of a skill, and the approach to reading either through a totally summational phonic attack or simply by adding word to word was tantamount to teaching a boy that the game of soccer is solely dependent upon how hard he can kick the ball, to the exclusion of all other contributory skills.

To illustrate this point only a few examples are necessary. The words *brown*, *bean* and *slightly* cannot be read by adding the individual letter sounds together; additional knowledge about the relationships between letters in a word and specific behaviours on the part of the reader in processing those letters is necessary. Mainly, in the above examples, the necessary knowledge concerns the degree to which the sounds of individual letters are subsumed within a different sound pattern when the letters appear in strings – /b/ and /r/ in /br/, /ou/ or /ɔ/ and /w/ in /braun/ – although there is the additional problem of choosing one of the nine or so sounds which could be attached to ea in *bean*; and in *slightly*, sl, ight and ly form the basic units beyond which any further breakdown of the component sounds would render the task of reading the word impossible.

When one looks beyond 'simple' word recognition, which obviously is not so simple as might appear at first, there are equally varied behaviours in interpreting a piece of continuous prose.

There is the fact that homonyms exist, such as *tears* with its two meanings; homophones, such as *pier* and *peer*; and that the meaning of individual words has to be related to the meaning of the full text.

One has only to read the following quickly to appreciate the pitfalls posed by the nature of English orthography:

'The boys' arrows were nearly gone so	1
they sat down on the grass and stopped	2
hunting. Over at the edge of the wood they saw	3
Henry making a bow to a small girl who was	4
coming down the road. She had tears in her	5
dress and tears in her eyes. She gave Henry	6
a note which he brought over to the group	7
of young hunters. Read to the boys, it	8
caused great excitement. After a minute,	9
but rapid examination of their weapons	10
they ran down to the valley. Does	11
were standing at the edge of the lake,	12
making an excellent target'	13

In the reading of the above text the reader's mind is centred initially on hunting with bows and arrows and hence there is a tendency to respond to *bow* in line 4 with /bou/ rather than /bau/. Similarly the word *read* in line 8 is frequently related to *note* in line 7. Many readers will respond with /ti:rz/ to *tears* on line 5, presumably on the assumption that little girls are easily turned to tears when confronted with armed boys, and the fact that the word *tears* can only be read correctly if considered within a text is demonstrated by its double use in this passage. Furthermore, the position of certain words and at end of lines may be seen as an extra hazard: would the tendency for confusion over *minute* in line 9 be so pronounced if the periphery of the eye could take in what followed whilst still momentarily dwelling upon the word *minute*?

This analysis of the behaviour of skilled adult readers pointedly emphasises the pitfalls facing less skilled readers. It shows clearly the complexities of the task and reminds us that it is not simply a question of using available cues but also a matter of knowing how to use them and how to employ a flexible and selective approach in their use. Thus it is essential that new entrants to the teaching profession should fully understand what is involved in reading before going on to consider ways of teaching children to read.

The first and essential thing to establish is something that was vividly demonstrated when we read the passage concerned with the group of boys out hunting: namely, that reading and thinking are inseparable, unless, of course, we are merely calling out unconnected words from a list. Whatever we read by way of text enters into our conscious thinking, and what we think influences our response to the text. This is so for readers of all ages and stages of proficiency. As proof of this, note the response of infant school children in the initial stages of learning to read to short unacceptable graffiti words; they are not merely content to say the word, their whole demeanour shows that they have processed the meaning of the letters and that they are placing the word in the context of what is acceptable and unacceptable to adults. Thus there emerges the first signpost for our teaching: namely, that in all our teaching we ensure that the texts we use are meaningful, otherwise the opportunities for distortion and error are multiplied.

Second, the selection of texts is something that requires careful consideration on our part. From our reading of the passage about the boys hunting it is clearly essential that children's texts should not contain elements likely to mislead, as you may have been misled in reading the words bow, tears and read. Neither should the sentences of a text be so loosely connected that the whole text lacks cohesion and thus prevents the natural flow of thoughts as the reader proceeds. Sentences which, although loosely connected with a topic, do not develop a line of thought and stand as isolated statements, pose severe problems for the learner. Such sentences as the following were frequently used in older reading schemes:

> The children are going to the farm.
> The farmer has many cows.
> The chickens peck at the ground looking for food.
> The farmer uses a tractor to plough his fields.

Children in the earlier stages of learning to read, finding something difficult about one of the above sentences would not be helped by reference to the other sentences even though they found no difficulty in reading them. In selecting reading material for children who are not proficient readers, we must be particularly careful to ensure that it is possible for them to build up the meaning of the text as they read so that they have a foundation of meaning upon which to build an interpretation of subsequent sticking points. Our purpose at any stage, and certainly in the initial stages, should be to ensure success, not failure. The closer we can attune the content and the format of children's books to children's thinking patterns, the greater the use they will be able to make of the textual structure before them. Strickland (1962) and Reid (1970) have dealt with certain aspects of the coincidence of written and oral patterns, whilst Roberts, T. (1978) has raised a note of warning about the assumption that children's oral language is spontaneously sequential and logically formulated. However, it is not the coincidence of language so much as corresponding patterns of thought that are so telling; it is the correspondence between the ideas and thought patterns within the text and those along which children most easily operate that is the essence of this problem.

The examples referred to so far in this chapter illustrate the fact that the reader has to contend with three aspects of language – the semantic, the syntactic, and the phono-graphemic (Osgood, 1957). All three have their part to play and if it is difficult to get far in reading English without the interpretation of semantic and syntactic cues, then it is impossible even to begin to read if one is unable to recognise words. Just imagine for one moment being able to recognise only a dozen English words. The task of reading any normal text containing words additional to those known twelve would vary from the very difficult to the impossible, and this would be so even though you knew the sounds of all the individual letters of the alphabet but did not know how to use them. To take a simple word like *cat*, even knowing the sounds of the separate letters poses a tremendous problem until the learner has 'acquired the knack' of running the sounds together and producing a composite sound, which admittedly has certain similarities with the three separate letter-sounds but which requires certain vocal adjustments before it can be pronounced as an entity of its own: $/k/ + /æ/ + /t/$ does not equal $/kæt/$ – try it by recording yourself. It is very important for teachers to realise that to talk of blending is an oversimplification. Blending is more than simply attaching sounds to letters and slurring them closely together. Blending requires the further and separate step of creating a separate composite sound.

In addition to learning the behaviours associated with blending, children have to come to realise that many letters and letter strings have more than one sound, and thus they have to acquire a disposition for experimentation with sounds that can be attached to letters, and this has to be done at a time when the dangers of confusion are great. Is it any wonder that many of our finest teachers still find the task of teaching children to read such a delicate and uncertain one?

Hence, our third consideration is that readers must be accomplished in certain forms of acquired behaviour which will enable them to use the store of factual knowledge that they have acquired. They must be able to blend sounds, select options whilst rejecting others, and they must be prepared to compensate for inability to use one set of cues by using another set. This latter point, which is often referred to disparagingly by teachers and parents as guessing, should in most instances be more accurately defined as the consideration of plausible hypotheses and is a vital part of the armoury of skilled readers. We all meet on occasion unfamiliar words, but we rarely fail to have a reasonable notion of their meaning gained from the context in which the word stands. All of these behaviours, although general in nature yet specifically applied to aspects of reading, have to be learned within the context of reading, and incidentally it is in this sense that it is possible to accept Smith's (1971) well-rehearsed assertion that one can only learn to read by reading.

Before leaving this initial consideration of reading, it is important to remind ourselves that reading is closely related in many ways to spoken language and that young learners will be helped considerably if they are able to relate what they read to what they say. Their ability to do this will depend to some extent upon their ability to reflect upon what they say, and this ability will in turn depend upon the ways in which spoken language is used in the home and upon the part played by reading and language amongst family and friends. If attention is given to what is said and how it is said and if importance is attached to the interpretation of print, then there will exist an awareness of the interconnection between the two, even though the child may not have any specific knowledge concerning that connection. However, it must be stressed that the existence of a literary background is not in itself pertinent; it is the use that is made of that background that affects the development of the young child. The existence of books and good conversation amongst the adults may have no effect, or even a negative effect, on the young children. What affects them is the degree of relevance of books and conversation to their lives.

This suggests a further factor affecting the development of reading, and that concerns the possession of a disposition or need for reading. Reading to please an adult soon wears thin, whereas reading as a pleasurable and worthwhile activity is something of far greater substance.

Already it must be clear that to study the teaching of reading, it is necessary to consider related topics such as the development of an awareness of spoken language, the inter-relationship between speech and print, and the influences of the child's background. It is also necessary to look more closely than has been the practice in the past at ways in which the child learns to construct texts and all that this implies in learning to write and to spell. These may have appeared separately from the teaching of reading on school timetables in the past, but they cannot be regarded other than as an integral part of the child's appreciation of the significance of the various elements of print. Just as adults can appreciate the working of something that they have themselves constructed, so it seems reasonable to assume that learning to formulate letters, to spell words, to assemble clausal complexes as approximations to texts and, finally to formulate sentences and construct texts, will all enhance the child's appreciation of all the elements within written text.

Further reading
Smith, F. (1985) *Reading*, (second edition). Cambridge: Cambridge University Press.
Whilst there has been a tendency for many people to interpret this book superficially, nevertheless, if read with care, its full significance in turning people's minds to a consideration of the true nature of reading can be appreciated.

Gollasch, F.V. (ed.) (1982) *Language and Literacy: the Selected Writings of Kenneth S. Goodman*, Volumes 1 and 2. London: Routledge and Kegan Paul.
Goodman's miscue analysis does much to emphasise that readers employ a multi-cue approach to reading and that they react in the light of what they perceive.

Perera, K. (1984) *Children's Writing and Reading*. Oxford: Blackwell.
This book should be regarded as an essential source for studying the elements of communication, and it should be used for further background study of all the issues raised in the following text.

Huey, E.G. (1908) *The Psychology and Pedagogy of Reading*. Cambridge.
  Mass: MIT.
The introduction by P.A. Kolers gives a clear interpretation of Huey's
incredibly advanced thinking on the reading process.

For those who wish to make a deeper and further study of reading, the
following texts are recommended:
Reading Research Quarterly, 7, No. 4, 1972.
Harvard Educational Review, 47, No. 3, 1977.
Gibson, E.J. and Levin, H. (1975) *The Psychology of Reading*. Cambridge,
  Mass: MIT.
Coltheart, M. (1987) *The Psychology of Reading*. Attention and Performance
  XII. London: Lawrence Elbaum.

Children's literature
It is essential that all who intend to teach in primary schools should
develop an understanding and appreciation of children's literature.
Hence, in the teacher training course an early start should be made on a
programme of private study, which includes a selection of the following
books and journals and is accompanied by reading and rereading a
selection of the children's books referred to in the texts.

Beard, R. (1987) *Developing Reading 3–13*. London: Hodder and Stoughton.
  (Contains an informative chapter entitled 'The experience of
  literature'.)
Benton, M. and Fox, G. (1985) *Teaching Literature: Nine to Fourteen*. Oxford:
  Oxford University Press.
Bettelheim, B. (1976) *The Uses of Enchantment*. London: Thames and
  Hudson.
Bolt, S. and Gard, R. (1970) *Teaching Fiction in School*. London: Hutchinson
  Educational.
Calthrop, K. and Ede, J. (1984) *Not 'Daffodils' Again: Teaching Poetry 9–13*.
  London: Longman.
Cass, J. (1967) *Literature and the Young Child*. London: Longman.
Corbett, P. and Moses, B. (1986) *Catapults and Kingfishers: Teaching Poetry in
  Primary Schools*. Oxford: Oxford University Press.
Egoff, S. et al. (eds) (1969) *Only Connect: Readings on Children's Literature*.
  Toronto: Oxford University Press.
Fisher, M. (1964) *Intent upon Reading*. London: Brockhampton Press.
Fox, G., Hammond, G., Jones, T., Smith, F. and Sterck, K. (1976)
  Writers, Critics, and Children. London: Heinemann Educational.
Fry, D. (1985) *Children Talk About Books: Seeing Themselves as Readers*.
  Milton Keynes: Open University Press.
Heeks, P. (1981) *Choosing and Using Books in the First School*. London:
  Macmillan.

Huck, C.S., Hepler, S. and Hickman, J. (1987) *Children's Literature in the Elementary School*. Fourth Edition. New York: Holt, Rinehart and Winston.
Hughes, T. (1967) *Poetry in the Making*. London: Faber.
Klein, G. (1985) *Reading into Racism*. London: Routledge and Kegan Paul.
Meek, M., Warlow, A. and Barton, G. (eds) (1977) *The Cool Web: The Pattern of Children's Reading*. London: Bodley Head.
Townsend, J.R. (1987) *Written for Children*. 3rd Edition. Harmondsworth: Penguin.
Tucker, N. (1981) *The Child and the Book: a Psychological and Literary Exploration*. Cambridge: Cambridge University Press.
Zipes, J. (1979) *Breaking the Magic Spell*. London: Heinemann.
Zipes, J. (1983) *The Trials and Tribulations of Little Red Riding Hood*. London: Heinemann.
Zipes, J. (1983) *Fairy Tales and the Art of Subversion*. London: Heinemann.

The following journals should also be included:
Children's Literature in Education. Published by Ward Lock Educational.
Signal. Published by The Thimble Press, Stroud, Glos.

An important discussion of the hitherto disregarded effects of reading matter upon children's attitudes and beliefs can be found in:
Lobban, G. (1975) Sex-roles in reading schemes. *Educational Review*, 27(3), 202–10. (The remainder of the volume is devoted to other aspects of sexism in education and its impact upon children and society. Thus the semantic content of children's readers, and indeed all children's books, becomes part of a larger and more serious problem than the apparently superficial one which describes the activities of males and females in story form. It becomes part of the training that a child receives to live in society, present and future.)

A useful basic list of books for children, classified by age, can be found at the end of Meek, M. (1987) *Learning to Read*. London: Bodley Head.

PART II
PREPARATION FOR
READING AND WRITING

2 Towards awareness of reading, writing and spelling

Several terms have been used to designate the period before a child actually begins to read, amongst them the pre-reading stage, the preparatory stage, and the stage of emergent reading. The latter is a term used by Clay (1959), McKenzie (1986), Teale and Sulzby (1986), and Sulzby (1987) and seems to be a more apt description because learning to read, write and spell does not happen within a prescribed period. Each gradually emerges, first as a hazy notion in the child's mind, and then imperceptibly develops as a stumbling type of behaviour which the child gradually improves and refines until the full attainment of the skill is achieved. No one would wish to claim that one minute a child cannot read and the next minute that child is a reader. There are times when looking at a page of print and illustrations is equated with reading (an activity in itself indicative as an emerging idea concerning the nature of reading), when letters can be vaguely recognised or written in some form or another, and when words or parts of words can be read or written. These phases vary in length with each child.

Furthermore, even before a child begins to learn to read by identifying some words, there is every reason to believe that the child is noticing and gradually becoming aquainted with certain patterns of spelling. For example, some research by Read (1971) showed that pre-school children who could not yet read had nevertheless acquired a notion of spelling. This notion varied according to the particular word in its degree of approximation to English spelling. These children developed their own system of spelling which may have looked implausible to adults, but the spellings were roughly the same system for all the children. Examples were: DA (day), KAM (came), LADE (lady), FEL (fell), MI (my), FES (fish), ALRVATA (elevator), PANSEL (pencil), ACHRAY (ash tray), EGLIOW (igloo), CLIK (clock). The sample of children may be regarded as somewhat exceptional in that they all came from literate backgrounds and had been provided with alphabet blocks, movable letters and writing materials, and had parents who were willing to answer their questions concerning the spelling of words in a straightforward way. In other words, the parents were not inhibited by the dubious notion that an early start in learning to read, write or spell is necessarily harmful. However, the achievements of these children illustrate what is possible under favourable conditions by children who were not, so far as the research suggests, exceptional in any other way. It is reasonable to conclude from this research that children do begin to abstract spellings from the phonetic contrasts that they are able to make.

This is one instance of the early emergence of aspects of literacy, and this particular instance will be linked later in this book with the development of writing. There is other evidence of the emergence of skills apposite to learning to read and write. Pre-school children frequently show interest in individual letters. For example, a three year old, whose first name began with S and whose mother's first name began with T, arrived outside their holiday hotel, the St Elmo, and responded to the sign by saying, 'Oh look, they've even got my name *and* mummy's name up.' There is the obvious evidence that children progress gradually but resolutely towards writing through scribbling, painting seemingly endless lines which nevertheless display approximations to the basic patterns of letters, and eventually they try to write a note to someone or to record a personal happening. Many examples of the emerging propensity to recieve and convey communications exist; so many in fact that when the movement to introduce the initial teaching alphabet into schools was at its height, several prominent educationalists, Molly Brearley, the principal of the Froebel Institute, amongst them, expressed the fear that its introduction would mean that the experiential learning that children had acquired from the traditional orthography of their home environment before coming to school would be wasted.

The compensatory role of the school

Thus we are led to consider the pre-school influences on a child that will affect subsequent progress in school, because in many cases an absence of certain experiences will prevent children from making any sense at all of what schooling is about (Francis, 1982), with resulting bewilderment and lack of progress on the part of the child.

ATTITUDES TO SCHOOL

The first and foremost requirement in learning anything is an understanding of what is required and the desire to achieve success in that activity, and one has only to consider the different attitudes of adults to education to realise that there will be a wide range of attitudes to schools and schooling fostered in children by parents.

The Newsons (1986) in their study of four-year-old children in an urban society illustrated the wide gap that could exist between parents in their approach to a children's quarrel. Not only was there a gap in the responses of the parents, but the parents' requirements by way of response from the child differed. At one extreme was the category of parents who gave the following answers when asked what their responses would be to a quarrel between their own four year old and a playmate:

> I try to be very fair.
> I try to see both sides.
> Find out who is in the wrong.
> Help them to see reason.
> Talk it over between them.
> Go into it and work out what it was all about.

At the other extreme:

> I usually turn a deaf ear.
> Say 'Now don't come tittle-tattling'.
> Take no notice.
> Say 'It's no use running to me'.

and there was a general expectancy that the child should

> Hit 'em back.

Not only are these two categories illustrative of two extremes of indoctrination in social behaviour, but they have implicit within them different approaches to the use of language. In the former the child is being taught to talk his way through, and possibly out of, the problem; in the latter, language plays little part – what language is used is terse, dismissive and not intended to resolve anything, except to get rid of the problem so far as the parent is concerned. Here we have a good example of how some children get an exquisite training in the use of language in resolving their own problems, whilst others do not.

We must remember this when children enter school at the age of five; some will have had a long training in the use of language of the type that is appropriate for solving problems in schools, whilst others will have had little training that is apposite to their subsequent needs in school. Some children will be aware that language is useful to them and they will have the confidence to use it that comes from meaningful experiences, whilst others will have neither the awareness nor confidence to operate successfully in a language-based, as opposed to an action-based environment. All of them will have had experiences that affect in one way or another their attitudes to future learning and towards the institutions of learning in which they will find themselves.

Tough, in a lecture to the UKRA Conference in Manchester, (1973) reported some interesting experiments which looked at the behaviour and language of parent and child whilst waiting for an introductory meeting with the child's prospective head teacher. Here again differences emerged. At one end of the spectrum the mother discouraged her child from playing with toy cars which were left in an open cardboard box in the waiting room, whilst at the other end of the spectrum the mother gave positive encouragement to her child. The reactions of the parents to the appearance of the head teacher were also significantly different: the one type of parent, being taken by surprise, because of her embarrassment admonished her child for playing with something that wasn't his, whilst the other parent showed an easy, confident and friendly recognition of the head teacher and included her child in the initial greetings. Children are very sensitive to such situations and neither response would go unnoticed by the children concerned. The former would appreciate that he was about to enter an alien environment full of restrictions, 'don't do thats', and rules to be obeyed, whereas the latter would regard it simply as an extension of the friendly atmosphere of home, but with the addition of new toys and plenty of children to play with plus a head teacher who is 'big friends with his mum'!

What a difference all this will make to the attitudes of the children towards entry into school and towards learning, and what problems it will pose for the teachers to whom these children are allocated! For on the one hand they will have willing entrants to their classes, whilst on the other they are faced with the task of obliterating fears and prejudices, often deep-rooted because of a cumulative anti-school and anti-learning effect, which cannot be dealt with other than over a long period of time.

Young teachers should not fall into the trap of regarding pre-school prejudices, attitudes and fears as superficial feelings that can easily be eradicated or changed in the first few days of schooling. Not only are they deeper seated than may be super-ficially appreciated at first glance, but these fears are being reinforced by the alien environment and by the continuing attitudes of the parents, as, for example, in the questions,

> I hope you behaved yourself in school today?
> Did you learn anything today?

spoken in a disparaging or doubting tone of voice.

LANGUAGE DIFFERENCES

Another factor affecting children's ability to cope with the early years in school is the forms of spoken language in which they are most practised in the years before entry into school. Bernstein (1970) has alerted us to the fact that spoken language emanates from situations, some of which require more formal kinds of language than others. Not every child is talked to regularly in such a way as to require elaborate sentences in reply. The type of child referred to earlier who was required to explain the situation in which she quarrelled with her friend does not belong to the majority entering school. Many children find themselves in a majority of situations at home requiring only a terse unelaborated statement. Halliday (1969, 1973) has pointed out that the latter type of child has a tacit understanding of what Bernstein called the elaborated code, but it is impossible not to believe that such a child, devoid of practice in the elaborated code will find the language of teaching both unfamiliar and unsettling during his early school experiences. No one can therefore hold that these two types of children are equal in their ability to take advantage of the new school-learning situation in which they find themselves.

ATTITUDES TO BOOKS AND THEIR USEFULNESS

In addition to these differences in the uses of language and in attitudes to school, there are obviously great differences amongst families in their approach to books. For some, books are central to all aspects of life – work, pleasure, help in needful circumstances – and are constantly in use, whilst the written word is regarded of little value in other families. Some children will be read to daily from very early in their lives, whilst others will never experience the pleasures of a bedtime story. This might be thought to be a trivial matter by those who naively regard the bedtime story as consisting solely of the transmission of a story line. The research of Wells (1985, 1987) should dispel this simplistic notion, because reading to a child not only provides an example of some aspects of the nature of reading and shows the child how to use books, but it helps children to learn how to 'use words to create hypothetical worlds . . . Stories are the bridge to abstraction,' and abstract thought is the height of human achievement. Also it begins to familiarise the child with the patterns and structure of written language.

Furthermore, children who hear stories read to them every day are usually the same children who see their parents using books – consulting a gardening manual, looking up a recipe – and who are frequently allowed to participate in the exciting tasks that result from referring to reference books, again demonstrating the purposes of reading, so that they do not arrive in school wondering what the fuss over books and reading is all about. They accept books as an essential integral part of life. Unlike the children referred to by Francis (1982), they are prepared in such a way that they can make sense of what school is about.

The need for experiential learning

All the aspects of learning mentioned so far, including many other things such as the development of skills in using pencils and paint brushes and making judgements about space and balance through playing with Lego and blocks and other educational toys, are not things that can be picked up in a few lessons; they are behaviours and attitudes and skills that can only be acquired gradually over a long period of time. It is through these activities that children learn to think about what they are doing, to develop ideas, to review what they have done and to plan further activities – albeit at a simple level, but it is the basis of development. What is more it is a development which underpins the development of thought in speech form, and hence these activities are a basis for language development. They are an essential element in helping children come to terms with and learn to cope with and prosper in their environment. A child cannot be expected to acquire new ways of using spoken language in the space of a few days or weeks. Time is required and learning has to be based on need, on example, on practice and on the gradual development of unusual skills through a variety of activities.

Yet, what happens in reality? Many children enter schools where the teachers have acquiesced in the parents' demands for an early start in the more formal aspects of the teaching of reading and even writing – some misguided parents want their children to start on *the* reading books the moment those children enter school, regardless of whether the children are adequately prepared for such a step. Some children are ready, of course, but many are not and an early start on the formal aspects of the teaching of reading can mean that those children who are not adequately prepared are going to miss some vital aspects of their education and are going to find their new learning unnecessarily difficult.

This point is significant whatever the age of entry into school, but its potency is emphasised when it is realised that approximately sixty percent of our children enter school before the age of five, so that even with an ideal mixture of pre-reading activities they are very young to be pitched into the more formal aspects of learning to read. They need to repeat in a social setting many of the experiences that they have had at home, so that they will have time to come to terms with school, its ways, its demands and its rewards. Such children, even though full of rich and varied language experiences gained through oral activities and from hearing stories in the home, still need to practise their communicative skills – talking, listening, drawing, scribbling, making things and, above all, playing – in a school setting, so that they begin to understand the significance of schooling and to come to terms with experiences in a social environment.

Of course, much can be gained from nursery education where the emphasis is on experiential learning and where play is not undervalued. My only fear is, that where nursery education exists, some teachers in the reception classes of infant schools may be tempted to think that the children have had all the play and experiences they need and that they can now move on to a more formal methodology of teaching the children to read and write. This would be highly detrimental for the children in infant classes, because our objective should not be simply to teach children to read and write, but to help them to prepare themselves to use reading and writing as part of their development, and the sounder the preparation for this the more effectively it will be realised.

Further reading
Wells, G. (1987) *The Meaning Makers: Children Learning Language and Using Language to Learn*. London: Hodder and Stoughton. (This book is more prescriptive than the 1985 book in its discussion of the application of the research to classroom teaching practice.)
Goelman, H., Oberg, A. and Smith, F. (eds) (1984) *Awakening to Literacy*. London: Heinemann Educational.
Newson, J. and E. (1968) *Four Years Old in an Urban Community*. London: Allen and Unwin.
Rosen, C. and H. (1973) *The Language of Primary School Children*. Harmondsworth: Penguin.
Wells, G. (1985) *Language Development in the Pre-School Years*. Cambridge: Cambridge University Press. (This book is an account of the research done by Wells in Bristol).
Trudgill, P. (1976) *Accent, Dialect and the School*. London: Edward Arnold.
Tough, J. (1976) *Listening to Children Talking*. London: Ward Lock Educational. (Illustrates the underlying principles of observing children's use of language).
Tough, J. (1977) *Talking and Learning: A Guide to Fostering Communication Skills in Nursery and Infant Schools*. London: Ward Lock Educational. (An account of teachers working with children in various curriculum areas, with examples of how to foster communication skills through dialogue.)
These eight books provide an excellent basis for the study of early linguistic and literary development in children, and the first two should be regarded as essential reading for all primary school teachers.

Francis, H. (1982) *Learning to Read*. London: Allen and Unwin.

The final chapter of this book should be regarded as essential reading for all those who intend to teach in primary schools.

McKenzie, M. (1986) *Journeys in Literacy*. Huddersfield: Schofield and Sims.
This book gives advice on dealing with the emergent stage of learning to read and is one of the first books to acknowledge the important contribution that writing makes to a child's development in reading skills.

McTear, M. (1985) *Children's Conversation*. Oxford: Blackwell.
Romaine, S. (1984) *The Language of Children and Adolescents*. Oxford: Blackwell.
These two books provide further evidence of the essential nature and composition of language as does:
Perera, K. (1984) *Children's Writing and Reading: Analysing Classroom Language*. Oxford: Blackwell.

Finally, in order to understand the early development of children a very useful starting point would be to read the following books:
Bruner, J.S. (1980) *Under Five in Britain*. London: Grant McIntyre.
Bruner, J.S. and Haste, H. (1987) *Making Sense*. London: Methuen.
Curtis, A.M. (1986) *A Curriculum for the Pre-School Child: Learning to Learn*. Windsor: NFER/Nelson.
Cohen, A. and L. (1988) *Early Education: the Pre-School Years*. London: Chapman.

3 Growing awareness of print and of reading and writing behaviour

Having considered the evidence presented in the previous chapter, it is essential that the teacher in a reception class of infants should give serious thought to the appraisal of every child's position in the long process of development towards being fully prepared to commence learning to read. If she begins the more formal processes too early the child suffers; if she delays unnecessarily then valuable time is wasted and the dangers of boredom setting in are very real. Either way, the child suffers.

This assessment of each child presents a very real and formidable problem for the teacher. Unless she has auxiliaries to help her, she cannot do the task even moderately well. Even with one auxiliary helper, fully trained, and anything over a dozen children, it is difficult to visualise any worthwhile assessments being made.

Reading readiness profiles

Attempts have been made in the past to devise a test of readiness for reading (Downing and Thackray, 1971, and Thackray, 1971), but few teachers would place full reliance upon them. This is not to criticise the tests as such, but simply to suggest that the assessment of all those factors mentioned in the previous chapter cannot be incorporated into a short test which concentrates upon a child's responses to written symbols and pictures. For example, the use of the Thackray Reading Readiness Profiles (1974) will provide a partial picture covering the ability to recognise the drawings of familiar objects, which involves knowing the names of those objects, but it is difficult to see this part of the test as anything other than a simple test of visual recognition, although it purports to test concept development. The profile also tests the ability to identify spoken words which closely, but not totally, resemble each other in sound and to distinguish them from other sounds, and the ability to match words visually. All three aspects of the test have a place in any profile a teacher might draw up connected with a child's ability to begin to learn to read. It will not go unnoticed, however, that this particular test does not indicate anything about the child's general linguistic development that would be revealed by the types of games and exercises that are suggested in Thackray's manual of instructions – developments in the construction of ideas and thoughts into sensible sequences, or the interpretation of what the child sees visually in the form of patterns of language, as is the case when describing a drawing or reading a text. In other words, this test simply reveals a limited amount of information, and it is dangerous to make assumptions on too little information, especially when they concern the behaviour of children.

The Linguistic Awareness in Reading Readiness (LARR) Test constructed by Downing et al (1983) does attempt to give a more complete picture of those things that would suggest a child has certain basic abilities and is aware of certain behaviours that contribute to the act of reading. For example, it tests children's ability to recognise what can be read, and to interpret representations of the acts of reading and writing by other people (Part One, Recognising Literacy Behaviour), so that teachers will know whether children in their classes can distinguish between visual images of text and other visual images, and between people who are reading and writing and people who are not. Part Three tests knowledge of the technical language of literacy: the ability to recognise numerals, letters, writing (although item 10 in Form A in this section of the test is dubious in its formulation), texts in the form of a story, words and the numerical placement of letters in those words (first letter, first two letters, last letters and last two letters), capital letters, punctuation marks, and the use of capitals in real nouns, all essential aspects of a child's armoury for understanding the teaching that she is receiving. Part Two of the test, however, gives cause for concern. This is supposed to test the understanding of literacy functions. Unfortunately, many of the items of the test are ambiguous, and in the case of Form A, item 5, it must be argued that the child must either be able to read with a fair degree of skill or he must guess that what writing there is concerns the objective mentioned in the question. It is impossible to interpret the responses to many of these items with any degree of certainty.

Thus, the LARR test will give indications of a knowledge of behaviours related to reading and familiarity with the terminology used by teachers of reading, together with some recognition of the manifestations of the terminology. What it does not test is the motivation, the desire and the disposition on the part of a child to read, and thereby it does not indicate whether a child really wants to read. Neither does it give any indication of the importance of books to the child's life out of school, nor does it say anything about the child's facility in the use of language.

OTHER ASPECTS OF READINESS

All of these omissions concern aspects which are basic and central in considering readiness to begin the process of learning to read. Underlying everything else the child must have a love of stories, a desire for books, a disposition to interact with stories, often in a creative way, and the child must be inquisitive about the interpretation of print and the information that can be obtained from it.

These are assertions that do not require experimental proof, for the simple reason that for children to accomplish anything so complex as reading they must need to do it in the sense of wanting to master something for the thrill and joy of doing it and for the satisfaction of completing the task even though the final goal may be some way distant. Thus we might venture towards the assertion that when a child wants to read is the time to begin to teach him. Whether he reaches this point naturally and of his own accord or whether the need and the desire have to be created for him by the teacher is another matter.

Observation and intervention by teachers

The preceding sentence raises the whole question of teacher intervention and the concept of compensatory education. A child who is articulate, interested and interactive with his environment, who wants to participate in learning of all kinds, who turns readily to books for enjoyment, who gets satisfaction from stories and from information read to him (remember not all children who are ready to read relish the thought of another story; they may be keener on more practical information such as how to build things or make things), who tries 'to write', and who can show readiness on the above mentioned tests is obviously ready for further help in learning to read. Unfortunately, a majority of children entering school at five years of age are not ready on these criteria. Consequently, having assessed all the children it is the task of the teacher to set about trying to compensate for what is lacking in awareness amongst that majority.

Starting from the assumption that for the foreseeable future the teachers of reception classes in infant schools and departments will not have the auxiliary help necessary to check all the aspects of each child's disposition, attitudes and awareness so far as reading and learning to read are concerned, then any check that the teacher makes is bound to be superficial and to some degree inadequate. (A checklist for the teacher to use can be found at the end of this chapter.) However, one of the great strengths of a more highly educated teaching force is its ability to adopt a flexible approach to all that is done in the classroom. This means that although the checks that are made on a child's readiness to learn to read may be inadequate, the teacher can make necessary adjustments and alterations in her teaching as the child's weaknesses or strengths reveal themselves. Thus a vigilant teacher will have in mind all that should have been done towards the development in literacy and emergent reading before entry into school; she will plan a tentative programme based upon what a child should have done; and she will adjust that programme as it evolves so that it matches the needs of the actual children that she is teaching.

The basis of her planning must be the inculcation of favourable attitudes to school, to books and to learning. Children must feel welcome, and this means that they must be wanted in the classroom and not required merely to be there. A vast difference in atmosphere can readily be detected by children between the teacher who likes children in her presence and the teacher who does not really like them. Children's fears must be allayed by involving them actively in the joys of classroom activities. Blocks, sand and toys all have their educational purposes, but they also provide the basis for enjoyable interactivity.

Books as a central feature of the classroom

Another and vital aim of the teacher's planning must be to make books and their use central to the classroom. A tatty bookcorner is a disgrace and nearly as bad as an unused spotless bookcorner! Respect for books is important, and is evidenced by the care with which they are regarded; but the way in which they are used is also an essential example to the children. There must be books for the children's use, but the teacher must also be seen to respect, like and use books for her own purposes. The children must know that she goes to the public library, and they must see her reading for pleasure at some time during the school week.

Guidelines for action surely lie in what is done in the ideal home. There children have stories read to them, they are encouraged to make up stories, to participate in labelling activities and to talk *with* adults (not to be confused with being talked at or to). This all forms a neat English syllabus for the reception class, and the limits of each aspect of that syllabus can be adjusted by the teacher from her reading readiness check list, and from her continuous assessment of the progress that the child is making.

The importance of spoken language as a basis for development

From the moment of entry into school, activities should be planned which encourage talking and, remembering Bernstein's point that the form language takes is largely determined by the situation or context, the teacher should plan to be involved as a participant – not as a supervisor – in the discussions centring on the activity. In this way the children will practise their use of appropriate forms of language: forms that tend towards the more formal and universalistic in Bernstein's terminology because of the formality with which the situation is necessarily imbued by the presence of the teacher, or any adult for that matter. The child has to become accustomed and practised in these more formal types of language for they are the basis of texts and of the language of teaching.

The basis for this emphasis on the practice of spoken language already exists in the normal activities of a modern infant classroom: sand and water play, modelling, painting and drawing, building blocks, constructional toys, clay modelling, and play in the Peter and Wendy House and in the 'dressing up' area. All of these can be the basis for oral discussion, imaginative and descriptive talk, the use of questions and instructive talk by the children, and the general enjoyment of talking about an activity in which everyone in a small group is engaged. The teacher should not see herself as teaching the group and giving instructions. Rather, she should enter the work in a participatory capacity. In this way the children will be exercising their language whilst their consciousness of the teacher's presence as an outsider will constrain them to use language in a particular way: elaborating their sentences so that she fully understands what their intentions are. The variety of normal activities of the infant classroom provide ample opportunity for the exercise of all the types of language covered by Halliday's seven models (1969, 1973). These are instrumental, regulatory, interactional (covering control of events and of people and including social interaction and communication) personal, heuristic, imaginative and representational (covering exploration of self and the environment, the creation of a personal world, and the communication of thoughts, ideas and information).

Reference to these seven models or types of language serves to remind teachers of the essential variety in language that needs to be activated in order to ensure all-round language development, so that gradually the children become more and more adept in the full range of uses of language.

One useful pedagogical model for the teacher is that all activities in the reception and infant classes should involve discussion *before* the activity (frequently the time most conducive to the production of expectant language and thought that veers towards the abstract – language that conveys the imaginative spirit and penetrative thinking of the child), *during* the activity (language that is personal, heuristic and instructional in Halliday's models), and *after* the activity (language that encourages evaluative, reactive and possibly, prescriptive thinking). According to this model, children will not be told to go and do this or that; the teacher or auxiliary will open a discussion about what may, or even will be done, she will encourage the children to raise possibilities for action, and as the children learn to get involved in discussion of this type, there will emerge gradually the ability to draw up plans for action. Similar progress can be achieved in discussion after the activity. At first it will be simplistic, direct and barely descriptive, but later it will become more analytical, evaluative and prescriptive for future action.

Reading to children

Another normal classroom activity – reading to children – took on a new significance following an important piece of research with three reception classes in 'downtown' Edinburgh schools (Reid, 1966). These children did not come from literary or educationally inclined home backgrounds and two very important points emerged: the children understood very little of the nature of print and they did not understand accurately the terminology of reading, such as *letter*, *word*, *sentence*, *story*, etc. Furthermore, their plight was compounded by the fact that they had some inaccurate knowledge, in that they had heard the terms but did not know exactly to what they referred. Hence, they confused letters with words, with stories, with figures, and this alerted us to the confusion with which many children approached the complex task of learning to read. How could children possibly cope if they didn't know, or worse still wrongly thought they knew, what the teacher was talking about when teaching them to read? Yet not all children entering the reception class are confused in this way, so to resolve their problems we must ask what has happened in their case.

Again we must look to their home experiences with books and print before entry into school, and keep in mind that much learning that is abstract in nature and concerned with complex things, such as the constituent parts of a text (letters, words, sentences, paragraphs, stories and the like) can only be achieved gradually over a long period of time and through persistent and regular interchange.

Children who have acquired this familiarity with the terminology of print and an awareness of the nature of print have done so mainly through their experiences of being read to at home. There they will have been able to witness how an adult handles a book, determining which is the front and the back, see what sequence to follow from start to finish, and will have noted the actions in response to statements like, 'Let's read the title', 'Let's turn to the first page and begin here', 'What does it say under this picture?',

'There's Teddy's name again', 'Let's look for the puppy's name', 'Oh there it is', 'Now, which line was I up to?', 'There's a long word. It says . . .', all accompanied by pointing with the finger and simultaneously responding orally. Hence the child over a long period of time and very many sessions of 'being read to' acquires a familiarity with books, learns something of their construction, and obtains insights into the nature of print. But it is only done by the child seeing the book the right way up and from the appropriate position facing the page as a reader. This is what the succeeding child gets and this is what the rest of the children must get in one way or another.

Naturally the teacher cannot read to each child individually except occasionally, so she must improvise in such a way as to approximate as closely as possible to the situation set up by the parent. Readings must take place with small groups in attendance, six at the most, and with the children standing *behind* the sitting teacher looking over her shoulder and following her actions. They watch as she turns the pages, follows the lines with her finger and points to words selected for special mention. This form of placement is not ideal, because the children cannot see the facial, lip, and eye movements of the teacher as they can when sitting on a parent's knee or alongside a parent in bed. Nevertheless, it better suits the purpose of learning about the use of books and the treatment of print than the form of placement wherein all the children of the class sit in front of the teacher, looking at the back of the book, and simply listening to the story that is being read. This is not to say that this latter procedure and arrangement does not have its uses – it does for the purpose of allowing children en mass to hear a story that is being read to them, but we should not delude ourselves that children are learning much about books under such procedures.

A further point to bear in mind is that not all children are equally capable of listening to and following a story, so procedures have to be varied to suit the children. For those who find difficulty, the smaller the group the more chance the teacher will have of making suitable adjustments, such as using the greater intimacy of the small group to instil a higher degree of motivation through pointing the story more firmly at the children personally, by encouraging responses from the children and by sensitive readjustments to reading speed, stress, emphasis and repetition in the reading matter. Children who have had enough should be allowed to wander off and do something else, and subsequently they should be tempted to listen to another story. Do not make story time 'a matter of life and death'! It should be relaxing and enjoyable, and not a test of endurance.

Sensitive parents allow their children when listening to a story to interject with reactions to the story, the book or to words vaguely familiar or in some way noticeable to them. Likewise in school, it should be the teacher's aim to encourage participation in the story time. Reactions show involvement, which indicates learning. Many interjections lead to the early stages of word study and spelling:

> Child: I've seen that word before.
> Teacher: Let's find it then.

and thus we have the beginnings of word study, word matching, visual discrimination and word identification, or we have the child asking, 'Show me Teddy's name,' whereupon the teacher points out the word, possibly in more than one context, and she subsequently writes the word *Teddy* on a separate piece of card or paper for the child to keep. Another instance occurred:

> Child: That word has got a tail, (pointing to the *y* in *baby*).
> Teacher: That is the word for baby; let's look for some other words on this page that have a tail.

All of these instances should be accompanied by pointing and, either then or subsequently, the teacher writing the words, so that we have the beginnings of letter identification and even the study of the boundaries within words.

There is a further activity connected with hearing a story: that of anticipating the outcome. This should be encouraged because anticipation is an element of reading that we want to foster as the children learn to read. It will be an essential element in their eventual ability to read quickly, to become involved in what they are reading and to use the semantic cues obtained from what they have read in order to help in the interpretation of the text that has still to be read. Hence, the sooner we encourage anticipation as a normal reaction to print the sooner and more easily will it be established as a reading habit.

All of this learning can be done as an incidental part of listening to an adult reading from a book. Always have a pad, set of blank cards and a blackboard available, so that in addition to seeing the words in print the children will see them actually being written. From this they will begin to learn to look at words in a specific way. It need not spoil the enjoyment of the story; in fact the interventions and participation help to alleviate the difficulties some children find in sitting silently and passively. Stories read with this more intimate arrangement heighten the intensity of them as shared literary experiences. Children in the vast majority of cases react well and sensibly to it. If they do not, then the teacher should consider whether the stories chosen are appropriate and whether the reading is done in the most professional way. A special study should be made by students of their ability to read aloud in a manner appropriate to the text, first by recording themselves reading aloud a variety of stories and comparing their reading with a reading done by professional broadcasters and actors, and subsequently by practising and preparing all readings before they do them in front of children.

Just a few words of caution at this point. In their desire to create interest in and enthusiasm for books, teachers frequently use the illustrations in the book as bait: 'Here's an interesting book,' we say hopefully, pointing to the pictures. Think of the possible confusion inherent in this if the child then understandably regards the pictures as the central feature of the book, carrying the message, with the printed text as subservient to the pictures. Herein could lie a source of bewilderment for the child who is unfamiliar with books and their usage. One has only to think of the situation described by Reid (1966) to realise how devastating such a misconception could be in terms of the emergence of such children as readers.

Traditionally, story time has been regarded as an important part of the school day. Unfortunately, in all too many cases it has occurred at the end of the day, when many of the children are tired and restless, and it has been seen as a severely limited activity in terms of the teaching of reading, in that it is simply a way of conveying a story to a group of children. In this book it is regarded as the opportunity to share a literary experience and to introduce children to the study of texts as well as introducing them to good literature, and therefore, it should not take place when the children are tired.

Labelling as an introduction to word study

Having raised the issue concerning the early beginnings of word study, the next activity of the infant classroom that springs to mind is that which is commonly referred to as labelling, an activity whereby the teacher attaches written names to various objects in the classroom, and, where appropriate, includes in the label a sentence or phrase about the object. For example, a label for a chestnut on the interest table may have the word, *Conkers*, followed by, *Conkers are chestnuts, but we cannot eat them*. In this way the teacher relates directly to the word most likely to be used by the child, goes on to add its correct name and then places the words in a language context. Thus she is proceeding from what is a concrete concept – the conker – to its symbolization in print and to a demonstration of how that word may appear in the context of written language. Nelson (1974) provides evidence that the sequence should be from concept to written word rather than from print to concept, and in labelling we have an early opportunity to establish a procedural principle in our teaching of attaching print to the actions, thoughts, intentions or findings of children as they occur. In this way the young child can begin to understand the purposes and nature of print and begin to learn that print can be closely related to what is occupying his attention and can express in a permanent form his thoughts, no matter how trivial or fleeting or profound they may be. Furthermore, if the teacher makes a habit of syllabifying vocally these words as she writes them, children will gradually become aware of the pronunciation boundaries within words, such as *pen/cils* and not *pe/nc/ils* and *bis/cuits* and not *bi/scuits*.

This activity has tremendous potential for an early introduction to the study of words but as an activity it must be carefully thought out. Otherwise, in an oversimplified form, it can make an insignificant contribution to learning or, if regarded as an opportunity for the formal study of words, it can be overpowering at an early age.

To clarify this issue, it is important that we should distinguish between instruction in some aspect and the study of that aspect. Instruction implies an imposed way of doing something, whereas to study something implies freedom for the learner to see it his way. This distinction is very important when dealing with young children who are confronted with the complexities of learning about the symbolic representation of ideas in the form of print. Frequently we do not know exactly how children will perceive things, and, because of their limited experience, we find it very difficult to provide precise instruction. Hence, we are on safe ground if we provide them with opportunities to perceive things in their way. For example, Smith (1971) has pointed out that letters have distinguishing features, otherwise they could not be differentiated one from the other, but we as adult skilled readers with all our experience of print and reading cannot really appreciate how children make their distinctions. This does not mean that we should not provide children with opportunities to perfect and learn the distinctions they make; it simply warns us not to make the distinctions for them and then assume that they have learnt what we have taught them. It may be the case that our teaching has conveyed nothing, but the children have succeeded by their own means!

This suggests a sequence based on a study-model of learning. The first step is where the teacher labels the object; at the second step the teacher and child do it together; whilst at the third step the child alone labels the object. The inestimable advantage of this model is that the child observes what the teacher does, is then able to actively participate with the guidance of the teacher, and is finally allowed to put his observations to the test having already succeeded in doing the task under guidance. Thus the danger of failure with its concomitant loss of confidence is reduced to a minimum. Indeed the success inherent in this procedure has the more positive effect of increasing confidence, which is an essential ingredient in any learning situation. Furthermore, the oral interaction between teacher and child intensifies the relationship between them and helps to develop the child's ability to communicate through speech.

Having established the procedure for learning to label items, an element of selection should be introduced. First, the one word naming the object – for example, *desk* – is presented by the teacher at the first attempt, then 'chosen' by the teacher and child at the second attempt, and subsequently the child is asked to 'choose' or pick up the word. Following this the teacher will select the word *desk* from two word cards: *desk* and *wall*. This will be followed by the child choosing from the two words under the guidance of the teacher (the teacher making it clear to the child that she will help him to make the correct choice). Finally, the child will be asked if he feels he now knows which is *desk* and is prepared to select that word from two words presented to him. This is repeated on later occasions with an increasing number of words from which the target word is to be selected. As you will see there is a certain amount of 'kidology' involved in these sequences, all of which are designed to ensure success whilst providing the opportunities for the child to make his own observations and guided decisions with little chance of failure.

For those who feel that these observations by the child may be limited to momentary selection of a target word, it should be remembered that Read's research (1971) demonstrated how children with 'an unconscious knowledge of the aspects of the sound system of English . . . tacitly organise phonetic segments . . . and . . . base their judgements of phonological relationships on certain specifiable features,' and Stuart-Hamilton's research (1986) shows how phonemic and graphemic awareness is developing in children in reception classes and the effect that it has on their ability to learn to read. Hence, children are learning unconsciously as well as consciously, and it behoves the teacher to provide opportunities for both unconscious and conscious learning through the above mentioned activities with words and the frequent labelling and re-labelling activities. Young teachers should assume neither that what they teach is learned nor that the provision they make for learning is ignored. Furthermore, they should keep in mind that labels are of little note in themselves; it is the active selection of labels, repeated frequently, that causes children to look at them and to note, either consciously or unconsciously, the features of the words on those labels.

Transcribing thought into print

Yet another activity common to many infant classrooms is the teacher writing under a drawing done by the child. Sometimes this is done in a hurry and too little attention is called to what the teacher is doing. However, this basic activity suggests a range of possibilities for language experience. Discussion between teacher and child as to what should be written should precede the actual writing. Simultaneously with the act of writing, the teacher should vocalise the words as she writes each one, and she may add comments, such as 'We used that word on so and so's drawing,' or 'That is a word that is already on the blackboard,' or 'How can we spell that word? It begins like so and so which we wrote under your last drawing,' each of these being attempts to draw comparisons for the child, or rather to suggest to the child that she draws her own comparisons.

When the writing under the drawing is completed, teacher and child should 'read' what is written together, and then the teacher, being sure that the child is well rehearsed in what is written, can suggest that the child alone reads the statement. Naturally, at the early stages in the reception class, children will not be able to read in the true sense of the word, but the object of this exercise is to get them into the habit of 'reading', so that we are teaching them certain types of behaviour, whilst at the same time building up confidence.

But we should not let the matter rest there. Further work can be done, such as later in the day referring back to the drawing and seeing whether the child has remembered what was written, again helping children to acquire habits: in this case, the habit of trying to retain things in their minds and showing them that to memorise things is an important part of schooling.

The emergence of children's 'writing'

Allied with the activity of the teacher doing the writing the children should be encouraged on occasions to 'write' their message or statement under the drawing themselves. Sometimes they will have discussed what they will 'write' with the teacher, whilst at other times they will just go ahead as they think fit. This, in some instances, can then be transcribed by the teacher, not in the sense of correcting the child's work but in the sense of, 'Now look how I would write what you have written.' Again this gets away from the idea of testing a child and promotes an atmosphere of studying together and learning from one another; it promotes and helps to establish a disposition for the emulation of others and for self-improvement.

Until very recently little notice was taken of children's early attempts at writing. It was accepted that children went through a scribbling stage, but all too often this stage was considered as a discrete entity little related to printed texts. However, there has been an important change in our thoughts on this matter: teachers have begun to accept the idea that scribbling and 'writing' are manifestations of attempts by children to 'sort out' the problem of print. Vygotsky (1978) suggests that there is a clear pattern of behavioural development from the use of gesture and visual signs, to the use of symbolism in play, followed by the use of symbolism in drawing, and arriving eventually at the use of symbolism in writing. He calls this developmental sequence 'the history of sign development in the child'. Apart from anything else this emphasises the importance of provision for play, interactive activity and drawing in the core curriculum of the infant school. It also suggests that during the early years the child is emerging as a writer as well as a reader, and hence the development of writing in all its aspects must be considered as it relates to all aspects of reading development. Admittedly, when children begin to scribble, their purpose is partly the joy obtained from the motor action, partly the experience of seeing marks appear on the paper, and partly the zest for acquiring new skills no matter what they are. As children are introduced to behaviours that contribute to reading, and at first it seems to them that reading is simply a unitary skill, so they acquire a desire to explore the possibilities of writing. And it is in this way that letter-like shapes begin to appear amongst their 'scribbles'. Look at the following examples which indicate a developmental progression. Figure 3.1 is an attempt by a four year old to write a letter to her mother, taken from Newman (1984). The message reads: 'To Mommy, we all love her very much. Love, Susan.'

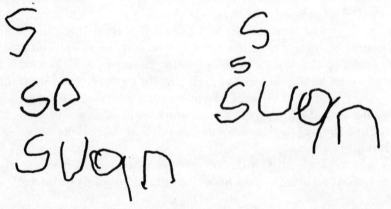

Figure 3.1

Jonathan, aged four years nine months and in his third week in the reception class, made a gingerbread man and then wrote, *I made a Gingerman*, accompanied by an illustrative drawing of a ginger-bread man (Figure 3.2). The child having produced this work uninhibitedly and specifically for the teacher, it would be churlish and foolish of the teacher to mark or alter the work. Such a reaction would be discouraging and dispiriting. However, there is a way in which the teacher can take advantage of this opportunity to promote further development. All she needs to do is to take up the letter or word-like form, comment upon the child's skill in producing it and then write that letter or word in its usually

Figure 3.2

acceptable form without comment. This approach will allow children to make comparisons, and it will not have the effect of showing them where they have gone wrong or even how they could improve on their original. Leave that to the children at this stage. They are bound to notice what you have done, because the very fact that they have produced letters or word-like forms in the first place demonstrates some awareness of what is required.

Implicit in the work of Bissex (1980) and Graves (1979) is the fact that children go through the motions of writing in the first instance and then begin to imitate print as they see it. This underlines what is said in the previous paragraph and it points to the importance of letting children witness teachers and adults in the act of writing. Although Goodnow's study (1977) of children's drawings found that there was no strong desire to communicate through the earlier graphic activities of children, nevertheless the above samples suggest the emergence of such a desire as the activities progress. Ferreiro (1978a and 1978b) noted similar developments, whereby three to five year old children experiment with the layout of shapes that approximate in varying degrees to handwriting. This she found occurring before the children began to use the alphabetic principle of phoneme–grapheme relationships. She also found that children at this early stage are parsimonious in their use of symbols to convey their message, a fact beautifully illustrated by Bissex's son when he wrote her a note asking 'RUDF' (Are you deaf?), and by Moira McKenzie in a lecture in Manchester (November, 1985) showing a child's response to a request to identify in writing a meat tenderiser (Figure 3.3).

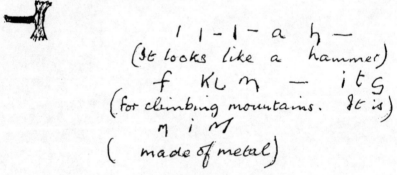

Figure 3.3

Responses to these two pieces of writing that would be in keeping with our desire not to discourage by implied criticism but nevertheless to provide opportunities for further progress would be, in the case of the first message, for the mother to reply in writing, *No, I am not deaf. Are you deaf?*, accompanied by the spoken form of this message, and in the case of the second example to accept the child's version as it stands, but soon afterwards find an opportunity to gather together a small group of children who have each written something and tell them, 'Now I am going to write on separate sheets of paper what each one of you has written. We shall read each piece of writing together and I shall ask you to try to remember your story so that you can read it back to me later.' Through these types of guidance and the opportunities they provide for study, the children will, in Ferreiro's words, 'formulate new hypotheses', so that they are gradually refining their ideas about the production of a written text.

When to this is added the natural propensity to search for ways of spelling (Read, 1971) before they have received instruction, then the teacher will appreciate what fertile ground there is for helping to illuminate some of these things for children in a reception class, remembering all the time that her teaching methodology should be illustrative rather than instructive.

For those teachers over-inhibited by adherence to the concept of readiness and wondering whether these activities could be prac- tised with children from non-literary or low educational back- grounds, it will be reassuring to note that Ferreiro found that children from both illiterate and literate families engaged in this experimentation and exploration of the possibilities of 'writing'. Thus the task of the teacher is made easier by the uniformity of children's urges to write and to spell as we do.

The emergence of spelling

To add to this battery of evidence in support of a gradual illustrative approach in our teaching consider the findings of Carol Chomsky (1979), Francis (1975) and Gibson et al (1970). Chomsky found a strong propensity amongst those children who knew their letter names to teach themselves spelling, and she presented a strong case for encouraging children to probe and experiment. Likewise Francis argues for allowing children freedom to discover for themselves the grouping of letters within words – a propensity for which was first suggested by Gibson and her colleagues – and she supports her argument by implying that what is discovered is more readily learned than what one receives through direct instruction. As teachers we have only to list the possibilities for an illustrative approach to appreciate the scope that exists for this kind of teaching:

writing under children's drawing;

writing under children's attempts at writing;

labelling with words, phrases and sentences objects of interest to
the child (remembering of course that *wall, window, ceiling, floor*
and *door* are not exactly enthralling concepts to most children, so
an interest table containing objects, toys, food, all appropriately
labelled, is an essential part of a language development
programme);

pointing out words in books and vocalising those words in a
deliberate manner;

displaying word cards that form sentences, thus:

| The | ball | hit | the | window |

in order to begin to wean children away from the assumption
that sentences are simply one long word (which is a reasonable
assumption if all there is to go on is what is heard, eg
'Howareyoutoday');

displaying word cards that have been bent to show the clustering of
letters and within-word boundaries, as in Figure 3.4;

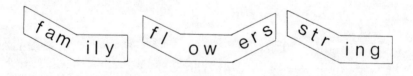

Figure 3.4

using colour to distinguish corresponding parts of words, eg *ight*
written in one distinctive and distinguishing colour on a chart
containing the words *light, fight* and *bright*;

writing words, phrases and sentences on the blackboard and on
notepads, not to be learned there and then, but merely to be
noted as appendages to what either the child or teacher has said.

Spoken language as an accompaniment to reading and writing

Finally, in our desire to help children towards the beginnings of reading and writing and through the early stages of the acquisition of these skills, we should not forget the part to be played by the use of spoken language alongside 'reading' and 'writing' activities. Britton (1983) says speech has an important role in the mastery of written language, suggesting that speech acts as a facilitator in each of Vygotsky's four stages and that there is a move 'from intimacy and immediacy of meaning towards constancy of meaning. Thus, while generalisation and abstraction, for example, have a role to play in the spoken language, it might be claimed that their homeground is the written language.' Alongside this move one can see the value of stories in helping children to move towards an appreciation of abstraction and to handle knowledge through the symbolic medium of language (Wells, 1987). Britton (1983) suggests a sequence that forms the basis for development: hearing stories, enacting stories in play, telling stories, dictating stories, and finally writing and reading stories. 'Dictating', he maintains, is a useful indicator of the internalisation of some forms of the written language in children who have not begun to read.

I do not think we should interpret the elements in Britton's sequence as discrete and strictly sequential, but rather we should use them as a rough guide to a general trend which teachers may note and for which they may make appropriate provision.

An interesting use of dictation was made in an inner city school in Leeds in the seventies whereby children who entered school before they were five years of age were taught to use tape recorders and were encouraged at their leisure to dictate into the machine any story or account of an event that came to mind. The headmistress, Kay Wiley, then transcribed the recorded message on a jumbo typewriter and together with the child read aloud the resulting text. This proved highly successful with children, and sooner than one would think with those whose acquaintance with books, stories and story-telling was minimal or even non existent, these children were able to see the outcome of their ideas and to begin 'to internalise' some of the forms that written language takes. The deliberate correspondence between what was thought and said and what emerged through dictation and transcription was the more noticeable to the child, because it was both immediate and relevant to him and, to some extent, a concrete manifestation of the nature of print based on his own thoughts. He could see the connection between what he had said originally and what he subsequently heard read back to him.

When we are told by researchers, Strickland (1962), Ruddell (1965), and Reid (1972) amongst others, that children in the early stages of learning to read will find it easier to deal with reading materials which approximate more closely to their own speech patterns than to a standard received form of English, I think we should have in mind the speech patterns used when the children are consciously trying to convey a message in the manner of the Leeds school children and not the patterns that they use in informal interactions in the playground as described by Roberts, T. (1978). Appropriate speech patterns will emerge when the teacher encourages children to participate in the group composition of one- or two-sentence stories which can be transcribed onto the blackboard and read together. There are many opportunities in the modern infant classroom for variations on this theme of the group composition of stories and messages: describing an activity that has just taken place such as dressing up, building a block tower, ladling water, gathering fallen leaves or trying to bounce a ball more than once; composing messages concerned with activities in the classroom; rewriting the rules of the classroom; noting what games can be played in the playground. All of these activities will produce the forms of speech that approximate more closely to written language and will be appropriate for transposing into print. At the same time, it must be stressed that the purpose of all the activities mentioned so far is to increase the range of the children's spoken language and to increase their awareness of print, not to increase their knowledge of specific items of print. That specific knowledge will emerge gradually as a by-product in the very early stages of schooling.

The composition and construction of texts

There is one other distinctive activity which has a firm place in the emergent reading and writing programmes. This is another form of presenting print, simplified by the exclusion of the need to spell words. It involves the use of word cards to construct written texts, and it is best exemplified by the materials referred to as *Breakthrough to Literacy* (Mackay et al., 1970). In its entirety the Breakthrough scheme is offered as the basis for actually learning to read, the general idea behind it being that children will first witness, then participate in and finally be responsible for, the reproduction, through the use of word cards, of their own thoughts as they emerge in speech. The child supplies the oral message, and in the first place the teacher transforms that message as spoken by the child into its written form by selecting word cards from a word bank and arranging them in the correct order. As the child's ability to select written words grows so that child begins to participate in the selection of words to conform with his message. Finally, the child develops an ability to select the words unaided and uses the children's sentence maker, a small version of the teacher's sentence maker.

The basis of this approach is the child's message and the child's way of saying that message, and hence the resultant written text, relates immediately to the child's contemporary interest and closely approximates to his speech patterns. Some of the words provided in the word bank are rather dated and there is an urgent need to provide a wider vocabulary than exists at present. This can be rectified, of course, by teachers writing extra word cards.

In the next chapter, when the actual process of learning to read is dealt with, reference will be made again to *Breakthrough to Literacy*, and it will be seen as a representation of the language-experience approach. At the moment, however, it is worth looking at as an excellent instrument for demonstrating those aspects of the nature of print that can be most easily understood by children who have not started to read. It should not be regarded as a replacement for the production of handwritten texts by the teacher but as complementary to her spelling out written language in the presence of children, as when she writes under children's drawing etc., because when actually writing out the message the teacher is demonstrating the fact that words are made up of letter forms. *Breakthrough* word cards do not demonstrate that aspect of written language, but they do demonstrate that a spoken message consists of discrete words and that those words can be arranged in a sequence that corresponds to the spoken message, and they provide opportunities for words to be studied and comparisons between words to be drawn by both teacher and child. Hence children who cannot read can nevertheless witness the production of a text which relates to their immediate activities and thoughts. Furthermore, that text can easily be changed in order to meet a slightly modified message on the same theme. For example, a child says to the teacher, 'It's m' birthday today. I'm 'aving a party.' The teacher then selects the appropriate word cards from the enlarged teacher's Sentence Maker, thus:

| It | s | my | birthday | today | . | I | m | having | a | party | , |

replacing 'm'birthday' with my birthday and commenting 'This is how we write "m'birthday" when we write: It's my birthday' with emphasis on 'my'. Similarly, having replaces "aving'.

When this has been done *by the teacher*, then some child is sure to add, 'It was my birthday yesterday and I had a party'. The teacher repeats the child's statement and proceeds to alter the previous construction, deliberately vocalising as she makes the changes in the card message: 'It was my birthday *yesterday and* I *had* a party.' Thus the children are witnesses to alterations in the grammatical structure to comply with the re-stated message. It is difficult to conceive of a more effective way of gradually introducing a child, who cannot yet read, to the composition of a written text, as well as arousing awareness of the possibilities for alterations in syntax and its effect upon meaning, and without ever having to refer to the technicalities of syntactical and semantic change.

Work of this kind with the Teacher's Sentence Maker is best done with groups of children numbering between two and six. This arrangement keeps the teaching unit reasonably intimate, it allows true interaction between members of the group and participation by all members in the work, and it enables the teacher to pick up all suggestions for changes to the original message. The group can be encouraged to make suggestions for extending the message.

The strengths of the *Breakthrough* approach are that it promotes work that is based on the children's activities and thoughts; it forces children to organise those thoughts in a coherent oral statement; it implants naturally an awareness of the nature of written language; it is language-based rather than word- or letter-based in its general approach; and by avoiding the need for word analysis, it does not require the children to be engaged in tasks which at this stage are beyond them (Piaget, amongst others, suggested that very young school children could not cope with the analysis of such complex structures as English words, whereas they can more easily understand the process of synthesis used in the construction of Breakthrough sentences). Sentences that have been compared and constructed in this way can be written for the children in a group book, and subsequently referred to frequently as a source for recalling bygone events in the classroom and for the children to be reacquainted with printed statements of which they themselves were the source.

Conclusion

A number of issues have been raised, and a number of activities designed to aid the emergence of a propensity for learning to read and write have been described. However, all will be diminished in their effectiveness if the attitude and personality of the teacher is not conducive to a happy, work orientated approach, and it must be remembered that frequently the most effective approach is through purposeful play and through activities that appeal to children. This is so throughout the infant school, and it is especially so in the reception class, where the teacher has to tread warily a path between encouragement and guidance on the one hand and a desire to 'get the children started' on the other hand. Those teachers who concentrate on encouragement, motivation and guidance are not necessarily those who are 'waiting for something to happen'. By the richness and quality of their provision, they display a deep underlying concern for development. They make school an exciting adventure for the children, and they realise that achievement, although relative to each child, is nevertheless the central thrust of the child's life. Children have learned to walk, talk and manipulate tools, such as knives and forks, through their own inner drive and perseverance; now on entry to school they are ready to begin to acquire new skills.

There follows a checklist which summarises all that has been written in this chapter. It will help young teachers to assure themselves that many of the seemingly mundane tasks of the reception classroom have an important part in the provision of a sound basis for learning to read and write.

Checklist for teachers who are preparing children for learning to read and write

A   SPOKEN LANGUAGE

The objective is to increase the range of uses of language.

1   Encourage discussion centring upon activities: art, craft, building blocks, water, sand and 'Peter and Wendy House' or den play. Participate *within* the groups from time to time to induce a disposition for 'universalistic' language (Bernstein).
2   Grasp opportunities to enter into a discussion with a child who has brought some object or toy to school. This may develop into a group discussion, which will add variety to the discussion.
3   Encourage discussions arising from stories, pictures, illustrations, films, events and artefacts brought to school by the staff. Allow children to intervene during the stories, the films and the showing of illustrations, remembering that language development is your basic objective in these activities.
4   Initiate games such as those devised by the Gahagans (1970). These included games such as: O'Grady says . . . , recognising voices of concealed speakers, spotting the mistake in a spoken sentence, repeating an unknown rhyme or poem, completing a known rhyme or poem, supplying nouns which belong to a class – such as fruit or animals, describing something before them and from memory, following oral instructions, using a battery-operated telephone to convey and receive simple messages, I-Spy, describing and identifying a concealed object, elaborating upon a story as a group exercise, describing regular and irregular shapes, and other activities proposed in this book.
5   Create and allocate jobs which require children to ask, to guide, to tell and to instruct others; use every opportunity to send them to ask the head teacher for information and materials and thereby gain yourself a supernumerary teacher who will get involved with the work of your class!

NB You should not dominate the conversations, neither should you rely upon question and answer techniques, otherwise the children may become constrained and inhibited in their use of language.

B READING TO A GROUP OF CHILDREN

1 Know the story before you read it to the children.
2 Prepare suitable illustrations and enlarged word cards of key words, both to be produced during the reading.
3 Allow children to see what you are reading and see how you turn the pages and how, occasionally, you follow the lines of print with your fingers. (Do not forget that the children must be behind and round you, so that they can see what you are doing from the appropriate angle.)
4 Select points from the story for discussion; write appropriate words or phrases on the blackboard, without necessarily dwelling upon them.
5 Refer back to previous stories and to actions, things, words and phrases in those stories. This helps to reinforce previous incidental learning and provides opportunities for further unconscious learning.
6 Encourage activities – dramatic play, art and craft, dancing, etc. – which can be developed from stories. This helps children to develop an ability to abstract themselves from thoughts about their immediate environment, an important side effect of hearing stories read, noted by Wells in his research.

C ACTIVITIES TO DEVELOP AWARENESS OF WORDS AND
WRITTEN LANGUAGE

1 Have copies of nursery rhymes printed in large type so that children may attempt to follow the text as they say the rhymes. Use the overhead projector for group work.
2 Label all objects brought by children – use individual words, phrases and sentences – and talk about those objects and labels, repeating the labelling process so that children have to make decisions about the choice of words.
3 Allow children to play with wooden cut-out letters (plastic are a poor substitute). Show them how to arrange the letters over word cards. (See Chapter 7 in Walker, C. (1975) *Teaching Pre-reading Skills.*) Treat this as a jigsaw-like game.
4 Encourage over-writing of words (this should be preceded by a practice in the use of pencils – scribbling, drawing, pattern making), but do not be over-zealous in demanding exactness.

5   Discuss their drawings and paintings and write underneath what the children say about them. Refer back to these repeatedly.

6   Construct sentences from word cards based upon the children's activities and the spoken language which accompanies or arises out of those activities. The children should be encouraged to participate in the choice of words. (*Breakthrough to Literacy* provides cards and troughs for this purpose.) Make alterations to these sentences so that children can witness the manipulation of printed language, as suggested in the Teacher's Manual to *Breakthrough to Literacy*.

7   Encourage children to record on tape stories which they have composed or descriptions of their activities. These should then be transcribed in written form by the teacher (use a jumbo typewriter) and subsequently the texts should be read to the children.

8   Make up envelopes of words taken from their stories, referred to in 6 and 7 above. These can act as sources to which the children can be referred on subsequent occasions so there is reinforcement of learning.

9   Encourage children to try their hand at 'writing' their own stories, and subsequently transcribe their story so that they can draw comparisons between their 'writing' and yours.

Further reading
Kroll, B.M. and Wells, G. (eds) (1983) *Explorations in the Development of Writing: Theory, Research and Practice*. Chichester, N.J.: John Wiley.
This book contains two very important chapters, by James Britton and by Marie Clay, in which clear evidence is produced to show children's disposition for organising their own learning.

Six developmental stages in the ability of two to five year olds to tell stories ending up with the stage of 'centering and chaining' – ie being able to produce a central core to the story and to link events within the story – have been suggested by:
Applebee, A.N. (1978) *The child's concept of story*. Chicago: Chicago University Press.

Storying, or the construction of stories, as a fundamental way of making meaning, is described in:
Wells, G. (1987) *The Meaning Makers: Children Learning Language and Using Language to Learn*. London: Hodder and Stoughton.

Francis, H.(1982) *Learning to Read: Literate Behaviour and Orthographic Knowledge*. London: Allen and Unwin.
The last chapter in this book should be regarded as essential reading for all who are about to teach, because it gives a clear indication of the difficulties an unprepared child will face upon entry to school.

For theoretical arguments that support the idea of the child as explorer and experimenter, setting up hypotheses and then attending to instances that confirm or deny those hypotheses, see:
Duckworth, E. (1979) Either we're too early and they can't learn it or we're too late and they know it already: the dilemma of 'applying Piaget'. *Harvard Educucational Review, 49*, 297–312.

For examples of exercises and tasks that can be given to children to develop 'pre-reading' skills, see:
Walker, C. (1975) *Teaching Pre-Reading Skills*. London: Ward Lock Educational.

For a useful graded series of 40 children's books at eight levels containing most of the nursery rhymes, see:
Southgate Booth, V. (1985) *Star Series*. London: Macmillan.

PART III
THE EARLY STAGES OF
READING AND WRITING

4 Conscious efforts to read: the early stages

As the child begins to get a clearer notion, but still only a notion, of the nature and some of the conventions of written English, it will be necessary for the teacher to begin to show the child words in ways which will call attention to their similarities and differences and to call attention to the settings in which these words are placed or can be placed. Thus the pupils must be helped consciously and deliberately to seek out the letter patterns within words and the sentence patterns within texts.

In an earlier chapter the inadequacy of a summational approach to word building was mentioned. Gibson and Levin (1975) demonstrated clearly that the critical units for reading the word *cleats* are three and not six: *cl, ea, ts*. To identify and attach sounds to each of these letters individually would be quite inadequate, and it is the teacher's task to establish in the child a disposition for seeking the letter-cluster boundaries within words. Indeed, many years ago comics for very young children were written with the majority of words hyphenated by syllables. This may have been undesirable for universal use, but it did suggest that teachers should assist the child to acquire the habit of seeing words in terms of letter clusters rather than in terms of individual letters.

Learning to read as a problem-solving activity

However, it is not simply a matter of identifying the letter clusters within a word, because these may have two or more interpretations. For example, the *ea* in *cleats* must be considered within the context of that particular word. Without prior knowledge of that word, syntactic and semantic cues will have to be employed to help determine which of the nine or more sounds can be attached to *ea* in this instance (*ea* has different sounds in *bear, ear, beautiful, ocean, great, head, pleats, creation, bean*). Thus the learner must acquire both a knowledge of the various possibilities in letter–sound relationships and a flexibility in behaviour to experiment with viable responses based on that knowledge, combined with the employment of cues from the context in which the word stands.

A STUDY APPROACH TO LEARNING

This suggests a study–problem solving approach, in which it is primarily the intention of the teacher to get the child to study words and texts and to find out for himself how they are constructed. This implies a radical difference in emphasis from the methodology wherein the teacher instructed the learner and assumed that the learner saw things in exactly the same way as did the teacher. The latter methodology was the one that tended to be widely used in the first forty or fifty years of this century. However, the work of Gates (1927) in America and Schonell (1945) in this country gave us our first glimpse of a study type approach to initial word identification in what came to be called the 'Look-and-Say' method, whereby children were presented with words, they were told what those words were, and it was then left to the children to take in the word as they perceived it without any attempt at overt analysis. (Both these writers proposed that subsequent to this initial introduction to words, and after the learner had become familiar with a small stock of words through looking at them and saying them as complete words, the teaching method should change to one where the emphasis was placed upon the phonic analysis of words. This fact is frequently forgotten or ignored by their critics.)

The language-experience approach

The work of Gates and Schonell was followed by Stauffer's language-experience approach (Stauffer, 1970), in which the child's spoken language was transcribed by the teacher and used as the basic reading texts. In these developments we see emerging the idea that in the first place what the child is asked to read is text based on what he already knows, ie he knows what the word confronting him is because the teacher has named that word, and he knows what text he is being asked to read because he has formulated the ideas which that text expresses. In other words, the print is matched to the ideas in the mind of the child at that moment, rather than the child having to identify the word or text without having any prior notion of their meanings.

This approach has been manifested in another form through the use of *Breakthrough to Literacy* (Mackay et al., 1970), whereby the teacher and children compose oral statements which are then represented by the appropriate sequence of word cards. The idea behind this scheme is that learners will more readily learn to interpret print if they participate in its construction, and if they see how print is constructed they will become familiar with the constituent parts of written language in ways which allow them to draw their own conclusions.

Clay (1980) more recently has expressed some reservations about a total reliance upon *Breakthrough to Literacy* in the early stages of learning to read, arguing that, with an absence of actual writing, children will not witness the construction of words, only of sentences, and will thereby be deprived of the opportunity of noting the detail of the parts of words as they emerge. There is much substance in Clay's arguments, not only from the point of view of word recognition but also when one remembers that the ability to spell is closely concerned with a familiarity with serial probability in letter formations (Peters, 1967). It is logical to assume that the more children see of the process of word formation, the more readily they will develop expertise in spelling. Hence, a compromise seems reasonable whereby both the language-experience and *Breakthrough* methods are combined. The majority of teachers who use the *Breakthrough* materials also make a habit of writing out texts based on what the children have said and requiring them, in the first place, to witness these texts being written by the teacher, and subsequently requiring the children to read them.

The inculcation of appropriate reading behaviours

In these developments we have a major principle: namely, that the texts which children attempt to read in the early stages of learning should closely reflect the thoughts and actions of the children as embodied in their oral statements. In fostering this practice we are training the children to formulate their thoughts and then to reflect upon them through the medium of print which they then see before them. Both the formulation of thought and the disposition to reflect upon what they read will play a major part in their educational development. In this we see the beginning of an ability to compose a text and an ability to learn through reading later on in their school careers (Lunzer and Gardner, 1979). Thus, the approach through writing and text construction has wider implications than simply introducing children to the early stages of reading; it prepares them for subsequent intellectual development by beginning to inculcate habits and behaviours conducive to that development.

Here then we have a framework to guide our teaching. But it is simply not enough to rely purely on children's ability to learn to read by reading texts they have helped to construct in one way or another. Children vary in their capacity to learn, to draw inferences, to make comparisons and to maintain a highly motivated desire to solve the problems of reading. Of course, some will succeed partly by their own efforts and partly as a result of other factors such as favourable circumstances of home, teacher–pupil ratio, and the like, but teachers have to be ready to create the opportunities for children to learn, and to do this they must be fully aware of all the contributory elements of reading so that, where necessary, they can intervene in order to facilitate learning. For this reason a list of elements that have to be learned is provided. This is a list which, in a rather formalised and segmented way, attempts to show the elements underlying reading skill. It should be obvious from what has been said already that this is not a step by step sequence; it is simply a statement of what has to be learned as integral parts of the total skill. In order to emphasise this, the teacher is referred to Clark (1976), whose research with normal readers led her to suggest that learning to read may differ radically from teaching children to read. Learning to read was not found to occur in a hierarchical fashion because all the aspects of language – semantic, syntactic and phono-graphemic – operate at all levels. McInnes (1973) pleads for reading to be seen as part of human language development, whilst Reid and Low (1973) see learning to read and write as part of something larger – ie learning to deal with the written aspects of language.

Jansen (1985) argues that in a complex skill consisting of many items it is impossible to deal with the items separately. His point is well taken in that the whole is more than the sum of its parts. However, this cannot mean that those items cannot be taught in one way or another in conjunction with a number of items or within the context of the complete skill. For example, letter sounds can be learned, but only effectively within the context of words; letter clusters can be learned, but only effectively within the context of words; and syntax can be appreciated, but only if associated with meaning. It is particularly important to remember this these days, when there is a tendency for some people to assume that reading together, teacher and child, is the predominant success-producing element in teaching a child to read. For one thing, such a procedure would be impracticable in a large class with one teacher and no assistants, and with children who do not read along with their parents at home. To wait for these children to get sufficient familiarity with, and practice in the interpretation of print through reading together with the teacher would mean waiting several years!

The elements of reading

One of the earliest things a child must learn, when starting to learn to read, is to recognise that the different letters vary in shape and that the shape of each letter is invariable. This can be achieved in a variety of ways – alphabet books, playing with wooden letters, matching individual letters, tracing with the forefinger letters made of velvet and tracing on a sand tray – much of it incidental and unstressed as part of learning to read. This can be as much fun as counting and chanting, rhyming and singsong. However, there should be as little vocalisation of the individual letter sounds as possible. Any vocalisation that does take place should be within the context of a meaningful word or closely associated with a *familiar* word.

The other elements are enumerated below, and I repeat yet again, the order in which they are acquired by the child does *not* necessarily follow the listed order. The child must learn, in one way or another, the following elements:

*Background
awareness*

That the printed text tells a story or gives information, ie that the visual symbols convey a language
message.
That the various shapes of letters and words are
cues to the various sounds we make when speaking,
although the child need not be able to identify
specific letters or words at this stage.
That there is an *exact* correspondence between the
order of sounds spoken and the left to right
sequence of *words* as printed – with the spaces
between printed words corresponding to (possible)
minimal pauses in speech: /ə/,/kæt/,/sæt/,/ɔn/,
/ə/,/mæt/. = a cat sat on a mat.

*Facts to be
learned*

To differentiate visually between the letter shapes: **i**
and **p**, **t** and **m**, **b** and **d**, and so on to include all the
letters.
To identify letter shapes by their sound: **c**=/k/,
a=/æ/, **t**=/t/.

*Behavioural
process to be
acquired*

That there is an approximate correspondence
between the left to right sequence of the letters as
written and the temporal sequence of phonemes
(sounds which make up the word).
c a t = /k/, /æ/, /t/.

*Facts to be
learned*

To differentiate visually between the digraphs (*ea,
ai, ch, sh, ie*, etc.).
To identify the digraphs by their sound: they must
learn the various alternatives, eg *ea* in *beat, idea,
beautiful, ocean, great* . . .

*Behavioural
process to be
acquired*

To form a meaningful word by synthesising, in their
correct order, meaningless vocal syllables: /ai/,
/den/, /ti:/, /fai/– /aidenti:fai/ (identify).

*Facts to be
learned*

To differentiate frequent letter strings, eg **-tion,
str-**, **spr-**, **-ing**, **un-**, etc.
To identify these letter strings by their sound: **-tion**,
= /ʃən/; -ing = /iŋ/.

Behavioural   To employ a variety of strategies for analysing and
process to be   recognising unfamiliar polysyllabic words.
acquired

The   To become familiar with acceptable syntactical
interpretation of formations in texts, realising that what sounds right
print in terms of usually is right, eg /ðə bɔi gɔ:l ðə kist/ does
meaning: a   not stand, whereas /ðə bɔi kist ðə gɔ:l/ does.
mixture of   To understand that syntax determines meaning, eg
knowledge and in *the boy bit the dog* and *the dog bit the boy* the meaning
process   is made clear by the function of the words and their
               juxtaposition in the senctence.

To respond with increasing facility to all the demands made in the
above strategies so that the whole process becomes more and more
automatic, effortless and fluent.

SOME IMPLICATIONS FOR THE TEACHER

What the young teacher must keep in mind when helping a child to
learn to read is that independently these elements deal with aspects
of reading that are meaningful in different ways: letters intimating
sounds and hence how to formulate those sounds; words intimating
sounds and conveying meaning in a semantic sense. Letters are
abstract in nature; whilst words are abstract in that they refer just
to sounds, many are also concrete in the sense that they refer
directly to some thing or being, whilst others – the function words
in particular – need to stand alongside other words in context to
convey semantic meaning. In any event words are the basic
element in communication, and indeed, word recognition is the
main distinguishing mark between good and poor readers (Underwood, G. and J., 1986) However, the learning of words in isolation
can be soul destroying. Furthermore, Ehri and Wilce (1980) show
that if you teach children to read using words *in* sentences then they
learn about the syntactic and semantic functions of those words.
Thus they acquire a fuller understanding of words than they would
if the words stood in isolation. The danger of the latter would be
that the children would acquire solely a phonic response to the
word in isolation. Donaldson and Reid (1985) emphasise this point
by suggesting that a child's first encounters with print should be
through texts, and they propose that the only single words in

isolation that a child encounters should be 'public print' – for example, words like *litter, hospital, school, door, window*. The context of the learning determines what is given priority in the learning.

These distinctions between the nature of the various elements and their treatment are important for the teacher, who must keep in mind the principle that is posed by them, namely, that because young children find the abstract more difficult to deal with than the concrete, it follows that whatever is taught should start from the concrete and that which is semantically meaningful. Furthermore, as Jansen puts it: 'that the child develops, grows, emerges, becomes more experienced, we know ... What is right at one level of teaching reading may be insufficient at another level of teaching reading and wrong at yet another ... In consequence we must listen when we teach.' He goes on to argue against using one approach and pleads instead for a combination of 'bottom-up' (letters and sounds → words → meaning) and 'top-down' (meaning → words → letters and sounds) approaches. In other words, an approach towards learning to read by one route only is inadequate simply because the task is complex and entails the employment of semantic, syntactic and phono-graphemic cues, each to make a contribution in its own way to resolving the problem of interpreting the printed symbols.

LEARNING FACTS AND UNDERSTANDING PROCESSES

A second factor which will not have gone unnoticed when reading the above list of elements is that in the case of facts that have to be learned it is one thing to learn those facts and another thing to employ them. This is frequently forgotten in the eagerness of the teacher to make rapid progress. Facts are easy to teach and easy to learn, provided there is a reasonable degree of application. How to employ those facts is something less tangible and involves knowledge of those facts plus an understanding of the possibilities of their use. Here the children have to acquire a procedure for responding to those facts.

Now it is much harder to devise ways of ensuring that the learner understands the processes involved in the use of facts. It would be hopelessly optimistic to assume that a young child trying to read a three letter word such as *cat* for the first time would understand the statement '/k/, /æ/, /t/ says /k æ t/', a statement frequently heard in classrooms. Children have many things to learn and understand before they know, really know that is, how to respond to the word *cat*. They have to know the word cat as relating to an animal, they have to know that in some way the print refers to that animal, and then they have to begin to understand how the printed word represents the sound /k æ t/. From this point onwards it will be a matter of picking out letters and letter clusters. At first, although they may give the response /k æ t/, they will be relying heavily upon the fact that they have been told that the word is /k æ t/, or, at best, they will *begin* to associate some feature of the word with some part of the sound; but they will do so with little real certainty. This is why encouragement is so important and so productive, because it reassures the child that the attempt is worthwhile. We cannot be sure of the features that will be noticeable to the child (Smith, 1971), even though Marchbanks and Levin (1965) and others have found that in general the beginnings of words are the most noticeable and the middle parts least noticeable. What we can do is to show the child another word with which he can draw comparisons. For example, *cat* and *cap* and *cat* and *hat*. Each of these words has some similarities and some differences and each is likely to be a word that is known to the child (as opposed to being simply recognised by that child). From the comparisons they make, children will begin to learn about the nature of printed words and begin to see certain correspondences, such as /k æ/, and /æ t/ in the above pairs. And, of course, as always the teacher will write these words on a pad in the presence of the child so that he witnesses the words being written. Then the child can be asked to overwrite or copy, as appropriate, the words.

This approach is the reverse of the traditional hierarchical sub-skills approach to learning to read, in which children were confronted with the printed word and expected to analyse it into its pronounceable segments and then to synthesise those sound segments and arrive at the total word. That approach is now thought to be inappropriate for the beginning reader, although it is acceptable at later stages when the reader has a much better grasp of reading behaviour, has a greater knowledge of the units of words, and is simply in the process of adding to his store of recognisable words. As adult skilled readers, we employ that approach when we encounter an unfamiliar word.

However, we shall look at that approach later. For the present, it is important to revert to a multi-faceted approach – one which allows the child to use a variety of cues including his knowledge of what is actually the meaning of the message which he has picked up from the context in which the print has emerged.

A multi-cued approach to the teaching of reading

Reading is many things and cannot, as yet, be encompassed in one all-embracing model. We cannot say that a reader's behaviour when reading a text always corresponds to a set pattern. Words that are taken in at a glance in one context will require sub-vocalisation in another, suggesting that reading is not a response to words per se but a response to a sequence of thoughts suggested by the words. (Thus Gibson and Levin (1975) can assert that 'reading is an adaptive process', both active and flexible, with texts being processed in highly variable ways.) The processing of letters, words, and strings of words is continuously being subsumed in the thoughts evoked by these symbols. At times the symbols provoke undue attention, but only to the extent that their processing is taking longer and their place in the sequence of thoughts that has been triggered by the rest of the text is somewhat unclear momentarily. Thus it is the accumulating semantic cues that predominate, and the reader proceeds to fit and adapt the letters and words and phrases that he sees and hears in varying degrees to the emerging information suggested by the text.

For this reason the flow of thought about a text becomes a prime consideration, and it is this belief that has lain at the heart of the search for means to achieve cognitive organisation for the child who is beginning to read. Illustrations, introductory stories read to the children, preparatory questions and discussion have all been used as advance organisers (Ausubel 1968), but none with such incisive success as those approaches whereby the reading matter stems from the child's actions and experiences transposed through his own speech and transcribed into print. *Breakthrough to Literacy* is the exemplar *par excellence*. Here we have a means whereby the child's thoughts are organised through speech and presented as text; his task is to associate the printed form with those thoughts and the speech patterns that he has adopted. Later when he has acquired a store of readily recognised words and phrases, he will be able to come to an unfamiliar text, and from the words and phrases that he recognises begin to build up a sequence of thoughts, so that virtually from the first word he recognises, the semantic cues begin to accumulate and lead into the emerging message.

Learning to read as a group

1   The group-composition of texts
The use of *Breakthrough* was referred to in the previous chapter and in particular to the initial use of the teacher's Sentence Maker for the group study of text construction based on the contemporary activities of that group or some of the children in it. The use of this device should be continued but now with greater emphasis on all aspects of text construction: how something should be phrased – can it be expressed thus or is there a more effective or better way of expressing it in speech; whether what we have to say needs to be expressed differently in writing; what words are necessary – and here there is emphasis on the selection of those words from a word bank; what the word looks like – does it compare with any other word in sound or in letters; whether we can remember from a previous occasion the word we want; whether we can remember this word by tracing over it with our forefingers, writing over it with a pencil and copying it onto our note pad; where in our word files we can store a copy of the word we have just encountered.

   This group composition of texts should be followed by the teacher writing out the story from the cards and sticking copies in the children's folders or personally constructed reading books, whereupon the children attempt to read back the texts to the teacher or to one another, trace over the sentence with a forefinger, overwrite and subsequently copy the text.

2   Word and phrase study
Using the texts constructed in this way as a basis, various activities connected with word and phrase study can be initiated. The children can be asked to reselect the words from the word bank, they can make a declared effort to remember the word, and to learn it by comparing it with words which have similar features. For this latter purpose it is useful if the teacher has a duplicate set of word cards which have the usual letter clusters 'highlighted' in colour, eg *string* would have *str* in one colour and *ing* in another. This is not to

advocate a rigid adherence to a colour coding system such as *Words in Colour* (Gattengo, 1969); it is merely an ad hoc device for alerting children to the boundaries within words, and for familiarising them with the letter clusters of English spelling. Additionally, the teacher should not miss opportunities to write these new words, using coloured pencils or pens, so that the children can see the boundaries within words actually appearing and being noted by a change of pen or pencil.

Various games connected with the words that have arisen in the texts can be used to call attention to the constituent parts of words. A useful source is Hughes (1970, 1972) with games like the following:

Print ten words on the blackboard and ask the children to write them down in groups according to word families. The list may be:

cake	tail
coat	goat
bell	bake
sail	same
game	shell

The groups will be as follows:

cake	coat	bell	sail	game
bake	goat	shell	tail	same

Other games described by Hughes are illustrated in Figures 4.1 to 4.8.

Figure 4.1   *Find the missing vowels*

Figure 4.2   *Find the missing digraphs*

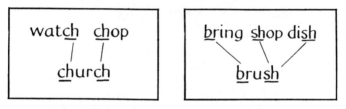

Figure 4.3   *Look for identical sounds*

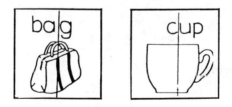

Figure 4.4   *Jigsaw make-a-word*

Figure 4.5   *Make-a-word from syllables using syllable cards*

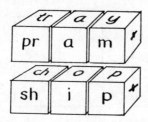

Figure 4.6   *Make-a-word with blocks (no pictures as aids)*

Figure 4.7   *Complete the word*

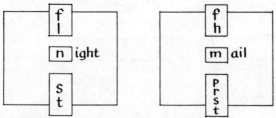

Figure 4.8   *Word family cards*

Reprinted with permission from: Hughes, J.M., *Aids to reading/Phonics and teaching of reading*, Unwin Hyman Ltd

These are but a few examples of the type of games and exercises which, if used discriminatingly and only for short periods of time, and to meet specific needs, will induce in children a sense of problem solving and give them considerable pleasure if their achievements are noted and commented upon. Such exercises should not be over used or used as 'run of the mill' work unnoticed by the teacher. They are not meant to be used as occupational exercises but as learning and practice exercises. Obviously, the examples used by teachers should be made to comply with the topics and words that form the *Breakthrough* compositions and other texts used by the class, because these exercises must be considered as supplementary to the main objective, which at this stage is to get children 'reading' texts whose storyline the children have created or that they know from oral repetition (nursery rhymes) or from having heard them read by the teacher.

3 Reading nursery rhymes and folk tales as a group
Running parallel with the group construction of texts, *Breakthrough* style, there should be group 'reading' of nursery rhymes and any other short stories, such as the folk tales – Goldilocks, The Three Bears, The Three Little Pigs, Red Riding Hood, and others – that are well known and well rehearsed. (They must be well known and well rehearsed if they are to conform to the pattern of requiring children to compare the printed form of the story with the story as they already know it.) These nursery rhymes and folk tales should be shown on the overhead projector, with the children having printed copies for subsequent reference. However, the main activity should centre on the overhead projector, because this enables the teacher to point to each word as it is 'read' by the group. The teacher may use the occasion to emphasise correspondences between sounds. For example, in reading together 'Little Bo-peep has lost her sheep', the teacher may encircle *peep* with the pointer, pass lightly over *has lost her*, and encircle *sheep*, thus stressing the correspondence between *peep* and *sheep*. After 'reading' the complete rhyme, the teacher may then return to those two words and write them on the transparency whilst simultaneously saying them with emphasis on the /i:/ sound. This may be followed by giving the children in the group copies of the words and asking them to trace them with their forefinger (*not* using tracing paper). At first they may be asked to trace over the words two or three times, but

eventually they can be asked to continue tracing over the word until they can form the word without copying. Naturally, the teacher will have to keep a close eye on this and ensure that she guides the child who stumbles; this exercise should not be regarded as a test of memory, but as an achievement of learning. Looking to see if the child gets the tracing right in the first place and that the word is formed or written correctly without copying in the second place should be done unobtrusively by the teacher, whilst her response when she finds that the child is doing it correctly and succeeding should be obtrusive, congratulatory and should convey admiration for the achievement.

LEARNING WORDS: FINGER-TRACING

Finger tracing is an exceptionally useful tool for learning activities. It enables children to develop a kinaesthetic sense of letter shapes and letter formations (Fernald, 1943); it ensures that children look at the word and its parts long enough to have some chance of remembering it (Roberts, G.R., 1969); and it is basically an activity which children turn to naturally, as witnessed by their inability to resist the temptation of writing or drawing on windows that have become steamed up. Older teachers will recall the emphasis placed by Montessori on tracing as an aid to learning. Unfortunately, she suggested that the letters that the children traced should be made of sandpaper, an impractical idea which fortunately has not caught the imagination of teachers. It would seem that Montessori did not like children with long fingernails! Perhaps if she had recommended using some form of cloth – a substance frequently used as a comforter – the idea might have been attractive. Another misuse of tracing involved the use of tracing paper. There are three disadvantages in this: it is difficult to use; the formation of the shapes of letters is distorted by an over attention to following the lines exactly, a distortion that does not occur when only the index finger is used because deviations from the exact shape are not recorded or noticeable; and the tracing paper itself tends to partially obscure vision.

LEARNING WORDS: CUT-OUT LETTERS AND OVER-WRITING

Although finger-tracing is something which should be encuraged whenever children are attempting to learn to recognise and eventually to spell words, there are other activities which follow on naturally. As the children develop an ability to formulate letter shapes they can be given, both as part of the development of handwriting skills, and as part of the effort to learn to recognise and reproduce words, exercise in writing over the letters in a word, using a soft graphite pencil. Also they can be encouraged to make up replicas of words using wooden cut-out letters, the type made from plywood and sold by Galt's of Cheadle (plastic letters are unpleasant to touch and sweet letters form part of the law of diminishing returns). First the wooden letters would be placed over the actual written letters, a close matching exercise, whilst after some practice the children would be able to select and arrange the wooden letters apart from the original written word. In this latter form of the exercise the children would have to carry in their minds, momentarily, the positioning of the letter as demanded by the word. Direct matching should be regarded as an easier first step than copying. In the former, self-checking is built into the whole exercise as it develops, whilst in the latter, things have to be carried in the mind and any self-checking follows the completion of the task.

All the activities associated with the teacher-led group composition of texts, followed by reading, as a group, those texts, as well as reading familiar nursery rhymes and folk tales, first as a group and subsequently individually, and all the word study exercises which emanated from those texts, should in the early stages be regarded as developing a closer and closer association in the minds of the children between texts and the themes of thoughts that already exist in their minds at the time of confrontation with those texts. The whole emphasis should be on studying – looking at and observing the actions of others whilst they are dealing with words and texts, and being shown how things synthesise. The direct analysis of words, the breaking up of words and the primary intention of looking for inter-word boundaries, should be delayed until the children have become familiar with the fact that correspondences do exist between words, that words can be segmented (as opposed to identifying in sound those segments), and that letters, groups of letters and words represent sounds that can be associated with the ideas that are in their minds.

The reasons for these assertions are manifold. At this early stage in the reception and middle classes of infant schools, children have a strong innate inclination to concentrate upon their immediate and specific activities. From Piaget (1953) we have seen how children centre upon what they are doing to the exclusion of all else and have a propensity to react intuitively to things in their environment. This would suggest the importance of basing language development and the teaching of reading and writing immediately upon the activities of children, and the modern British infant classroom is ideally organised to provide the opportunities to do this. Supplementary to this, we can use what children are largely familiar with and can recall at will: the nursery rhymes and folk tales. Where these are not familiar it could be argued strongly that teachers should give time to ensuring that they quickly become well known to the children.

A further reason is that children at this early stage find analysis of words a difficult thing to do (Roberts, T., 1975). Hence the need to use word cards and word exercises that require a synthetic approach rather than one which is analytical, remembering of course that in writing the children's dictated thoughts, as in Stauffer's language–experience approach and in writing out words that arise in any of the group composition sessions, the teacher is demonstrating, although not explaining, the constituent parts of words.

Finally, there are strong justifications for group reading. In the first place, it can be teacher-led and thus avoids failure by any of the children. Secondly, it provides opportunities for the children to observe the reactions of others, both teacher and children, and to learn from them; it gives children time to think. Thirdly, it allows for mistakes to be made openly and to be corrected either through the correct responses of the other children or by the teacher in a spirit of support rather than of correction. Hence the learner does not run the risk of feeling isolated in his difficulties. He sees others making mistakes and struggling to respond, and he witnesses these mistakes and difficulties being resolved. There is a further very important point: having practised reading a text as the member of a group, the individual child can proceed to practise the same reading behaviour on his own, confident that he will succeed. The behaviours acquired in group reading will act as an example for his subsequent behaviour and as pointers in the use of his skill.

Further reading:
For those who wish to make a detailed study of the skills of reading and writing, there are four very important works of reference:
Perera, K. (1984) *Children's Writing and Reading: Analysing Classroom Language.* Oxford: Blackwell,
which clearly explains the linguistic bases of reading and writing;
Gibson, E.J. and Levin, H. (1975) *The Psychology of Reading.* Cambridge, Mass: MIT,
which is an interpretation of much of the research done in the U.S.A. prior to 1976,
Coltheart, M. (ed.) (1987) *The Psychology of Reading.* London: Lawrence Erlbaum,
which describes and evaluates experiments in major areas of reading: and
Clark, M.M. (ed.) (1985) *New Directions in the Study of Reading.* London: Falmer Press,
which contains short but highly informative chapters by people who have a keen awareness of current trends in our thinking about language communication.

For some basic considerations in early word identification skills see two papers:
Ehri, L.C. and Roberts, K.T. (1979) Do beginners learn printed words better in context or in isolation? *Child Development.* 50, 675–85.
Ehri,L.C. and Wilce, L.S. (1980) Do beginners learn to read function words better in sentences or in lists? *Reading Research Quarterly,* 16, 452–76.

These two papers should be read alongside a chapter by:
Underwood, G. and J. (1986) Cognitive processes in reading and spelling, in A. Cashdan (ed.) *Literacy: Teaching and Learning Language Skills.* Oxford: Blackwell.

For a collection of games and exercises concerned with learning to read, there are two books by the same author:
Hughes, J.M. (1970) *Aids to Reading.* London: Evans.
Hughes, J.M. (1972) *Phonics and the Teaching of Reading.* London: Evans.
Furthermore, Scholastic Publishers have introduced a series of books under the general title, *Bright Ideas.* Students and newly qualified teachers will find the volume on reading – *Reading Activities* – extremely informative and useful, containing a wealth of ideas about exercises and games related to reading.

5 Teaching children to write: the early stages

Running alongside, and intermingled with, the work described in the previous chapter and continuing from the work described in chapter 3 will be the processes of teaching children to write.

Differences in spoken and written language

It is important to keep in mind that there are differences between speech and writing and that the influence of the former will constrain the development of the latter to some degree (Kroll, 1981, quotes evidence of this from several sources, amongst them Britton et al., 1975, Lundsteen, 1976, and Shaughnessy, 1977, and his model describes a developmental relationship between spoken and written language in which they begin as separate processes, come together as almost 'talk written down', are subsequently differentiated in the child's mind and eventually used discriminatingly in their various forms to meet a variety of situations).

In the first place there is the difference between the production of speech and writing. This difference has been clearly stated by Vygotsky (1962). In speech there is usually, although not in monologue, an interlocutor who responds to the speech as it emerges, either with interjections or periodic responses, or with body language in the form of facial expressions, movements of the head or changes in stance. These responses serve to encourage or deter the speaker and he in turn is able to adjust what he is saying as a response to the signals from the interlocutor. In writing, any response that the writer may receive usually comes after the completion of the task and may be minimal. For example, it is common practice for many teachers to respond to children's writing with simplistic remarks such as 'good', or 'good effort' (which means 'it is not very good but reasonable for you'), or even less effectually, merely by giving a numerical mark. Hence the writer has to rely largely upon his own motivational resources whilst writing.

This difference in the production, or motivational aspects, of the two activities can be mitigated to a certain extent in two ways. Piaget (1960) brought to our attention the part played by monologue in the young child's life – a form of speech which accompanies action and thought on the part of the child and which in some measure is akin to writing in that it does not rely upon an interlocutor. Obviously, monologue is allowed during children's play in nurseries and well run infant classes, but it has not been seen as being an essential link between social speech at one extreme and the individual pursuit of writing at the other extreme. During monologue the child is going some way towards the role of the writer; the only difference being that monologue is always connected with the immediate actions of the speaker whilst writing is, at best, one step removed from the writer's immediate actions. Nevertheless the linkage is there, so monologue should be seen as preparatory to story telling which in turn is one of the bases for writing. It should be encouraged through the provision of challenging play situations which need to be thought out in terms of constructional play, dramatic play, fantasy and problem solving. In this way, by providing the bases for monologue, the child will edge slowly towards anticipating his future role as a writer.

A further way in which the difficulty of the writer can be reduced is for the teacher to assume partially and intermittently the role of interlocutor. She can do this by intervening whilst the child is writing, reading what has been written up to that point and reacting to it in some way. The reaction may be in the form of agreement or disagreement with the written statement, it may be to suggest alternative ways of expressing the thoughts of the writer, or it may be to suggest or discuss what should come next. In other words the nature of the task of writing is altered so that it approximates in some measure to the nature of social speech. The child is given feedback during production rather than after its completion. New forms of spoken language are fed in as part of the composition of the text and ideas are turned into fresh forms of expression, so that there is development of spoken language hand in hand with the production of written language.

Yet the matter does not stop here. There is the added difference in the form of speech and writing. This the child will learn by several means. As he hears stories read to him and as he begins to read for himself he will gain a subconscious awareness of the differences in form. Similarly, through language-experience approaches he will see differences between his speech and what is transcribed for him. Thus the child will learn from seeing the teacher produce written language. Just as he has learned to speak in the presence of speakers, so he will learn to write in the presence of writers. Thus it is essential that the teacher writes for the children in their presence and that she calls attention to her writing. Writing on the blackboard, writing labels for classroom objects, writing under children's drawings, transcribing their oral stories, writing instructions and making work cards and, more importantly, actually writing stories and poems in the presence of a group of children, are all occasions when children will see teachers engaged in various aspects of the craft of writing. Graves (1983) pointedly remarks that 'we don't find many teachers of oil painting, piano, ceramics or drama who are not practitioners in their fields', and he goes on to say that in demonstrating their craft as writers teachers take the mystique out of writing and children cease to believe that writing is handed down 'like the Tablets'.

Although many of the suggestions made so far are implemented already in many schools, their importance needs to be emphasised and our objectives in using them need to be clarified so that what we do is explicit and pointed in its effects. A new step for many teachers, but one that is well worth taking, is to make group composition and construction of texts, with the teacher participating fully in the group, an essential element in the English syllabus. This activity will involve group discussion, individual oral contributions, further discussion, transcription into written form sometimes by the teacher and sometimes by each individual, followed by further discussion as to an acceptable written text, and a final review of the text. Through this process comparisons will arise between speech and writing; children will see the teacher make alterations to speech patterns that would be unacceptable as text. Furthermore, children will be introduced to the craft of writing through working with a craftsman. They will not be left to the difficult and haphazard task of learning to compose and construct texts in isolation.

A programme for the development of writing

THE COMPOSITION OF STORIES AND COMMUNICATIONS

A first consideration must be to foster and to practise an ability to think out stories, statements and descriptions as a mental exercise manifested in the form of spoken language. Teachers cannot assume a developed ability or a willingness on the part of children to do this. It is something that must be encouraged through the provision of 'props', through rewards for effort and through a general expectancy by the teacher that this is something that is done. 'Constructing stories in the mind – or storying, as it has been called – is one of the most fundamental means of making meaning' (Wells, 1987). In the early stages it will be a case of accepting the story as it emerges, but it is hoped that there will be developing during the junior school stage an ability to plan before writing. It will not be easy for teachers to foster this ability, and a determined and prolonged effort is essential. One device for achieving this is to ask children to say briefly what is in their mind and to insist on brevity. This has the effect of forcing children to commit themselves before presenting orally or in writing the elaborated message.

Thus there needs to be a basis upon which ideas can be composed. That basis may be an activity in or out of school: describing some process in art or craft, a team game or, even in the junior school, a mathematical process; it may be an experience in handling clay, scoring or missing a goal, hitting a rounder, dropping a catch, coping with frustration, or completing a task; or it may be the repetition or recall of a previously heard story. (Kress, 1982, shows how children call up plots and episodes from previous reading, and the example of a story by a five year old boy printed below shows that at that age they can integrate and synthesise past experiences of literature.)

It is not sufficient merely to give the name of a topic for the composition of an oral response; the source of the idea must be thought about by the children, discussed and thought about further. Many children will not be familiar with such intellectual pursuits and, therefore, it is necessary for the teacher to suggest how thoughts can develop and show by example how an activity, experience or story can be developed and how ideas can be put together with the resulting outcome of something that is interesting to hear. Patient work and persistence will be necessary and only through a great deal of encouragement will many children develop a facility for producing spoken language of the desired extended nature.

This preparatory work is essential, if one accepts Neisser's (1967) proposition that skilled writing results from 'thinking with a pencil in one's hand', as it leads to an ability to reflect, edit, revise and rewrite in order to achieve exactness. Admittedly, these activities will be more fully developed later on in the junior school, but the foundations must be laid early on, so that children develop a disposition and a propensity for the composition of a sequence of thoughts about a topic.

The following passage of transcribed speech and the way in which it was delivered suggest certain procedures that teachers could follow, and it shows the value of a background of experience of stories and their construction. It is an orally dictated story, told by Jonathan, aged five years and three months:

> Once upon a time there lived a king with a beautiful princess called Alaminta. One day a dragon came to the castle where Alaminta was playing by the fish pond with her brother. Her brother was called Brave Knight. He went in the castle and put a hat on his head and went to his father. He said, 'Father will you find some metal because I want to dress up as a knight?'. He rushed out in the garden with his Daddy's sword. He was astonished. There was a dragon with the princess. He drew his sword and started fighting. The battle began. All the other knights came out with their weapons, with shields and lances and swords and spears and bows and arrows and missiles. One knight was very brave and climbed on the dragon's back and took off his lance's case and he stuck his lance in the dragon. Alaminta dropped in the moat. All the knights made a boat called a submarine, and they started the engine and down they went to save Alaminta's life. They brought her back. The queen was very happy to hear the knight's news saving Alaminta's life from the dragon. One day Alaminta was very sad to see the dragon dead. She went to tell the knight with the lance that he was very mean to kill the dragon. The

queen came out and saw Alaminta crying because the dragon was dead. The queen took the dragon inside the castle and put a plaster on the dragon's back. The dragon was very happy when he was able to talk again.

This story was dictated to Jonathan's father, who was just beginning to learn to type at home. The father was not fully conversant with the keyboard so his typing was slow, and he continually got so far behind that he had to ask the child to stop and wait until he had caught up with the narration. Many people would have thought such breaks in the flow of the child's speech would inhibit him and jeopardize the sequence of the story. In fact the contrary was the case, and the father realised that what was happening in the breaks was that the child was thinking ahead and sub-vocally, as evidenced in grimaces and whispers, organising his thoughts and developing the story in his mind.

This example has important implications for teachers, many of whom have assumed too readily either that the thoughts would be there and would emerge instantly or that the thoughts were not there and would not emerge at all. Not only did the above instance prove this to be at least partially wrong, but also when we realise how newspaper columnists, novelists and other adult professional writers prepare, develop, edit, revise and rewrite their texts, it seems foolish that we do not accept that children need to learn to do this before they can produce anything worthwhile in terms of their ability. And when one thinks of children who lack basic ability, then the need for training over a prolonged period is all the greater!

Children must be required to think from the earliest school years about the stories that they are about to produce. This can best be done through the teacher waiting upon the child's story as was the case with the father and child above. The reason is that the very presence of the teacher waiting and listening will encourage the child to try to put in that little extra effort. A variation of this can be adapted from the interactive approach to storytelling of the Athabaskan speakers in Canada and Alaska (Scollon and Scollon, 1981) whereby listeners participate in the build-up of the story. Sulzby (1987) suggests that judicious interventions, designed to support the emergence of a story as the child is telling it, has a teaching effect in that it helps the child to learn how to maintain an oral monologue that is sufficiently clear for other children to understand and is thus in a form more closely akin to a written text. This helps in the development of a child's growing awareness of the difference between utterance and text (Olson, 1977).

Furthermore, if this story as it emerges is written on an overhead projector by the teacher in the presence of a group of children, they will witness the construction of a text which corresponds to what they hear from the storyteller, and this will give them excellent reading practice. Also they will be exercising their own thoughts on the topic of the story, and the storyteller will be responding to the audience. Thus they will receive the beginnings of a training in reading comprehension as well as in the composition and construction of texts.

Following the completion of the story, other members of the group can be encouraged to tell their version. Thus we can see the possibility of a snowball effect, each storyteller feeding upon the stories that have gone before, adding to them, altering them, improving them in some cases, but in any case benefiting from the models that have gone before and, hence, utilising a form of group interaction through the 'build-up' of thought. In this way we can see children's minds being exercised in the composition of trains of thought; they will experience how others are thinking about a topic, and they will be getting further practice in thinking that is abstract in nature. All of these are experiences which will complement those aspects of thought that Wells (1987) suggested were the product of hearing stories read by an adult.

The following stories were recorded orally on tape (unaided and unsupervised) at Brudenhall Infants School in Leeds some years ago. They are told by children from homes less educationally endowed than Jonathan's, and, in the case of Fakhara, by a child whose mother tongue was not English and who had been in England for less than a year. Nevertheless, these stories, recorded so that the head teacher could type them out and include them in each child's 'reading' book, show an emerging ability to weave a story.

Story told by Fakhara, aged five years and three months:

> Once there was a little boy. One day the little boy was in
> his house, he was sad because his little mouse was lost.
> His mum had gone out, so he went out too – went out –
> he went outside and he saw his little mouse and he was

pleased. He said yesterday to his mum, 'Can I play with my mouse again?', and then he was lost in a witch house. And next in the forest he was trying to find him quickly because the witch was coming. The witch saw the mouse, but then the mouse went out of the forest. When the boy got home he went in and saw the mouse. The little mouse said, 'We shouldn't go out, little boy,' so the little boy stayed home with his mouse and that was the end.

(Notice evidence of the range of thought even where the child does not develop those thoughts fully in language.)

Story told by Jane, aged five years:

There was three bears, mummy bear, daddy bear and baby bear. They all lived together. Mummy made some porridge. Daddy said it was too hot, and then mummy said it was too hot, then baby did, and daddy decided to go out while it was cold, while it went a bit cold. And then a girl come round and tried daddy bear's porridge, the mummy bear's and then the baby bear's. Then she tried daddy's bed, and then she tried mummy's bed, and baby's bed was just right. That was the end.

(Notice the economic use of language compared with the deliberate repetition of many reading books).

Story told by Wayne, aged four years and eight months:

Once upon a time there was a little boy. He had a rabbit. He said 'You are getting older. You will have to go tomorrow,' but the rabbit cried and cried. Tomorrow the rabbit got his clothes all packed and went. He said that he was going to East America. The boy said, 'I hope you enjoy yourself,' but Mother said, 'Mind you don't get killed.' He said, 'I might go to Jamaica. I might not go to America. If I don't go to America, I ring you.' So he ringed her and said he had gone to America. The first thing he did he went to a pub.

All of these stories bear evidence of potential for telling stories and varying degrees of understanding of the form that texts should assume.

As a form of comparison, and to show the extent to which a child's ability to compose a story is concealed when he has to write his story directly, the story in Figure 5.1 was written and illustrated by Jonathan, aged five and a half years, three months after he had told the Alaminta story.

Figure 5.1

VARIETY IN LANGUAGE

It is worth considering for a moment Halliday's model (Halliday, 1973) suggesting the seven uses of language: instrumental, to get things done and to achieve the satisfaction of material needs; regulatory, to control and regulate the behaviour of others; interactional, as between self and others; personal, as the expression of the speaker's individuality; heuristic, for the exploration of the environment and for learning; imaginative, for the creation of a world of the speaker's own making; and representational, for the expression of propositions. This list of the uses of language reminds us of the variety of experiences that are necessary if an adequate basis is to be laid for the complete development of language. It is not sufficient to provide for the development of some of the types of language; all must be developed if the child is to cope with the demands of later schooling and learning

Table 1, derived from Halliday's models, suggests that the primary school and its normal curriculum provide an ideal setting for the development of all forms of language.

Halliday's seven models	Intention	Subjects and aspects of the curriculum as bases for language experiences
Instrumental Regulatory Interactional	Social control Interaction; Communication	Small group work in art and crafts, play, hobbies, skill training for games and physical education, projects in history, geography etc.
Personal Heuristic	Self Exploration Environmental	Dramatic play; literature and poetry: reading and writing; mathematics, science, nature studies
Imaginative Representational	Creation of own world Communication of thoughts, ideas and information	Literature; dramatic play; oral and written composition. Research reports for topics of all kinds including science, nature study. Mathematics, history and geography.

Table 1: *Language across the curriculum*

It is necessary to utilise the stimulants for all-round language development that are provided by the modern primary school, whilst remembering that the provision of activities alone is not sufficient in itself to ensure progress in learning. Indeed, Katz (1977) has argued that many children suffer 'from insufficient adult help in making sense out of their rich environments'. There must be provision for specific and conscious learning through the actual teaching programme that is invoked, so that the children not only

produce appropriate language, written or spoken, but are consciously aware of what they are doing in terms of language. The
end product is important but its value in developmental terms will
be severely diminished if produced unconsciously, because the
child will not be aware of the use that he is making of language.

Finally, it must be remembered that there needs to be a recipient
or a purpose of which the speaker, or writer, is aware. Hartog and
Langdon (1907) reminded readers of this, except that in their case
they were referring only to writing. In the case of Jonathan and his
story of 'Alaminta', there were probably several purposes: to
provide his father with something to type, to please his father, and,
from the exuberance of the story, it was probably to satisfy the
child's desire, at that moment, to engage in an imaginative
adventure. Because of the lack of such intimacy in the classroom as
existed in the situation which produced 'Alaminta', it is all the
more necessary for teachers to be ever watchful for opportunities to
respond at all stages in the production of the children's thoughts,
either by responses, advice, interjections, contributions to the
theme, anything by way of reaction rather than no reaction. It is
only through such reactions that the desire to proceed is boosted
and encouraged. Those teachers who use some form of the
language-experience approaches to the teaching of reading will be
keenly aware of the effects of teacher response and of some form of
visible outcome to the spoken thoughts of children. Those who
enrich the school day with stories, well read and presented, will
know the effects this has in providing the children with models of
thought processes connected with the compilation of stories, and
they will be aware with Wells (1987) that they are helping the
children to think in the abstract, away from their immediate
environment. They are also familiarising the children with the
patterns of written language.

THE CONSTRUCTION OF TEXTS

A second consideration in a programme for the development of
writing is the promotion of actually writing down their thoughts.
Awareness of this process will have been started through the
experiences of the children with *Breakthrough* type activities and/or
other language experience approaches that are used in the very
early stages of learning to read. They will have witnessed teachers

constructing texts using either word cards or by writing words and texts under the drawings done by the children. They will have noted teachers writing labels for objects in the classroom, or providing explanatory notes to items on the interest table. This observational study of other people writing will have been supplemented by the children being allowed to try their hands at writing – apparently scribbling in the first place, with scribbles beginning to approximate more closely to written English as illustrated by Bissex (1980) and Clay (1983), and referred to in an earlier chapter. The writings and researches of Bissex and Clay encourage teachers to be less sceptical about the value of scribbling as a preliminary to writing.

Preparatory activities
As with learning every other skill, there must be a preparatory period during which the child engages in activities which will prepare him for the task of learning to perform handwriting. During this period the child must be given opportunities to handle objects, to manipulate them, and, eventually, to do so for particular purposes. These activities will include handling and manipulating toy cars, toy trains, dolls, dolls' clothes, playing with constructional toys – especially those involving the use of tools – playing with rods, blocks, counters or any other materials which can be handled and manipulated, and handling Plasticine, clay and sand. In all these activities the objective should be to encourage the children to control these objects and materials by using their hands. Placing a train on a railway track is not an easy operation for many infants; neither are the more involved tasks of dressing a doll, using a spanner in the constructional toys, constructing a precariously balanced building made from wooden blocks, making something from Lego, or performing the tasks of mother at a dolls' tea party. Skill develops over a period of time and although it can be hastened with practice, it cannot be taught in a trice. It must be given time to evolve.

As these activities proceed, gradually it will become obvious to the teacher that it is time to introduce actions which are more closely connected with the skill of handwriting. This is not to say that they should supercede the above activities, neither does it imply that they are more important. They are merely part of the developmental process in the acquisition of handwriting.

Finger tracing and the basic patterns

Perhaps the most important of these activities will be tracing with the forefinger in sand and in paint or glue. The movements in finger tracing should be free, bold and flowing, so that the child gets the full kinaesthetic sensation and enjoyment from the movement. The children should be encouraged to make the types of movement which are basic to our graphic system: anticlockwise and clockwise circular movements, humps, troughs, vertical and horizontal lines. All the letters fall into these five categories. The anticlockwise letters are a, c, d, e, g, o, q; the clockwise letters are b and p; the hump letters are h, m, n, r; the trough letters are u, v, w, y; and the line letters are f, i, j, k, l, t, z, plus some of those already included in the other categories. The letters x and s fall into the two categories of clockwise and anticlockwise. Obviously, therefore, the teacher will encourage such movements as those in Figure 5.2, which are basic to the formation of the various groups of letters.

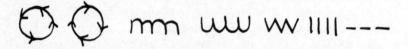

Figure 5.2

A development of this type of activity is tracing enlarged letters, either cut out of material stuck on card, or written with a felt pen in clear type. This type of activity should be done in very short sessions; perhaps as short as it takes to trace one letter half a dozen times, and certainly no longer than two or three minutes. It is extremely important to emphasise that the tracing is done with the forefinger. Tracing paper should not be used because its use will impede rather than enhance the learning process. After all, the sole purpose of tracing is to engage the tactile and kinaesthetic senses by making the child use the senses of touch and movement in his efforts to learn. Using a pencil or pen is one stage removed from direct touch, and it is impossible to move freely over a piece of tracing paper: the enveloping circular movement of an O becomes a hesitant when tracing paper is used.

Of course, alongside this there will be attempts by the teacher to show children how to formulate letters of the alphabet. This is best done in close relationship with the children's attempts to write messages. From these the child becomes more ego-involved in learning to formulate letters properly, because in this way he improves his own work and his standing as one who can write. At first it is wise to employ finger-tracing as a means of learning the movements necessary to produce a given letter. This avoids compounding the difficulty of the task by insisting that a pencil is used. However, do not overdo the practice, otherwise tedium sets in. What is required are short frequent practice sessions, so that the loss of learning between sessions is not excessive and there is positive reinforcement of learning (Reed, 1969).

Over-writing and copying
From finger tracing of words and sentences, will develop short exercises and tasks in over-writing words, such as labels on objects belonging to the child and on objects in his environment. Later the child will copy sentences onto the bottom of his drawings, and he will copy into his personal story book oral stories which he has composed and which the teacher has written out for him. And if he is fortunate enought to be learning to read through the construction of his own stories (Roberts, 1970), he will copy out the stories he has made with word cards.

A lot of the work during these early stages will be repetitive, but this need not deter the teacher. Children love repetition, provided that it is not imposed upon them for long periods. Usually it is safe to say that repetitive tasks should, where necessary, be initiated by the teacher, and the child should be allowed to drop the activity when he wishes. Nevertheless, there are occasions when it is necessary for the teacher to insist upon a little more persistence than the child is prepared to give voluntarily.

Within all of these activities, there are times when precise instruction is imperative if the child is going to make optimum progress. The child needs to be told and shown how the teacher can do these things, and this should be followed with help in actually doing it himself. Only by combining the two aspects of instruction will the child be able to understand what is required and what is involved in the accomplishment of the particular task. When he has received help, he will need the opportunity to practise the skill or part-skill that he has learned, so that the learning will be reinforced.

Letter formation

The most important thing to learn during the early stages of actual letter formation is the starting point for each letter. If the child acquires the habit of starting at a specific part of each letter, he will find the transfer from print to cursive writing much easier and he will develop more readily into a quick and legible writer. The start places, as described in Roberts (1972), are shown in Figure 5.3.

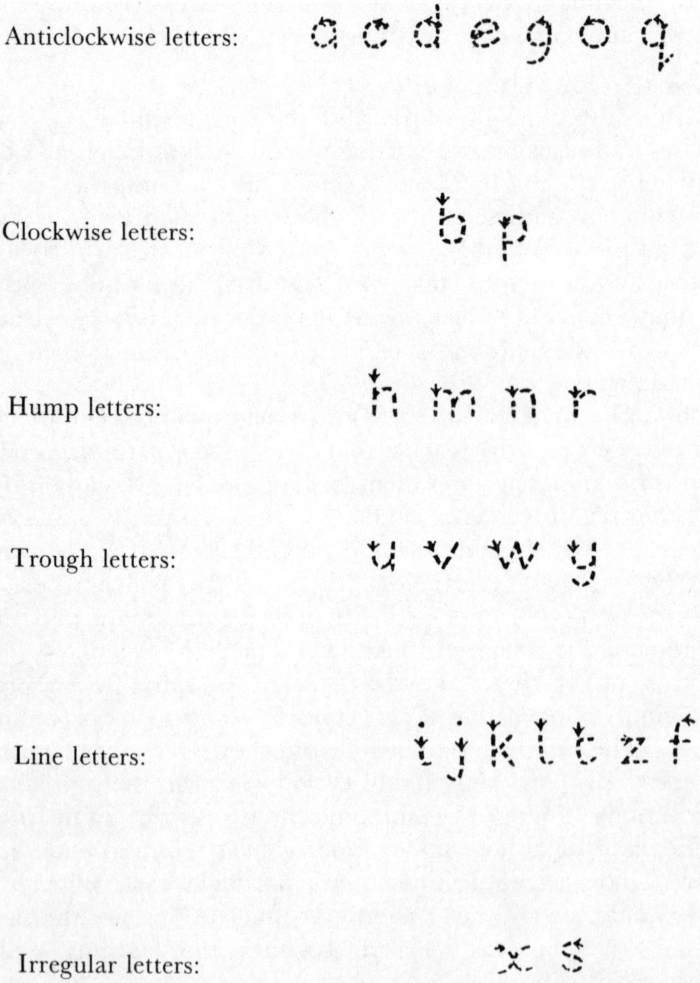

Anticlockwise letters: a c d e g o q

Clockwise letters: b p

Hump letters: h m n r

Trough letters: u v w y

Line letters: t j k l t z f

Irregular letters: x s

Figure 5.3

A useful device produced by the Learning Development Association which provides children with the opportunity to check the procedure they should use in forming the complex letters is shown below in Figure 5.4.

Figure 5.4

Posture for writing
When the children are developing some facility in the formation of letters, the teacher should begin to pay some attention to the sitting posture of the child. Handwriting is not a natural activity, and therefore it is not possible to assume that the child will automatically adopt the posture most conducive to the activity of writing. It is important that he should, because his posture determines his style to some extent. Hence the teacher should show the children how to sit and she should remind them of the correct position when they are writing. The guidance should not be too demanding and slight deviations should be allowed where the child appears to be developing his handwriting clearly and without impediment. Generally, the points to emphasise are that the child should sit well back on the chair, both feet together on the floor, body at an oblique angle to the paper, elbow of writing arm well in, and body at a slight angle to the perpendicular with the spine straight (too often these days children have to write at desks or tables that are either too high or too low in relation to the chair and the size of the child's body).

Naturally the teacher will avoid pestering the child unduly, but help given in an unobtrusive manner during the early stages will avoid later discomforture.

Sooner or later every teacher of infants has to decide whether or not to use lined paper. Recently the vogue has been to use plain paper for all types of practice in handwriting, but this hardly seems sensible. Few adults can write in an even and level form on plain paper! Yet lines can be inhibiting. So what is the teacher to do?

Like so much else connected with primary education the answer depends upon the immediate objectives. Plain paper is ideal for general practice with patterns and large letters during the very early stages. But lined paper – say one-inch lined – is useful when the child begins to write short stories. In the latter case, it would be unwise to emphasise the need to write exactly on the line; in fact the teacher could well be continually impressing upon the children that the lines are merely a rough guide, just as motorists use lane lines as a rough guide, some keeping nearer to the line than others. Occasionally, for very brief periods of practice, narrow lines could be used to control the size of the middle parts of letters, for example ‾‾bag‾‾ . This should not be laboured or overdone in any way; it should only be used to demonstrate and achieve some idea of the proportions of letters.

Connecting the letters

The change from separate letters to some form of connected handwriting usually occurs at the age of approximately nine years. There is no need to rush into this and there is no reason why all the class should transfer simultaneously, but when it does occur, the children should be helped by the teacher. They should be shown how she wishes them to make the connections between letters, and they should be required and encouraged to practise this for short periods. The old idea of complete uniformity in a cursive style has disappeared, and the uniformity of the italic and Marion Richardson styles is confined to a minority of enthusiasts. There is little to be said in support of uniformity, apart from an attractive appearance. The main criteria for a style of handwriting seems to be that it should be legible and that it should come easily to the individual child.

Thus the teacher should encourage each child to develop a style which to some extent evolves naturally, but she should frequently discuss this style with him. References should be made to clarity, shape, size and slope of letters.

Handwriting exercises should be periodically employed to remedy any malformations and to develop an easy flow, unimpeded by the constraints of story or other textual construction. The absence of any uniform style throughout the class or school should not deter the teacher from giving attention to the development of individual, legible and easy styles.

One further point about handwriting concerns the tools for the job and the use of those tools. No child can possibly attempt to formulate letters with pencils less than four inches long; every child should be shown how to hold a pencil for writing (so a fair proportion of trainee teachers need to re-learn how to hold a pencil) and should receive frequent reminders throughout the time spent in the primary school so that an easy unrestrained mode of writing is possible.

Initial steps towards spelling
From the reading and writing activities mentioned above there will gradually emerge some notions of spelling, such as those identified by Read (1971) and referred to in Chapter 3. This progress will continue beside the child's constant interactions with print, through looking at books, through seeing print around the classroom, through *Breakthrough* and language-experience activities, and through voluntary attempts to write. There seems to be little evidence, if any, that a more formal approach to spelling would be beneficial during the early stages in the infant school, because the nature of the task is too abstract to hold the attention of young children, and they would find the complexities of the spelling system bewildering. What can be done to some effect is for the teacher to take up those words which a child attempts to spell, write them out clearly with the child watching, encourage the child to trace (with the forefinger) or copy those words, and finally to have them readily available and to refer to them frequently during the day or days following the encounter with those words and, where appropriate, draw comparisons with other words that the child encounters. In this way the child is being taught to look at words, to make a conscious effort in doing so, and to draw comparisons between words which he has encountered and needed to use.

TENTATIVE STEPS IN COMPOSITION AND CONSTRUCTION

The activities mentioned so far in this chapter are an extension of the first item – preparation – in Kroll's developmental writing sequence (Kroll, 1981), and will be found mainly in the early and middle infant classes. There follows what Kroll describes as consolidation, where children express in writing what they can already express orally. This phase of development is associated with top infants and lower juniors. (Perera (1984) does not regard Kroll's phases as discrete and suggests that they should only be used as a rough guide to the possibilities for development, and as such, of course, they are very useful. Kroll, himself, points out that his model oversimplifies development and should not be regarded as unidimensional and strictly linear.)

There is a danger that newcomers to teaching will find this so-called period of consolidation somewhat perplexing. On the one hand there is the consideration that the sentence is the basis of written texts, whilst on the other hand children's language, at this point in their development, tends to be clausal in structure.

Children up to this point are well practised in informal spoken language, which, 'typically, is organised on the basis of clausal complexes that are not sentences. They may be long chains of clauses linked by co-ordination or simply by being adjoined. While the sentence typically is a structure of main and subordinated and embedded clauses, the clausal complex is typically an aggregate rather than a syntactic structure . . . Consequently, learning to write has some of the features of learning a second language, including the initial "interference" from the first language' (Kress, 1982). Given the different social, educational and language backgrounds of children, referred to in the work of the Newsons, Tough, and Bernstein, Kress goes on to stress that 'children come to the learning of writing from different starting points, some much closer than others to the syntax of writing [see Chapter 2 above], some much further away . . . Writing and speech have their own textual and generic forms, which differ in their structures and in their characteristic functions. These must be learned by the child as part of learning to write.'

Hence, the child must move from utterance to text (Olson, 1977) and all that that implies in learning to treat text not simply as speech written down but as something which has its own form.

Thus a course of development suggests itself, whereby children proceed through developments in patterns of speech, to writing down a representative form of those patterns, and finally learning to construct texts which are sentence based.

Too often in the past this has been left by teachers to develop spontaneously and unconsciously, primarily because it was not realised what was happening. Nowadays, teachers would look to promote and even to enhance this development.

This can be accomplished best through allowing the children to see their utterances converted into texts, and this is what happens in group work with the Teacher's Sentence Maker in *Breakthrough to Literacy*. The children make oral statements which are transposed into texts through the use of word cards by the teacher. A further development of this is the group construction of texts, first, and perhaps most aptly because of its clausal nature, through the group construction of poetry, as in the following poem *The Tiger*, produced by older infants under the guidance of a student teacher, Helen Amor:

> The Tiger
> Moving through the dark trees –
> A tiger!
> Orange, black and white stripes,
> Going to catch and kill something.
> It has sharp claws.
> It looks very scary.
> It has sharp jaws,
> And it runs very fast.
> It roars and pounces.
> Footsteps creaking on the leaves,
> Walking very slowly.
> It is going to kill an antelope.

Helen read Blake's poem *The Tyger* to a group of infants. Then together they thought of as many words as came to mind as a result of hearing the poem. She then wrote the first two lines on a blackboard and the children supplied the rest of the text. Note the short staccato statements gradually giving way to a developing theme, showing the impact of that emerging theme upon the structure of the text. The children's part of the poem begins in a descriptive vein and then moves to a narrative theme. Thus, whilst

Sentence

one admires the variety and balance of the poem, it clearly
illustrates how these children, in a state of transition from reliance
upon utterance to an understanding and use of text, are constrained by their thoughts. If their thoughts are upon discrete
pickings from the subject matter then the structure of what they
produce reflects that discreteness. And as a theme develops so a
different language structure emerges. Hence the possibilities for the
group construction of prose texts, provided the subject matter
engenders appropriate trains of thought.

Kress (1982) suggests that learning to write is all about
establishing what a sentence is about, and Streng et al. (1978) states
that 'a child who has not internalised the rules of basic sentence
patterns really cannot read, although he may be able to associate a
written word with an object or a picture'. Obviously these rules of
sentence structure cannot be explained to young children, but they
can witness the formation of sentences as the teacher purposefully
and deliberately transforms their utterances into the acceptable
form of texts, keeping as close as possible to the thoughts of the
child but not necessarily retaining that child's exact wording. Thus
the children will hear what the child says yet see what the teacher
writes. In this way the children will be able to begin to draw
comparisons between their actual speech and the form it must take
when transposed into writing. This is another instance where
learning may take place most effectively through the opportunities
provided for the child to emulate the teacher. (This is one of the
major reasons why teachers should sensitise themselves to their
impact upon children by continuously evaluating their performance in terms of the response they get to their teaching.)

As the children develop their abilities to construct texts many of
these group composition and construction sessions should be
followed up by requiring the children to reproduce the text on their
own, and the teacher should then mark it with a view to imprinting
upon the child's text, and therefore upon that child's consciousness,
an acceptable adaptation to a sentence based structure. She can do
this by elaborating upon any clausal structures that may have
reappeared in the child's version of the text, putting in the
punctuation of capitals and full stops and by adding appropriate
connecting words. Children during these early stages will write in
lines, but occasionally they will overrun the line and in this way
they indicate that they are experimenting with line/sentence

formation and beginning to approximate to the sentence structure of text. By noting this overrunning of the line and commenting upon it approvingly the teacher encourages the child's tentative moves.

An additional activity is one in which the child is encouraged to solve the problem of jumbled strips of card, each card containing phrases or clauses that can be arranged so that they form a complex sentence. For example:

1 | The boy and girl
sat together
but they were not friends.

2 | The dog
who was very cold
sneaked into the sitting room
and lay by the fire.

3 | The big red double decker bus
which was taking us to the baths
swerved to miss a dog
which ran across the road.

4 | The boy
who was a stranger
went into the shop
and
opening the till
took the money.

5 | When we saw the policeman coming
we began to run away
dodging through the alley ways
although we had done nothing wrong.

(NB The capital letter and the full stop indicate to the knowledgeable the beginning and the end of the sentence.)

Naturally only the knowledge and sensitivity of the teacher can adjust these mini-stories to suit the abilities of the class, and at first many children will experience difficulty if these sequencing exercises are not done as a group activity, with the teacher playing a prominent part. The objective should not be to test the children but to allow them to participate in a problem solving exercise, possibly merely as spectators in the first instance, so that they can gain a growing awareness of what is possible with language. As the children's ability increases they will be able to do these exercises alone and the complexity of these exercises can be increased accordingly.

As an illustration of the need to adjust to different levels of ability and to different experiences Jane Brook, practising with a class of middle and top infants, made the following distinction. The middle infants, having participated in a project concerned with the story of Cinderella, were given the following three sequencing exercises, the cards in each instance being presented in random array:

1	"Fetch me two lizards", said the Fairy Godmother.	Cinderella brought two lizards.
	The Fairy Godmother waved a magic wand.	The two lizards turned into footmen.

2	Cinderella was dressed in rags.	She wanted a pretty dress to wear to the ball.
	The Fairy Godmother waved her magic wand.	Cinderella's rags turned into a lovely ball gown.

3	"Bring me a pumpkin" said the Fairy Godmother.	Cinderella fetched the pumpkin.
	The Fairy Godmother waved her magic wand.	The pumpkin turned into a coach.

These exercises were done after recalling the story of Cinderella and were carried out in a cooperative spirit, so that any child in doubt could seek advice from those around, including the teacher.

The upper infants would have found this exercise very easy, so they were given a more challenging sequence based on a folk story heard but not much dwelt upon. The cards were of the following kind where the order was somewhat ambiguous and thus led to discussion.

1 | The ugly duckling lay
in the reeds by the river. |

2 | He was very sad. All the other animals
laughed at him. |

3 | The ugly duckling ran away
and hid all winter long. |

In these activities we see a development parallel to that which occurs in spoken language. Just as we attempt to teach children to express themselves through speech that can be understood universally and which thereby approximates more closely to the syntax of writing, so we show children how to express themselves through text in ways which are divorced from the replication of sub-vocalised speech patterns. Just as there is a developing adjustment between the speech or sub-vocal patterns and the thoughts of a child that are particular to different situations and relationships, so there must be developing some degree of separation betwen the two in the production of texts, so that the writer can become detached from those patterns in order to produce different patterns, ones based upon a sentence structure rather than a clausal complex.

Naturally, in all this the teacher will be sensitive to the possibility of overdoing the pressure on the child to produce patterns of written language that do not initially come easily to him, but the very fact that they do not come easily suggests the child's need for help and guidance. So long as the teacher employs a study approach rather than an instructional–testing approach, the dangers are minimised.

Implications for teachers

As a guide to young teachers the following summary of the implications of all this should prove useful:

1 The importance of developing a string of ideas clearly in the minds of the children and demonstrating the transposition of these ideas into texts using the group as the teaching unit and not in the first instance the individual child. This enables each

child to witness the growth of a text.

2   The futility of over stressing 'correct' punctuation too early, but, nevertheless, the need to use the opportunity to prepare the children for the eventual use of punctuation by noting its existence in texts produced by the group and in books which they are using in learning to read.

3   The part to be played by the teacher in amending texts produced by children individually, including the imposition of a rudimentary form of punctuation, all to be done with a gradualness that will not overwhelm the child but which will nevertheless allow the child to see and learn what has to be done.

These three points are encapsulated in the statement by Kress (1982) that 'the most potent factors in the child's learning of writing are the models of written language which the school provides, and which it encourages the children to emulate.'

Supplementary activities to promote composition and the development of themes

Whilst all that has gone before in this chapter should be regarded as the basis for teaching children to write, there are many contexts in which this can be done. The majority of these centre upon group work, with no more than six children per group, so that each child has ample opportunities to participate.

Most of these activities are concerned with promoting and developing a theme by a group of children with the teacher in a supportive role. The texts which emerge are then dealt with sometimes on a group basis and sometimes on an individual basis.

Perhaps of all the activities that spring to mind the most basic is that of extracting a story from a wordless picture book, orally in the first place and subsequently transposing this into a text. A good example of what is required is a collection of books published by William Collins, of which *Rain* by Peter Spier is an excellent example. This book has a brief synopsis on the back cover and it can be used in three ways: to formulate a story from the pictures; to extend the synopsis using the pictures as a guide (this particular use of the book would be more appropriate with lower juniors); and as a discussion document whereby the children determine what each picture depicts. Another such book is *The Hunter and the Animals* by Tomie de Paola, published by Anderson.

A further development of this idea but with the emphasis on divergent rather than on convergent thinking was employed through the use of *Tom Badger Goes Skating* by Jean Gilder. Reading this story to a group of top infants, the teacher allowed opportunities for participation: for example, discussions of what happens in the seasons; what happens to Tom as he approaches the broken ice; what is and is not good behaviour – Tom's bullying compared with the children's help in retrieving him from the pond. This particular lesson was seen as part of the religious and moral development of the children, but it was equally an English lesson in which children were taught to react to a story, to analyse a situation, to consider the practical implications of a text and to formulate and realise thoughts emanating from the story.

Other activities of a somewhat similar nature, but less constrained in context and more abstract in nature, consist of developing a theme from two or three related pictures, composing a story from a series of highly evocative words – the type of high information words that could have formed the basis of the old fashioned telegram, for example, *bird, broken wing, cat, saved,* or *child, climbing, fell, cried*. Similar activities can be found amongst computer programmes like *Concept Keyboard* and others which present words categorised by a theme, which the children construct as with the *Breakthrough* cards.

Finally, one must not underestimate the effects of the class or group project upon children's ability to formulate themes or streams of connected thoughts. The following can act as a model for the development of language through a central topic. It was implemented by a student, Mrs Laura Theophilus, practising in a school in Gloucester.

The topic was *Night,* and it consisted of three elements: nocturnal animals, people who work at night, and Bonfire Night. Each item and its subsections were initiated as small group exercises. Individual work followed and finally the work was formulated for display by the groups.

An outline of the work done for the project is shown below.

1   Nocturnal animals

Group 1, Hedgehogs – story composed by the teacher with pictures and photographs;
– poems about hedgehogs, with interjections by children to both the story and the poems being taken up by the teacher as a serious contribution;
– word study whereby the children contributed *small, prickly, hibernate* as words relating to a hedgehog;
– phonic awareness which involved the search for words beginning with *h* and the construction of an *h* list;
– art and craft which consisted of a group discussion about a model garden with undergrowth and a hedgehog, its construction as a group participatory exercise, followed by opportunities for the other groups to comment upon and discuss the finished display;
– written work concerned with a description of, or a story about, the hedgehog.

Group 2, Owls   – story called 'Wise Old Owls'
– poem, 'The Owl and the Pussy Cat';
– word study: *hoot, claws, beak*
– phonic awareness: *ow* words;
– art and craft: a wall frieze of a night scene superimposed upon which were the children's cut-out owls and stars (the teacher had encouraged the children to get their parents to take them out after dark to look at the night sky);
– written work about owls

Group 3, Cats   – a similar pattern was followed as in the case of hedgehogs and owls. The emphasis in the language was more specific, concentrating upon the movement of cats, because it was thought that the children would be more familiar with cats than with hedgehogs and owls. The art and craft consisted of Plasticine models and drawings depicting the movement of cats. (It was interesting to compare the ability of a child to depict movement through drawing or modelling and his ability to describe that movement.)

During and following the completion of the work of the three groups there was a considerable amount of cross-group interest in various aspects of the work, and the teacher took advantage of this to avoid constraining the word study to each particular group. Hence all the children eventually encountered the words studied and the phonic awareness lists. The motivation was not always at its peak, but the inquisitiveness of young children compensated to some extent. Furthermore, this work provided the basis for counting and number exercises – counting the owls and the stars etc. – and environmental and nature study connected with the lives of the animals and their habitats.

2   People who work at night
Here the sequence of activities and the organisation was different from that used to study nocturnal animals. Three familiar neighbourhood occupations were chosen and following a general class discussion about a representative of each occupation – a nurse, a policeman and a fireman – the children were encouraged to ask their parents about the work of each of these people. This was followed by a visit from a nurse in full regalia and visits by the class to a police station and a fire station. Before each visit the children were alerted to some of the things to look for and questions to ask, and after each visit there followed:

– word study in which the children contributed ideas about what each of the three people – nurse, policeman and fireman – did;
– phonic awareness, whereby words were selected from the above discussion and written on cards depicting the pronounceable elements within the words, eg

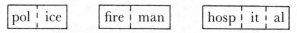

– mapping out a written text, as a group for some of the children and individually in the case of others;

– completion of writing;
– art and craft, consisting of the creation of a hospital centre in the classroom with various artefacts brought by the children, and contributions to wall displays for each of the occupations.

3　Bonfire Night

Advantage was taken of the build-up of excitement and expectancy *before* the event. Children were told the story of Guy Fawkes, and they learnt the poem 'Remember Remember the Fifth of November'. Discussion centred round the dangers and the care to be taken.

On the next day after Bonfire Night, whilst it was fresh in the memory, discussion in groups took place concerning the noise words connected with the festivities (word study) and lists of colour words were drawn up – the children suggesting the words and the teacher writing them down. Gradually some of the discussions began to link colours with feelings, red the colour of fire and danger, darkness and blackness with mystery and fear, and white sparkling stars with beauty. These colours were prominently displayed in the wall frieze made by the children, and the feelings associated with them began to appear in the children's writing. Finally, the class moved on to consider candles which were lit by the teacher, and discussion began about the flames, a topic which never fails to arouse interest and usually stimulates the imagination. In this case the children's imaginations ranged more widely than usual, probably under the stimulus provided by Bonfire Night. A series of experiments was carried out and some good descriptive language was used in subsequent discussions of these experiments.

This project is offered as an indication of the possibilities of extending the imaginative, and to some extent the abstract thinking of children, together with word and language study, in an engrossing and integrative manner. Although done originally with infants, a similar project with minor alterations of content could be used at any stage in the junior school. Its advantages were that otherwise tedious tasks, such as the various aspects of word study, could be accomplished within an interesting context which held the children's attention and allowed them to see words in a language setting which was meaningful to them.

Attainment targets and levels, key stage 1 (5–7 year olds)

Much still has to be done to develop children's ability to write beyond the infant school and consideration will be given to this much neglected area in Chapter 8. The Report of the Committee of Inquiry into the Teaching of English Language (DES, 1988) suggested targets of development in English for three age levels, seven, eleven and sixteen.

This report was followed by a report of the National Curriculum English Working Group (November, 1988) which proposed levels of attainment and programmes of study. After statutory consultations with interested bodies the National Curriculum Council itself produced a revised version (March, 1989) of the Working Group's proposals and the Secretary of State for Education and Science is preparing to set before Parliament Orders largely based upon the document of March, 1989.

The Secretary of State's proposed draft Orders, which cover Key Stage 1, ages five to seve, have again been sent out to various bodies for comment. They cover five targets: speaking and listening, reading, writing, spelling, and handwriting. There are three levels of attainment, which are summarised below.

At level 1 in speaking and listening pupils should be able to participate as speakers, listen attentively and respond to simple instructions. In reading they should be able to recognise that print carries meaning; begin to recognise individual words or letters in familiar contexts; show signs of developing interest in reading; and begin to talk about the content of stories and non-fiction books. In writing they should be able to use pictures, symbols or isolated letters, words or phrases to communicate meaning. In spelling children should begin to show an understanding of the difference between drawing and writing and between numbers and writing; write some letter shapes in response to speech sounds and letter names; and use at least single letters or groups of letters to represent whole words or parts of words, whilst in handwriting pupils should begin to form letters with some control.

At level 2 pupils should participate as speakers and listeners in a group engaged upon a prescribed task; describe an event, listen attentively to stories and poems and talk about them; talk to the teacher; listen and ask and answer questions; and respond to more complex instructions. They should read straightforward signs, labels and notices; have a working knowledge of alphabetic order; use a combination of pictures and context cues, sight words and phonic cues in reading; recall a story just read and predict what will happen next; respond to stories in an informed way; and read with increasing independence and skill a range of appropriate material. When writing pupils should produce short texts containing complete sentences, some punctuated with capitals, full stops or question marks; describe coherently and chronologically real or imagined events – displaying understanding of the rudiments of story structure; and produce simple non-chronological writing. Children should be able to produce recognisable, though not necessarily always correct, spelling of a range of common words; spell correctly common monosyllabic words which they use regularly; begin to show knowledge of spelling patterns in their attempts to write words unaided; and show knowledge of the alphabet. Their handwriting should enable them to produce legible upper and lower case letters in one style correctly oriented.

Level 3 requires pupils to relate orally real or imaginary events in a connected, meaningful narrative; convey accurately a simple message; listen, question and respond to other children and adults; and give and react accurately to precise instructions. Stories and poems should be read fluently and meaningfully; whilst children should read silently with sustained concentration, they should show interest in stories and show an ability to recall and discuss setting, plot and characters, including the use of inference, deduction and previous experience in the appreciation of texts which go beyond the literal, thus indicating some understanding of structure. In addition they should show, through reasoned questions, an ability to select and use reference books according to appropriate criteria. In their writing, children at level 3 should produce independently longer pieces of writing using complete sentences, reasonably punctuated with capitals, full stops or question marks, begin to use a wider range of sentence connectives than 'and' and 'then', such as 'but', 'when', 'after'; write more complex stories with a defined ending; produce a wider range of types of non-chronological writing; and begin revising, redrafting and checking for correct and consistent use of tenses and pronouns amongst other things. In spelling children should be able to spell correctly common polysyllabic words; recognise and use correctly regular patterns for vowel sounds and common letter strings of increasing complexity; become aware of word families, and begin to check the accuracy of their spelling. Their handwriting at this level should approximate to a clear and legible cursive style.

Accompanying these levels of attainment will be programmes of study. These will be issued to all teachers and they should be studied in conjunction with arguments of this book so that in instituting the National Curriculum, which teachers will be required to do by law, sight will not be lost of the underlying principles of teaching children in an enlightened manner to read and to write and to communicate effectively and confidently.

Further reading
It is imperative that those teachers who wish to understand more fully the ways in which children's writing develops should read:
Kress, G. (1982) *Learning to Write*. London: Routledge and Kegan Paul.
This book produces analyses of texts written by children and suggests ways of promoting development and of correcting scripts. In conjunction with Kress's book, it is also necessary for intending specialists in children's writing to study:
Perera, K. (1984) *Children's Writing and Reading*. *Oxford*: Blackwell in association with Andre Deutsch,
and to pay particular attention to the discussion in Chapter 4 of the differences between speech and writing, and to Perera's recommendations concerning the implications for teachers. The study of these two books alone will contribute significantly to a teacher's understanding of children's writing.

Those who intend to teach infants should read:
Clay, M.M. (1975) *What Did I Write?*. Auckland: Heinemann.
This book shows the progressive development of children's writing, whilst
Marshall, S. (1974) *Creative Writing*. London: Macmillan,
gives sound general advice on the motivation of children and the promotion of writing.

PART IV
THE DEVELOPMENT OF
READING AND WRITING

6 The development of reading ability

Word identification behaviour

Throughout the preparation for learning to read, referred to in earlier chapters, the teacher will have been creating a disposition in each child to look for the basic elements that form part of reading and to draw appropriate comparisons between what he sees before him and what he has already learned and knows. He will be looking for words within sentences from his experience with the *Breakthrough Teacher's Sentence Maker,* and he will be noting similarities between words, such as common initial letters and even common letter patterns. He will be acquiring both consciously and subconsciously a growing awareness of the relationship between the spelling and the sound system of English.

In this chapter I wish to deal with the further development of this particular behaviour, the full significance of which is something that has not been properly recognised before. It is not the simple matter it seems to be of teaching the word and letter elements of the language, because much more is involved, even in straightforward word identification. Children must be taught to actively engage in the search for, and the comparison of, elements. Hence, they must acquire a set for seeking out the boundaries within written language: the words within a phrase or sentence; the unitary and sequential nature of word strings in their clausal form and subsequently in the form of sentences; and, finally, boundaries within words. These can be both graphemic boundaries, such as blends (*bl-, tr-, -ld, -mp* etc.) and letter strings (*str-, -ight, spl-,* etc.), and spelling patterns, especially the basic patterns as defined by Fries (1964):

1 (c)vc: *at, bat, that, bath, all, back, span, clang;*
2 marker e: *bad, bade; pip, pipe; grip, gripe; strip, stripe; tub, tube;*

	hop, hope;
3 /e/, /iː/:	bet, beat; best, beast;
/æ/,/ei/ :	bat, bait; pan, pain;
/ɔ/ ,/ou/ :	rod, road; got, goat.

4 minor patterns: *shot, shoot; wood, stood, blood.*

Children must be brought face to face with all these elements that are found within words, and they must experience the sound values that may be attached to them in a natural way. A word must not be split up vocally in an analytical way, because that leads to distortion (ber-ar-ter for *bat*), but compared naturally with one or two other words – *bat, bad, cat; tree, trip; strong, string; splash, split; fight, light* – by looking at them and learning them pronounced as normal words. Then having determined the boundaries, recognition of what lies within those boundaries will depend upon the child's willingness to reflect upon what he knows that is relevant to recognition. This will involve recalling similar or near similar instances. It involves activating the memory and searching for a possible solution. This is not the type of behaviour in which we should expect the untrained child to engage readily; it is a mode of functioning which he may do in a subconscious manner but only to a slight degree. Teachers need to foster active searching behaviour as a developing habit and skill. Children should be challenged to recall past experiences with words and language, to draw comparisons and to use everything around them, such as wall charts, previous writing and reading materials. This form of mental behaviour is an acquired and highly developed habit and skill in adults but this is not the case in young children. It is an activity that they could find bewildering or unintelligible if explained to them didactically. Hence we are back again to a basic procedure in teaching: namely, of showing the child how it is done rather than explaining what it is that they should be looking for. To this end the teacher should be ever vigilant for opportunities to refer back to words and phrases that have gone before and to draw comparisons. In this way, for example, the child, confronted with the word *fight* which he does not recognise, should be shown by the teacher where he can find a previously known and recognised word, such as *light*, which has quite a lot in common with the word *fight*, both visually and phonically. From this the child will begin to recognise boundaries for himself – in this case the boundary between the initial consonant and the letter string *ight*.

It is this aspect of the teaching of reading that has escaped discussion in the past. There has been an over-concentration on the facts that have to be learned and too little attention given to the forms of behaviour necessary to retrieve those facts, and this omission on the part of teachers could prove to be a source of difficulties in learning to read. Facts can be 'drummed in' by a variety of reinforcement techniques, but it is not always easy for children to learn how to use those facts.

For example, it would be possible to teach a pigeon to recognise the letters of the alphabet by Skinnerian methods of reinforcement, whereby when shown a letter *A* it would immediately raise its left outside claw, knowing from painful past experience, that if it did not do so it could expect an electric shock in that claw, and similarly with other letters of the alphabet. (I suppose the only difficulty would arise when we had run out of claws.) However, the point I want to make is that it is not impossible to teach recognition of the letters and of grapheme–phoneme correspondences. What would be difficult would be to get the pigeon to understand what use to make of them. We have all encountered children who recognise and can attach sounds to the letters of a word yet cannot make up the sound of that word because they have not acquired the twin skills of blending the letters together into larger units within the word and searching their memory for a word which some or all of the sounds of that word suggest. They are not prepared to work at the identification of that word; they will pronouce the letter sounds individually and if the sound of the word does not occur to them immediately then they admit defeat. An important element in teaching is to inculcate in children a disposition for searching for clues, dwelling upon them and relating them to the known facts and learnt information, just as adults when doing a crossword dwell upon the clues in those instances where the answer is not immediately obvious.

This procedure is made much easier when the word that is the source of difficulty stands in a meaningful sentence, ie a sentence which makes a degree of sense to the reader. In that case the reader has a context from which he can draw upon semantic cues. These, when related to even small parts of the difficult word, help to make those parts suggestive of the actual word. This is the justification for Smith's statement that a person can only learn to read by reading (Smith, 1971). What he meant was that reading is a complex skill. It involves the use of many different cues – different in kind, such as semantic, syntactic and phono-graphemic, as well as in their form, for example, letter, letter string, or spelling pattern – and the performance of certain behaviours appropriate to the recognition and interpretation of texts. All these have their part to play, so that each contributes to the process of reading. Any fragmentation here detracts from the process and distorts it. Hence a child confronted by an unfamiliar and unknown word in isolation and out of any meaningful context is faced with a very different problem from that which would face him if the same word were placed in a meaningful text or a known context.

THE IDENTIFICATION OF WORDS STANDING IN ISOLATION

When confronted by an unfamiliar word standing in isolation, the child must look for boundaries within that word and do two things in the first place. He must search for spelling patterns, which, as Carol Chomsky (1970) has argued, carry the meaning in English (*heard*, is meaningful when compared visually with *hear* and *ear* but not if it is compared with those words in terms of sound), to see if these suggest some similar known word. He must also search for sounds, suggested by the letter formations, which give rise to notions of what the total word could sound like. Thus he may get various indications from different cues and different parts of the word, and these have to be considered in relation to one another and in relation to known words that may be indicated by some or all of the cues. Hence word analysis and identification requires an experimental, problem-solving approach in which various hypotheses are set up and tested. The question is how is this to be achieved?

Again it must be reiterated that this cannot be satisfactorily achieved by telling young children what to do. It can only be achieved through their seeing others do it and by practising it in the course of their encounters with words. Children must learn these behaviours through participating with the teacher or parent in analysing words and resolving their identity. For this reason, not only should teachers help or even take the initiative in sounding a word, they should draw comparisons with familiar recently learned words that have some similarity with the problem word by writing that learnt word again and indicating points of comparison. Colours may be used to emphasise or illustrate boundaries. For example, the *ight* in fight (unknown) and in *light* (known and recalled) could be written in red or underlined in red. Highlighting felt pens are even more effective. Such actions by teachers will indicate to children the elements within words as they see them, and eventually each child will acquire the habit of actively searching for elements that have some meaning for him simply by practising that habit.

Obviously this approach with words standing in isolation is not something that should be used in the very early stages of learning to read, simply because it requires too much of the child. It assumes he is capable, to some extent, of determining boundaries of different kinds within words and of considerable powers of thought in relation to an abstract intellectual activity. To identify an isolated unfamiliar word is an intellectual feat. It depends upon knowledge of grapheme–phoneme correspondences and all that means in terms of identifying boundaries within words; upon an ability to use the graphemic patterns to generate meaning from an internal lexicon; in most cases to associate both sources; and finally, to come up with a pronounced word which conveys meaning to the child. However, it is something that children need to learn, and the suggestion is that it is something that needs to be taught, not as the main approach to word identification but as an additional approach to that done through words in context, and one that should gradually be initiated once the child shows some facility for recognising words in context.

The half-sample of the experiment conducted by Ehri and Wilce (1980), which studied function words (*gave, might, very, while, which, must, both, from, should, enough*) in unstructured lists and then listened to sentences containing the words, remembered the orthographic identities better and could pronounce the words faster and more accurately in isolation than the half-sample who had studied the words embedded in sentences. This latter half-sample, on the other hand, learned more about the syntactic/semantic identities of function words, hence the value of a combination of these two approaches.

A Programme of Development

We can see in all this a developmental sequence in the acquisition of skilled behaviour in reading. Children have to learn certain behaviours and acquire certain habits in relation to the acquisition of responses to elements of written English. They have to solve a variety of problems, and they have to learn how to set about doing this.

In earlier chapters, we saw how children looked at print whilst adults read to them or labelled things. These activities indicated that print conveyed a message, and the children began to learn that print was associated with spoken language. Eventually they began to acquire the notion that there was a corresponding sequence between thought, speech and print.

Subsequently, they witnessed their own thoughts, frequently emanating from their actions or experiences, conveyed through speech and formulated as a text, either through the use of word cards (viz. *Breakthrough Sentence Maker*) or through the teacher transcribing what was said, as in the language-experience approach (Stauffer, 1970). They also saw that their own chants, rhymes, riddles and jingles could be represented in printed form (nursery rhymes, etc.).

From all of these activities in which they could observe and imitate superficially the behaviour of the teacher, they began to look at the details of the texts more and more closely. They became aware of words as discrete elements; they began to learn to compare words and thereby to discover the various elements in all their variety within words; and thus they began to learn the behaviours necessary for word identification. This was done with words whose meaning and context was known to them, so that words were not seen as something divorced from a context that was occupying their minds at that moment.

Gradually, work concerned with the texts increased so that children were required to take the initiative in drawing comparisons between words, searching out comparable or contrasting words, noting common phrases. They began to refer to the teacher's word charts containing word families, all based on the elements of words referred to in Chapter 4 above, to compare rhyming words in the nursery rhymes, and to pick out common phrases, such as *once upon a time, there once was. . .*, noting the words within those phrases and realising that they could be read quickly 'without hardly looking'.

From all this then, children would soon come to realise that reading was all about making sense of what was written, and so would begin to learn that part of reading behaviour was to think about what was read through having to read aloud. Faced with an unfamiliar word found amongst others that were familiar, the child would be encouraged to think what it could be and subsequently to check his 'guess' against a reiteration of the known text and finally against his, albeit, limited powers of word identification. Questions would be asked, such as: Does any part of the word remind you of another word? Can you pick up any sounds from parts of the word that suggest a word that you know? What sound do you think it begins with? Does this sound suggest any word you know?; and other such questions which instigate searching behaviour.

WORD IDENTIFICATION

At approximately this stage, with the child having acquired a reasonable sight vocabulary – enough to cope independently with the more common nursery rhymes and the introductory books of any reading scheme – there would be provision for a more systematic look at many of those words that he already knows, and words with some elements within them that correspond to those words would be introduced. For example, a list of *ight* words, *-ow* words, the blends and digraphs and common letter strings such as *-able, -tle,* etc. would be built up, in each case taking words that are known and adding new words (making sure, of course, that the new words are familiar in meaning by introducing them in a meaningful context). At the same time new words that arise should be related to familiar recognisable words of a corresponding or similar construction. In both cases it is a vital feature of the teaching strategy that there is always the known element against which the unknown can be matched.

In suggesting that a more systematic approach to word identification should emerge as the child shows some signs of developing reading ability, it is not envisaged that this should amount to a formal programme covering various aspects of word recognition carried out separately from the child's reading. Rather, the intention would be for the teacher to look for opportunities to attach some teaching in word identification behaviour to the child's normal reading programme. For example, with the list of the elements of reading described in Chapter 4 in mind, the teacher would look at what a child would be reading next and pick out one of those elements, write separately the word containing that element on a pad and produce or help the child to produce some corresponding words, as was the case with the word *fight* above. With an adequate system of recording, all the elements would be covered eventually, but they will have emerged in an order dictated more by the child's reading programme and the teacher's estimation of the child's capabilities than by some hierarchical sequence.

A word of caution is necessary here. The newly trained teacher should not be misled into thinking that once taught something the child will have learned it sufficiently to retain and reuse the information. Accordingly, there should be in the teacher's records a retrieval facility by which that teacher will be reminded to raise the matter at several frequent intervals until the child's learning is properly and adequately reinforced. Nor should the teacher be mislead into thinking that if the child forgets what he has been taught then the teaching has failed. The grounds may, and most probably have, been laid for further more effective learning and, after all, it is the gradual process of learning how to go about these things that is crucial, and not what is actually learned, so that subsequent teaching sessions should be welcomed by the teacher and should not be regarded as simply rectifying past failures.

WORD STUDY IN A LANGUAGE CONTEXT

Alongside this seemingly incidental word identification prog-ramme, there should also be a programme of word study and a study of language usage.

Word study is distinguished from word identification here in that the former is envisaged as a further development of the latter.

Children when reading can be encouraged to participate in a game of searching for a comparable word or an opposite word to replace a given word, by being asked when reading, *The knife was sharp*, for example, to say what would be written if the knife was not sharp, or if reading *The present was welcome*, to suggest ways of saying that it was not wanted. This type of activity can be done as a group reading exercise with the use of an overhead projector, so that there can be some discussion and interaction amongst the children. It can also be pitched at almost any level of reading and word study.

Through this type of activity the effects of prefixes and suffixes can be studied, changes caused by tense and number can be noted and eventually the foreign basis of some words, such as Anglo-Saxon, French, German and American, can be noted and discussed; naturally the latter only when the children are in the upper junior classes. It is mentioned here simply as a reminder that word study is a continuing process throughout our educational system.

Word study is frequently interwoven with language study and related to the uses of language: how language is used to describe, narrate, command, request and so on. It is all too easy to assume that children will pick this up naturally, and to some extent they will. However, it should not be left to chance. Attention should be drawn to the form that language takes to achieve particular ends by the teacher with such remarks as: 'That is a beautiful way to describe. . .', 'That gives me a very clear picture of. . .'; 'Why do you think the author makes a certain character speak so brusquely?'; 'Would you write it that way?'; all questions to call the child's attention to the style of the author. It is not too early even in the middle infants, in some cases, to begin this process. Children are sensitive to spoken language (Beatrix Potter used such tongue twisters as *mischievous, soporific, floundered,* and children loved them because they are unusual sonorous words placed in a context that children understand). Similarly, they are sensitive to pleasant ideas, to menacing situations, to beautiful descriptions and to ugliness, so why not call attention to the way those things are expressed in writing? Parents do this when reading to their children, admittedly often in a somewhat restricted way, when they say after reading their nightly story, 'Didn't it sound terrible!', or 'What a nice sounding little story that was!', which admittedly is rather patronising. It is a small step from that to the teacher suggesting that something read by the child is written aptly. In this way the teacher sets standards of appreciation which the children begin to emulate, and of course this development in the child's powers of appreciation and his sensitivity to the use of language and to the importance of the choice of words will also be greatly assisted through the teaching the child receives in connection with learning to write. Through consistent challenges to express his thoughts aptly he will experiment in the composition and construction of texts. Clay (1983) in another context, using Luria's theories of complex brain functioning in speech and writing, argues that writing helps to organise reading behaviour by 'slowing up the complex activity so that all the pieces can be interwoven'. By giving thought to how something should be expressed one is in a better position to appreciate what one reads on the matter. The two aspects of reading and writing development are inextricably interwoven and it should be the concern of the teacher to extract the maximum effect from their interconnection.

This argument for the teaching of reading through meaningful contexts is fully supported by Henderson's statement that 'successful identification of a word as a visual pattern is not the natural terminus of cognitive activity but a preliminary to morphological, phonological, semantic and syntactic processing' (Henderson, 1987), a statement that indicates the nature of the sub-skills of reading and thereby shows that only in context can all the necessary sub-skills be combined to achieve the necessary goal.

Two cautionary points

It will be seen from all that is written above that before children are asked to identify unfamiliar words they will have received, one hopes, a long and intensive introduction to texts and to the behaviours and, to some extent, the knowledge that is required for the interpretation of those texts. As a result they will be equipped to begin the more demanding acts in learning to read unaided. They will have been trained in such a way that they have a clear notion of what is expected of them, which will leave the teacher free to continue the process.

Unfortunately, many children enter school having no idea what is involved in reading. They have never had stories read to them, they have hardly ever seen their parents read, there are no books in their homes, and language plays a somewhat subsidiary or reduced role in their lives. Francis (1982) found that many children entering school had no idea what schooling was all about and did not know what was meant by reading. Reid (1966) in an earlier study in downtown schools in Edinburgh found what was in some ways a worse situation as far as teaching is concerned, namely that the children's ideas about aspects of schooling and reading were totally confused. Hence, these children not only had to learn new things, they had to unlearn things that they thought they knew and then relearn the true facts. There was particular confusion with the terminology of reading, such words as *letter, words, story and figure* being interpreted idiosyncratically.

Thus we should be very wary of those who make light of the preparatory period or who, from their educated middle class experiences, do not realise the gap that exists between those who have been through that preparatory process and those who have not. There is much to be said for the reading together of 'real' books – the unreal book is a whimsical concept – but there is so much more to learning to read than looking at books that it is easy to imagine children, such as those mentioned by Francis and Reid above, falling more and more behind their peers from educated, language-oriented homes. Indeed, in infant schools in general the worrying situation has arisen whereby all children from all kinds of background experiences are introduced to the more formal aspects of learning to read, such as starting upon the reading scheme and being expected to identify unfamiliar words, during the same twelve months after entering school at approximately five years of age. How can they all be ready for this within the space of such a limited time span? It is not surprising that the source of the problem of slow learning is based in the infant school. Some children are never adequately prepared for the language and learning experiences that are to come in the upper infant, junior and secondary classes and, therefore, they can never adequately benefit from them. Teachers in secondary schools confronted with children who can hardly read and who cannot use reading in order to learn should not waste time looking to see where these children have been 'turned off'; some of them have never had the chance to get 'turned on'!

The second cautionary point concerns the use of artificial exercises and games as an aid to word identification. I think that it is crucial that they are regarded only as aids and are not used in lieu of the teaching that has been described above. Teaching must be seen as the basis and the mainstay in the child's development of word identification skills, and the use of games and exercises should be regarded simply as supplementary activities.

Having stressed this point, it is convenient and helpful to use games and exercises as very short, crisp, extra activities, either as a means of discovery or a means of practice for the children. Stott (1962) devised a comprehensive scheme of games, through which it was alleged children would learn all the skills of word identification, whilst Hughes (1970, 1972) published many exercises with the same objectives in mind as Stott. Figures 6.1 to 6.5 show a few examples taken from one of the books by Hughes. If you intend to use them you should consult his two books, both mentioned in the bibliography. Figure 6.6 shows a domino game which should appeal to many children, produced by the Learning Development Association. Such games and exercises can be useful as devices for experimentation, and they can be used to ensure that rules have been generalised, but remember that their contribution to learning to read is minimal if used alone.

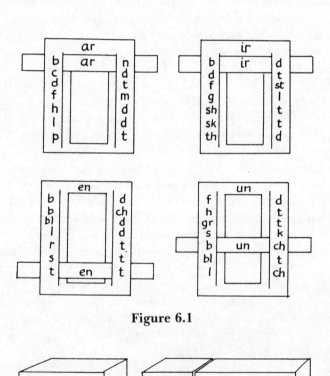

Figure 6.1

Figure 6.2

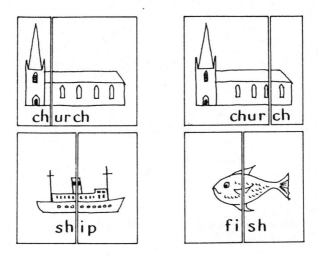

Figure 6.3

4. *Vowel Digraph Cards*
Use a piece of card, 16 cm × 12 cm, and prepare a vowel digraph card as illustrated below. Print words which cannot be illustrated at the bottom of the card.

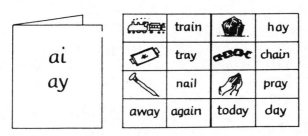

Figure 6.4

Individual Snap Cards

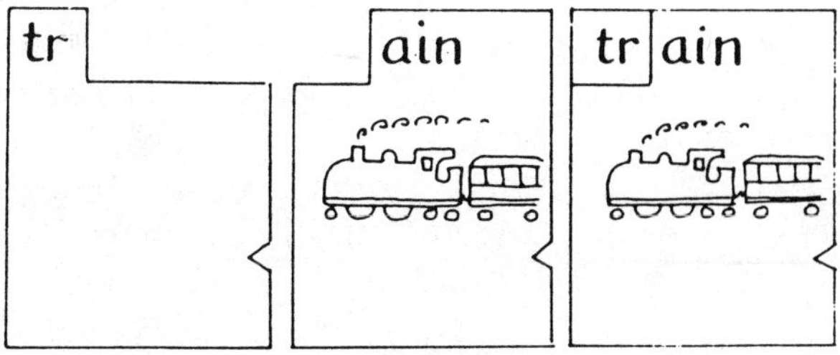

Figure 6.5

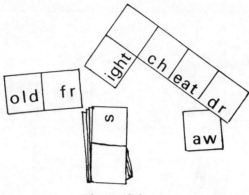

Figure 6.6

Reprinted with permission from Hughes, J.M., *Aids to reading/Phonics and teaching of reading*. Unwin/Hyman Ltd

The use of books

During recent years, there has been a positive movement towards providing children with better literature to use for the purposes of learning to read. Many people were worried by the restricted language used in the early books of the popular – ie popular with those who purchased them – published reading schemes. Such schemes as *Happy Venture, Gay Way, The Ladybird Keywords Scheme, Janet and John*, amongst others, provided children with stilted language along the lines of: *Peter. Jane. Here is Peter. Here is Jane. I like Peter. I like Jane.* Many people began to wonder at the hidden effects of such a spartan exercise.

Hence several people, some of them gurus of the little folks literary world, have proposed schemes whereby better literature may be presented to children in their early stages of learning to read. To get away from the confines of a graded scheme of reading books, they have proposed that a wide selection of good books should be offered, from which the children can make their own selections. This they called individualised reading.

Goodacre (1971) wrote about individualised reading and I used the idea myself with a class of very backward readers aged ten to eleven years at Wood End Junior School in Coventry in the 1950s. A variety of books, both good and mediocre in literary terms, were spread out round the classroom and the children were completely free to select a book, try it, keep it if they liked it or put it back if they did not. A noticeable procedure was that some of the children would select a book that caused them some difficulty but, because they were interested in the contents, they would struggle through it, asking for help on almost every line. Having completed that book they would then select one that was far too easy, read rapidly through it as though to reassure themselves of their ability to read, such as it was, and then select their next book for its subject matter and proceed with the struggle to read. So much for those who think that children do not have high levels of aspiration or a desire to apply themselves if given the chance and the encouragement! Of course it was fertile ground, for the children mentioned above had been subjected to years of Happy Venture Introductory Book and Book 1, the *Gay Way* early books, and nothing else because 'they weren't ready for it'!

However, I am sure that many teachers would not feel happy with such a loose arrangement of individual choice. Fortunately, two books on individualised reading have appeared in the last few years, B. and C. Moon (1986) and Bennett (1985), both of which, whilst adhering to the idea of individualised reading, have suggested ways of grouping the books in a loosely graded sequence. The Moons divided the books into four stages: picture books, introductory books, developmental readers, and bridging readers, and within these are thirteen levels, with books suggested for each level. As new books are continuously entering the market, this list is updated yearly and can be obtained from the Reading and Language Information Centre in the University of Reading.

Bennett lays great emphasis on the books that she recommends as being 'real', and she sets out a list in which the books are grouped into three stages: First Steps (34 books), Gaining Confidence (39 books), and Taking Off (51 books), together with a further list for six to eight year olds.

Apart from being a useful source of suggestions for good literature, these two texts suggest a form of organisation of reading materials that would be acceptable and reassuring to many teachers who do not like the rigidity of the graded reading scheme.

The movement of which these writers are, with Waterland (1985), representative has not gone unheeded by the publishers of graded reading schemes. Various schemes have appeared in recent years, amongst them the massive *Reading 360* (Ginn), *Link Up* (Holmes McDougall), *Language Patterns* (published in Canada by

Cassell), *Story Chest* (from New Zealand, Arnold – Wheaton), *The Oxford Reading Tree* (Oxford University Press) and *Open Door* (Nelson). These are more comprehensive and more carefully constructed than any of the older reading schemes, and their use of language and their style is more varied and less stilted than the early books in the schemes of yesteryear.

Whichever books are chosen or whichever reading scheme is used, the crucial question above all others that should be asked about the early reading materials is whether or not the texts of those materials cohere and form a developing statement. Do the thoughts expressed in a sentence relate closely to what has gone before and to what emerges in subsequent sentences? In other words, can the new reader anticipate what is coming, and, if stuck on an unfamiliar word, are the semantic cues sufficiently constrained to enable the reader to make reasonable hypotheses as to what the word could be? This question is tantamount to asking whether or not the books which are placed before the child who is beginning to read are worthy of the term literature and are written in a way that enables the reader to use a variety of cues and not have to rely upon one type of cue – phono-graphical – alone. Epstein (1969), by comparing the adaptation for young readers of Beatrix Potter's *Peter Rabbit* with the original, has demonstrated clearly the deadening effect of mutilated English. Compare the two versions – first the original:

> First he ate some lettuces and some French beans; and
> then he ate some radishes;
> and then, feeling rather sick, he went to
> look for some parsley.

with the new version:

> In the garden he saw carrots and beans and radishes.
> 'Mmm', said Peter to himself, 'Carrots, beans and
> radishes are what I like best'.
> He began to eat.
> He ate some carrots.
> He ate some radishes.
> He ate and ate and ate.
> Peter ate so much he got sick.
> He went to look for some parsley.

As Epstein points out, 'the value of this inane performance is impossible to grasp. There is nothing old-fashioned or obscure about Miss Potter's version and there is nothing in the new version to make it clearer or more interesting than the original. The pedagogical theory that is reflected by the repetition of words in this version of Peter Rabbit is that a child, in learning to read, has to encounter the same few words over and over again until he has mastered them: a perfectly sensible theory except that the modern adaptor in this case has misapplied it and her version is so dull that it is hard to imagine that a child would want to read it at all, whereas the original is so lively that one can easily imagine a child's reading it over and over again and encountering, as according to the theory he should, the same set of words repeatedly'.

Beck et al. (1979) in their examination of two commercial reading programmes suggest that simplification frequently adds to the confusion with which the reader is faced, because the limitation of vocabulary usage distorts the text and leads to ellipses in story structure and to the deletion of causal relationships between sentences. This imposes a heavy burden on inadequate readers by heightening the inferences that have to be made in order to resolve the meaning of the passage.

Furthermore, Stein and Trabasso (1982) have pointed to the fact that 'any two episodes in a story structure can be connected by one of three relationships: *and, then* or *cause*'. They explain them thus: an *and* relationship signifies two episodes in a temporal sequence according to narrative time, but where the episodes may have occurred in any order, or may have occurred simultaneously in real time; one episode is not a precondition for or a cause of the other. The *then* relationship is where one episode is preconditional to the other but is not a direct cause of it or where one episode occurs before the other but with no causal relationship to the second episode. The *cause* relationship indicates a direct connection where one episode ensures the occurrence of the second episode. They write that 'the type of logical relationships linking episodes and the number of episodes in a story are thought to have significant effects on the comprehensibility of a story.'

Mandler and Johnson (1977) and Stein and Glenn (1979) posit even more directly the idea that children are better able to remember stories in which the episodes are linked by a *cause* relationship than those in which the episodes are linked by either *and* or *then* relationships. This seems to be a reasonable proposition on the assumption that things which are interdependent are more memorable than things which are less closely interwoven. In the case of the former the relationship can be deduced logically.

When one considers the reservations posed by these researches, and when one thinks of the effect that a laborious style can have upon a reader, it becomes obvious that so-called 'scientifically designed' reading schemes should be examined critically and rigorously.

Furthermore, it is not merely a matter of what aids the child in the short run. If the children are denied the experience of language that is rich, stylistically attractive and which introduces them to highly developed forms of language, then they will not be prepared adequately for the complexity of language in the later books of the scheme, which are written in a more sophisticated form of English as a rule. Lack of such experience was identified as a possible cause in a falling off in standards of reading by all but the bright and well prepared children by Donaldson and Reid (1985).

ACTION FOR THE NEW ENTRANT TO TEACHING

The question for the young entrant to the teaching profession is not so much, which scheme or which approach should be used? It is, which scheme or approach will I be expected to use in my new job? So, what advice can be given?

The first point to be made is that the teacher can modify any scheme or approach so that she is at least able to approximate to her desired way of teaching. B. and C. Moon and Bennett have shown that even if there is no graded reading scheme and the method of individualised reading is in operation, it is possible to impose some constraints on the levels at which children read if this is so desired. And it must be remembered that the way in which the teacher operates using an individualised approach is similar in most ways to that in which effective teachers operate who use a graded reading scheme – *the* scheme as it is frequently designated. For it is a myth that the scheme has magic powers and that once entered upon the child will emerge at Book 16 or Level 12 or whatever, as a fully fledged skilled reader. Good teachers do not place such faith in any scheme and do a lot of things, additional to activities connected with the reading scheme, which contribute to successful development in reading ability. Southgate and Lewis (1973) looked at the time spent on reading schemes by teachers who were regarded as effective teachers of reading and who said that the reading scheme played an important part in their teaching plans. They found that of the time spent on activities which could be said to have some part in helping the children to learn to read only thirteen per cent of that time was spent on the reading scheme. The remainder was spent on word study, phonic activities, looking at and identifying individual words, labelling things and reading labels, and the like. These findings surprised even the teachers themselves, but they were salutory findings in reminding us that the reading scheme is not the crucial aspect in the teaching of reading. The crucial thing is the teaching we do, the kind of help we give, the effectiveness of the example we set and the way in which we monitor the child's progress with a view to being supportive where he is weakest. Nothing can replace the inventiveness of the teacher and the interventions she makes.

Thus there is plenty of scope for the teacher to improvise under whatever conditions she finds herself. All that was written earlier in this chapter and in preceding chapters falls in with the approaches suggested by B. and C. Moon, Bennett and Waterland, and an arrangement of that nature would be preferred by this writer. Having operated a scheme similar to that which they propose, I cannot see any difficulty in extending what they propose by introducing more group work and a greater emphasis on the study of language and its components. Similarly, what I have written could be considered as preparatory to the introduction of a child to a reading scheme and as supplementary to the use of the schemes once the children have started on them.

Reading from books

Whether the books that a child is expected to read are taken from a graded reading scheme or chosen from a collection of children's literature, it is important that the young teacher has a clear idea of how the child will approach the task of reading and interpreting the text.

It has been stated that 'we bring our experience to bear on any text.' Let us consider this statement. From the very first moment of encounter with a text, the readers must take their first cues from the graphic input, especially if the text is to any extent randomly chosen; that is, if the text is not directly related to the activities or thoughts of the readers at that specific moment.

To these cues they attach meaning, whether tentative or exact. The way they do this will depend upon their skill as readers: if they are skilled then the graphic input will usually suggest meaning in terms of context because the words will be recognised as familiar, and this will then originate a model of anticipation (Merritt, 1970, Smith, 1971), which will itself be checked against further graphic input; if, on the other hand, they are beginners then the graphic input will be associated with specific sounds and these phonological cues will suggest particular words. The words will implant semantic cues which will be built up into a model, and this model will be likewise checked against the ensuing graphic input and the whole cycle will be repeated.

This process of interpreting a text suggests a very different form of behaviour from that which assumed that reading simply involved the sequential decoding of discrete words accompanied by the automatic and simple summation of each word-meaning into the total meaning of the text. This naive and over-simplified view is disproved by the very nature of written language – its phonic inconsistencies, its syntactic structure, and the fact that its surface structure does not specifically represent its deep structure. The behaviour that is necessary in order to interpret a text is far more complex and is perhaps best explained in terms of coding at several levels. The graphic input in the first instance will depend upon the training that the child has received. If he has been trained to look at letters, ie if the teaching has proceeded from the hierarchical view that letters add up to words and words add up to comprehension, then the span of his initial input will be very narrow and may simply involve looking at the first letter of the first word. The temptation will then be to attach some form of sound, either overtly or covertly, to that letter, take in the next letter, attach a sound, add this to the previous one, and hope that a meaningful word will emerge. The pitfalls in this approach are obvious. However, if the child has been trained to take up an approach that is consistent with the nature of written language, then his initial graphic input will tend to be at least word based, and may even take in a string of words. (He will have been partially trained at least for this type of behaviour if labelling has consisted of phrases and sentences rather than single words and if a sentence approach – for example, through the use of *Breakthrough* cards – has been used in the period of emergent reading.) As the child takes in the initial input he will be trying to recall the word or words from his store of learnt words, using association of cues (graphic and/or phonic). If recall is successful it will serve as a reminder to him of something that he already knows (for example, *boys*, ie human beings like himself in their stage of development, or *the horse*, ie an animal with four legs such as that upon which the girl next door sits) and from that moment a train of thought will be established and the reader will then proceed to check his anticipatory thoughts against the subsequent graphic input. Hence there is a direct link from graphic input through the memory store to a train of thought. Put in another way, the words lead directly to the ideas. However, the child may not be able to recall immediately a word in response to the initial graphic input. In this case he will have to revise his behaviour and take in the graphic display in a different form, this time seeking not virtually instantaneous recognition of a previously identified word, possibly, or even probably, on the basis of reduced cues, but trying to transpose some of the graphic input into phonemic or morphemic cues which will themselves be chunked together to suggest some word sound known to the child. The difficulties facing a child in this predicament can be seen, because the chances are great that the first word in a text will be one which cannot be decoded on the basis of phonemic cues alone, words such as *which* or *once* or even a homonym such as *tears*. In this event it is essential that the young reader should be trained to look further than the initial word and to reserve judgement upon the meaning of that word until he has collected additional cues from the subsequent words in the opening statement.

It is at this point that the child's working knowledge of English will be crucial. If the child has been encouraged to experiment with spoken language and has seen its relationship with written language then he will naturally fall into an exploratory kind of behaviour. For example, in the sentence, *When boys and girls come out to play, the teacher stands. . .*, the child may not recall the first word and may not be able to attach a word sound to it by using what knowledge he has of letter sounds. If, however, he looks at the subsequent words he may well recall the graphic units, *boys and girls*, and he may also recall the sounds that can be attached to those three words. If he then proceeds further he will build up some ideas which emanate from his knowledge of boys and girls. These ideas will be modified, or even radically altered if necessary, as he checks his thoughts against the ensuing cues which he gains from the graphic input, from associated sounds and from his tacit awareness of grammatical structure. As his interpretation of the text builds up, so he will be able to eliminate certain possibilities and to verify others. Hence by the time he has sorted out the general theme of 'boys and girls coming out to play in (the implied) presence of the teacher', he is in a far stronger position to decode the word *when*, because his mind is now thinking along lines which more severely constrain the range of possible responses. To speculate, the child may be able to guess the word from the semantic cues which he has obtained from the rest of the sentence, and he will check his guess against those phonic cues which he can muster from part of the graphic input. For example, he may recognise *en* as the sound /en/ or even the letters *hen* as the sound /hen/, which would be enough to verify or reject his guess. A similar course of phonic interpretation may take place even if the child did not make the initial guess. In this event, however, he would be setting up sounds against which he would compare what message he has got so far from the remainder of the sentence, and he would be trying to build up a structure of sound out of which would emerge something that enabled him to make sense of the emerging message in total. Weber's research with first-grade children (1970) showed that where errors in reading were made and took the form of substitutions, 90 per cent of those substitutions were grammatically correct, showing a tacit understanding of syntactic structure and a propensity to read sense and not accept nonsense.

Hence, the whole process must be seen as the manipulation of cues, many of which are loosely constrained and many of which provide the possibility of alternative responses. These cues fall into three broad categories: graphic – with either a phonic or a lexical response or both – syntactic or grammatical and semantic. However, whereas in the past many writers have assumed that the graphic cues both initiate and predominate the reader's attempts to interpret the text, this can now be said to be the case only in the identification of unfamiliar discrete words standing in isolation (as in a graded word reading test). The argument of this book is that in reading a piece of prose, the cues used will vary according to the ability of the reader in relation to that particular text, according to the constraints of the text, and according to the point at which the reader finds himself in the text. As he builds up a store of knowledge about what is in the text, so the constraints upon his anticipation will become increasingly severe and his use of semantic cues increasingly potent, in which case his reliance upon grapho-phonemic and grapho-morphemic cues will dwindle.

In terms of behaviour, this implies a flexible approach by the reader based upon a familiarity with and an easy confident approach to the juggling of ideas within an increasingly confined framework. Where several responses to a word may have been possible at the beginning of a text, this number will frequently be reduced as the reader proceeds due to the constraints of the text. Flexibility is therefore essential. The reader must be given a general training which will encourage him to react in this way, using a variety of cues in a problem-solving manner. Thus a training which lays emphasis upon the use of a rigid hierarchy of skills and sub-skills would be a training which would discourage flexibility. The young learner must witness and experience an approach to texts in which variable types of behaviour are utilised openly. Hence, the type of group activities associated with the use of the *Breakthrough to Literacy* Teacher's Sentence Maker are an ideal way of indicating:

1 the possibilities for manipulating written language – sentences, phrases, and words;
2 the interchangeability of the separate classes of words;
3 the possibilities offered by the various types of clues which exist;
4 the possibility of compensating for lack of cues in one aspect of language by using cues from the other aspects.

Thus the Sentence Maker, along with the overhead projector and erasable pens, should be used well beyond the point when children begin to practise reading on books.

Teachers' roles

What does the teacher do to prepare and help children as they begin to read their first book?

The first step is to enhance their background knowledge concerned with the subject matter of the book. If the book is a story concerning or involving an animal then the children's thoughts must be directed towards that animal, its nature and its habits. If the story is concerned with the actions of children there should be some discussion of what children do, and so on.

The obvious implication of this is that there is an advantage to be gained if several children are beginning the same book simultaneously. Motivation and stimulation of ideas are easier to raise in a group than with an individual child, firstly, because there is no scope for peer interaction where only one child is concerned, and, secondly, because of the inevitable barrier that exists between teacher and child, between an unrelated (as opposed to family) adult and a child, which assumes greater proprotions and inhibits the individually taught child. (Don't assume for one moment that you can have such a close relationship with a child in your class as exists between a parent and child. To illustrate this, think what children will tolerate in school because of the authoritarian relationship between teacher and child which they would not tolerate for more than a minute or two at home!)

The second step is to ensure that each child has a sufficient sight vocabulary to ensure a moderate degree of success in tackling the book. The number of words that he does not know in the book should be minimal if any, and even then they should be of such a nature that he will be able to 'guess' them from the context, helped perhaps by reminders of the discussions that took place prior to reading the book. This type of preparation is not something that should be crammed into a few moments prior to reading. The words and phrases should be studied through what would amount to the teacher telling them the story contained in the book beforehand. Words and phrases can be written out and noted.

It is obvious that this is best achieved if the first book is a well known story – a folk tale or a nursery rhyme. The children will then know the story line, and the introductory preparations will be intent upon heightening their awareness of the printed form of the story they already know. This means that the learning of words and phrases will take place in a meaningful context and, of course, the outstanding advantage of starting children off on the folk tales and on nursery rhymes is that they are memorable. That is why they have persisted down the ages. Parents who read to their children know how readily and willingly children return again and again to these stories if given the option.

The third step occurs whilst the child is reading his book. The teacher's task will then be to support the reader, even to read alongside him to ensure success and to maintain a speed of reading that ensures that the immediate sense of what he is reading fits into a total meaningful pattern. Another advantage to be gained from folk tales and nursery rhymes is that the story line will be in the child's mind and this will help him to anticipate what is coming on the page. Hence, anticipation, an invaluable part of the skilled reader's armoury, is being instilled into the child's reading behaviour from the outset. What is more, knowledge of the story line will help him to concentrate upon the way that story is presented in print, that is, to concentrate upon looking at the words and phrases and taking them in, rather than having to do that and sort out the meaning of the passage simultaneously. Weber (1970) illustrated the difficulties first-graders have in attending to both the meaning and the graphic detail. Biemiller (1970) working with the same children that were used by Weber, found that children at this early stage in reading went through three phases: at the outset of reading the child would pay little attention to the actual text so long as what he said made sense; then he would realise that there must be a close relationship between what was written and what he said, and as he was not certain about the actual words in the text he tended to remain silent; and, finally, as his decoding skills improved or as he gained knowledge of more words, so he was able to pay closer attention to the words of the text and read the text as it actually was.

When we think about this sequence reported by Biemiller, once again the advantages of requiring children to read known material during their early attempts become obvious. The second, sticking, point in Biemiller's sequence would be overcome by avoiding the necessity for undue emphasis on text analysis and word analysis by encouraging semantic guessing. The child at this stage would not be forced to keep quiet; he would know the story and he could anticipate the text. To help children at this stage some teachers make tape recordings of the stories to which children can listen as they read.

Naturally the degree of non-response at this second stage will be determined and influenced by the kind of reading instruction that is given to the children. The more time that has been spent on the preparatory stages, the more time and opportunities the children have had to imbibe and consolidate a sight vocabulary, the more opportunities they have had to draw their own comparisons between words and to discover what are the distinctive features of words for themselves (Smith, 1971), and the more intense has been the preparation for the actual reading books that they will face, then the more confident they will be to 'have a go' at responding carefully to the text. It is interesting to note that Scottish children who had received more training in word analysis than American children, with less emphasis on meaning, gave more incorrect responses that changed the meaning of the text (Elder, 1966).

However, it is not perfection in reading that we are aiming at here. The goal should be primarily to ensure rising confidence, not falling confidence, in the child. Furthermore, one of our main objectives should be to inculcate the correct forms of behaviour, one of which is not to stumble through a traumatic session of attempted word analysis. Therefore, the child's limitations should be minimised and the obstacles he faces should be reduced. Should he not keep closely to the text but get the main gist of the story, no concern should be shown at this stage. It should be regarded as a good first attempt, even if the story is one that is known to the child. To repeat that known story in the presence of text is an achievement for a young child, and there will be plenty of opportunities as time goes on to draw the child closer to the text. This will be particularly easy if folk tales and well known stories are being used as readers, because the children will want to reread these stories, and then the opportunities will arise for the teacher to guide the children more closely towards the actual text. At a later stage it can be fun and a challenge to check that the story has been read properly.

Thus the emphasis is upon interpreting a text when reading, as opposed to rigorous word study, whilst at the same time matching the parts of that text to the meaning as it emerges. As the children do more of it so their attention will be called more and more closely to the details of the texts. Frequently they will be asked to use their story books as a basis for their writing, and thus they will need to pay particular attention, as time goes by, to the spelling of words, to the construction of phrases and to the composition of texts. Words that are required can be related back to their context, and they can be noted for their distinctive features. Passing comments by the teacher, such as 'Have you seen any other word like that?', or 'That word reminds me of . . . Can you find it for me so that we can compare them?', will help to focus attention.

In all of this we see training in anticipation, in checking one's thoughts against the text, in looking at words and phrases, drawing comparisons and noting the constituent parts of words; all of it designed to illustrate to the children that, if they are prepared to try to solve problems, if they try to draw comparisons, if they think about things previously learnt, if they are prepared to 'have a go', then they will eventually succeed in doing things that they thought were impossible. We will have changed their attitudes from 'I either know or I don't know the right answer' to 'I shall try various possibilities.'

The fourth step is a very important step in that it is preparing readers for the future and ensuring prolonged development in reading skill. It cannot start too early, and it is basically training in reflection upon texts, a skill found to be central to older children's ability to comprehend texts (Lunzer and Gardner, 1979). Right from the early books the children should expect to discuss what they have read. Goodman on numerous occasions has suggested that after a child has read a book he could profitably be asked to recall to the teacher what he had read. This, thought Goodman, was a more effective form of comprehension exercise than simply asking the child a series of questions. One thing to be gained is the training it provides in reorganising information received and presenting it again in a logical and ordered form. It could be considered as contributing to a child's development as a writer because it is requiring him to compose an oral text. Later he can be required to present it in written form. These are worthy benefits to be gained from recalling a story, but there is another and, so far as reading goes, one of great importance. It is that by requiring a child to retell a story the teacher is emphasising the necessity to think about what one is reading and to make a conscious effort to retain it. So many children in the past have been able to think that once the words were out of their mouths when reading aloud that was the end of the matter. If something had stuck in their minds, so be it, but if it hadn't then they felt no compunction to reread the text.

There is another aspect to the practice of reflection upon a text, and that is involved in the manipulation of textual details whilst reading in order to obtain the true meaning of a passage. When a child stumbles on an unfamiliar word, or one that he has forgotten, and the teacher suggests he go back over what he has already read to see if in doing so the meaning will convey a clearer clue to the identification of the word, or when asked to read on to see if that will help solve the mystery, or when it is suggested that a comparison of the problem word with one that the child already knows may help, the child is, in all these cases, being shown how to use texts. From this type of work the child will gradually become aware of many ways of approaching a text in an attempt to get the full message.

LISTENING TO CHILDREN READ

Much of the teacher's role in helping children with their early attempts to read a book has been dealt with in the discussion above. However, there are some further points to make.

Always have a notepad available whilst the child is reading. On this pad you can illustrate words, show comparisons with other words, emphasise phrases and so on. The typist's pad is excellent because pages can be ripped out easily so that the child can retain for reference what you have written by way of illustration.

Keep a record of any errors the child makes and any problems he has, so that you have a clear record of his strengths and weaknesses. Don't waste your time keeping the number of the pages that the children are on in their readers. If the book is worth reading they will remember the page they were on! In any case what are book markers for?

When you have sufficient records of the mistakes made by a child try to draw up a profile of his errors showing those to which he is most susceptible. From this you will be able to decide what to concentrate on when next listening to him read and what teaching needs to be done apart from listening to him read. A categorised list of reading errors can be found in Appendix 2.

Give children notice that you want to hear them read and insist that they prepare what they are going to read to you, that is if you are not going to prepare with them. Remember that adult skilled readers do not find it easy to read aloud unfamiliar texts.

SILENT READING

It is surprising how soon children reach the stage where they can read the simpler books unaided. There should be no pressure towards reading independently, but when it occurs it should be encouraged, because, after all, silent reading is the essence of the activity. Reading aloud is merely a means whereby we can teach children to read. So when a child shows willingness to read alone, even though vocalising, it should be encouraged. Ask a child to reread alone a story and then come and retell it to you. In doing this you will be giving the child a sense of purpose which will help to concentrate his mind on the activity.

Do not hesitate to challenge children to find out what story is contained in such and such a book and to come to you with the information. Sometimes they can be expected simply to tell you what they have discovered, and on other occasions they will be encouraged to write it down as a message for you. Do not worry if they are not too good at writing; the effort will be a useful part of the development of their ability to write. There is a close connection between pretending to write and the real thing, as was discovered earlier.

FOLLOW-UP TO THE FIRST READING BOOK

Unlike the old type of reading primers with one book, and possibly a couple of supplementary books, at each of the early levels, reading schemes of recent times tend to have many books at each level of difficulty. And of course those teachers who do not use a reading scheme similarly make provision for a number of books at all levels to be available. For those who use nursery rhymes as the earliest reading books, Southgate Booth (1985) has provided a graded list.

As was mentioned above, the children will have been prepared for reading their first books, and just as there was a need for preparatory work so there is a need for follow-up work to ensure reinforcement of learning. One way of doing this could be for the children to make a collection of all the words that they have learned and read in the form of a word index. There could be help with the alphabetical arrangement of these words, which would then form a bank of known words which could be displayed for parents to see and could be used for a subsequent stage in the progress towards reading independently.

Children could be encouraged to use these words, when working in a group with the teacher, in the reconstruction of the stories that they have previously read. This could be done along the same lines as was done earlier with the *Teacher's Sentence Maker* from the *Breakthrough to Literacy* scheme, except that now the children would be selecting the words from their word banks rather than having to rely upon the teacher to do it for them. Again one can see the advantages to be gained from having used nursery rhymes or folk tales as the earliest reading books, because in that case the children would not have too much difficulty in recalling the theme and would, therefore, be freer to concentrate upon the selection of words. However, if other stories have been used it will simply indicate a need for a little more attention by the teacher to recalling the story with the children before the actual reconstruction using word cards takes place. (The term 'children' is used purposefully because there are tremendous advantages to be gained from working in a group – children can see how others perform the required tasks, they can help one another, they can see others struggling and thereby realise that they are not the only ones to find things difficult, and, additionally, it is an economical use of the teacher's time.)

WRITING TO SUPPLEMENT READING

Alongside these activities with word cards the children should be encouraged to write the stories themselves. The fact that they may only be more or less able to scribble should not be seen as a disadvantage. They will be trying to represent in their own way the story that they have read, and as was the case with the examples of children's writing, about the meat tenderiser for instance, shown earlier in this book, the children will be making a serious attempt to approximate more and more closely to written English. Underneath the child's attempt the teacher should write in normal English what the child has attempted. This should be done unobtrusively and without detracting from the child's efforts. In this way the child will not be discouraged but will have the opportunity to note how the teacher does what that child was trying to do. These stories with child's and teacher's writing can be pasted into a personal story book which each child builds up and eventually takes home. Nothing can be more exciting at this stage than for the children to produce their own story books. Some schools place the child's photograph on the front of the folder or book in order to intensify the sense of personal achievement. At the same time the child, one hopes, will be recording on tape some of these stories so that the school secretary or head teacher can type them out on a jumbo typewriter, and these again can be used as reading matter. The children can be asked to read their own stories whilst listening to their recording of that story. This will guide them in their reading, freeing the teacher to attend to other matters, and providing a possible starting point for silent reading. As children do more and more of this reading whilst listening to the recording they can be positively encouraged to try to read silently, and it can be put to them that this is the first step towards 'reading like adults'! Apart from this, reading and listening will inspire confidence and promote greater fluency.

As a further aid to the writing of stories, student teachers should begin to build up word banks centred upon various topics. For example, eight by six inch index cards could contain a number of words and phrases relating to a topic. The words could be illustrated by line drawings to help the younger children, and additions could be made to the collection of words on each topic at the suggestion of the children through discussion groups. In this way they are being taught to build up resources for themselves and to utilise one another's knowledge.

There are several publications on the market based upon the classification of words by topic or theme, amongst them a collection under the series title of *Children's Britannica First Steps* (see further reading at the end of this chapter). Many children will find these much more helpful than dictionaries, simply because the words that they need are more readily accessible in a classified form.

If this recording of stories based upon the children's immediate experiences and the retelling and rewriting of stories is continued, one can imagine the amount of reading material that will accrue in addition to the early reading books. In addition to this one would hope that material specifically written for the infants would be arriving from older junior school children. If this is approached thoughtfully by the junior teachers, it can result in some excellent reading material for the infants. The juniors will find it exhilarating to write for the infants and the infants will appreciate such personal attention by their elders. (The implications for junior teachers will be raised in the next chapter.)

Finally, there is another source of literature which infants could profit from, and that is the stories which teachers write for children. These can centre on subjects or events that are of particular and pressing interest to the children at any particular time: the death of a hamster, a school break-in, the arrival of a new member of the class, the misbehaviour of some older juniors. Children see things from a personal point of view and can resolve problems so much more readily if they are posed in a child's way of looking at things rather than an adult's. Donaldson (1978) has shown how different the results of Piagetian experiments can be if posed from a child's standpoint. Similarly with reading: if the text is written in a way that reflects their experiences, then so much the better. The opportunities for personalised stories or stories of particular and specific relevance to a class, group or even an individual child are manifold, so every new entrant to teaching should have learned to type so that they are able to produce stories quickly and at will.

The development of reading beyond the early stages

From all that has been written so far, it will be obvious that the objective has been to create an environment in which reading and writing are activities enthusiastically and willingly entered into by the children with support from the teachers that reduces failure to a minimum and ensures relative success for all the children. Under these circumstances it should not be difficult to ensure that children develop a habit and a desire for reading and writing. Hence, the main task of the teacher is to promote reading as a central feature of all aspects of the curriculum. No opportunity should be missed to make the children rely upon reading to resolve problems, whether in art and craft, control design technology, science, nature study, history, geography, the appreciation of literature or the resolving of mathematical problems.

A moment's thought will indicate the variety in styles of texts that will be encountered in these various aspects of the curriculum. This means that children must be trained to cope with a variety of styles and to adjust their reading behaviour accordingly. Mathematical and scientific texts frequently take the form of precise instructions tersely written, whereas much of the literature that the children read at this stage will be expansive and at times discursive or even rambling.

The best way to get children to adapt their reading behaviour to suit a variety of purposes is to place them in situations which require them to read in ways that are apposite to the task. Students on school practice frequently complain to their tutors that children do not read the work cards or written instructions carefully and that they expect to be *told* what to do. This often says more about the training the children have received in the school before the student's arrival than it does about the work cards. The children have learned that there is an easier way than working out the meaning of the written text, and that is to ask the teacher! The answer to this problem is to check the work card or the instructions to ensure that they can be interpreted and, if satisfied that this is a reasonable possibility, refuse to tell the child what to do and make a determined effort to insist that children make repeated attempts to understand texts. Many children suffer at the secondary stage from never having been taught that in order to understand some texts it may be necessary to work at them, reading and rereading the text and making a conscious and sustained effort to organise mentally the message of the text in a manageable form. On some occasions it will be helpful to write out salient points from the text to aid mental reorganisation. Children need to be taught how to go about this practice.

To quote one such instance where more than a superficial reading is necessary, Henderson (1987) made the point that phrasal idioms cannot always be understood straightforwardly from the meanings of their component words and that this suggests that units larger than words may require lexical representation. *It is raining cats and dogs* is something that must be learned in its entirety, as must the phrase *a shadow of the real thing*. Children must learn by having such statements pointed out to them and by being shown how they fit into the text.

As an aside to the argument for training children to rely more heavily on what they read and not to turn too readily for oral elucidation, I do not wish to give the idea that work cards, home produced or published, are invariably easy to understand. In many instances they are written by people who fully understand the subject matter and who inadvertently make unwarranted assumptions about the reader's background of skill and understanding. Hence, work cards frequently do not give adequate information, they assume knowledge and they assume that the reader is familiar with the logical processes that may be required in the solution of the problem that is set. Students when writing work cards should ask themselves the following questions:

1 What knowledge or skill is assumed?
2 Does the card set out the problem clearly and in an appropriate style of language?
3 Is it necessary to provide extra information, such as a reminder of necessary background knowledge, or an example of how a similar problem may be solved, or guidelines for the analysis of the problem?

Just as the student teacher will learn much about the development of reading skills through the attempts made to produce adequate work cards, so children who have to produce written work for others or use texts to achieve their objectives will learn much about the construction of texts and, consequently, about their interpretation. The work sheets in Figures 6.7 and 6.8 were used by a student, Katherine Schofield, with a junior one class of eight year old children. Notice how precisely the children had to follow the written instructions.

The Tuning Fork
1 Draw a tuning fork very carefully.
2 Hold the tuning fork like this:

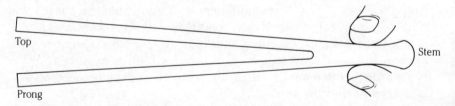

Figure 6.7

3 Strike the top of the tuning fork against a book or the floor. Listen to the note it makes.
4 Strike the tuning fork again, and gently touch one prong with your thumbnail. What happens?
5 Strike the tuning fork, touch one prong against the edge of a sheet of paper. What happens?
6 Strike the tuning fork, touch one prong of the tuning fork against the surface of some water. What happens?
7 Strike the tuning fork and put the stem onto a rubber, a pencil, the desk, your hand. What happens? What makes the clearest sound?
8 What is a tuning fork used for?

Science Workcard 5
Ticking Watch
Equipment you will need: a blindfold, a ruler, a watch, a cardboard tube.
Work in 2s
1 First decide who is to be Number One and who is to be Number Two.
2 Number One is blindfolded. You put up your hand when you can hear the watch ticking.
3 Number Two – put a ruler on the table.
4 Ask Number One to put his ear to one end of the ruler.
5 Now slide the watch along the ruler towards Number One.
6 Stop when Number One can hear the watch ticking.
7 Now each of you in turn put your ear to one end of the cardboard tube, put the watch at the other end.
8 Can you hear the watch tick now?
9 Measure the length of the tube.
10 What is the tube doing to the sound of the ticking watch?

Figure 6.8

In addition it can be argued that writing reports on science and environmental experiments for others to read is as important a factor in learning to read competently as is the writing of stories and the interpretation of texts from all aspects of the curriculum, so long as the reports have to be read and understood and the stories appreciated by others, and so long as the interpretation of the text is central to the solution of the problem. Just as the teacher gets feedback from the children who use her work cards, so the children must get feedback from their writing and reading behaviour.

PROJECTS AND TOPIC WORK AS AIDS TO READING AND WRITING

Project work can be a wonderful exercise in thinking, reading, writing and decision making. It can form preparatory training in problem solving, researching, reporting and critical appreciation. However, like so much else in teaching it has to be carefully planned and executed with clear purposes in mind.

Two essential points to remember are that projects and individual topics in primary schools are vehicles for the development of study techniques and they are intended to provide scope for individual interests and talents. If these two points are missed then project and topic work can become activities which merely keep the children occupied.

To be more precise, the purposes of project and topic work are that they provide training in the use of books, in the organisation and reporting of information, and in the evaluation of the work done, and that all this is done through the pupil's personal association with the subject matter. The idea behind such work is that these study skills can best be fostered whilst using them and in so doing improve them. In other words, the children must learn whilst doing the job, and this necessitates working either in small groups or individually and with a fairly high degree of teacher intervention. If the children are left to their own devices they will lose much that can be gained from skilled guidance and purposeful discussion.

The following teaching programme suggests itself:
1 Either the topic or a portion of the project must be selected by each child during individual or group discussions with the teacher. If the choice is not to originate with the children, the

teacher should be at pains to stimulate *real*, not forced, enthusiasm in each child, otherwise there may be little initial enthusiasm for the work.

2 There must be discussion of the search procedure and the research work to be done. The value of this discussion in terms of language usage, of thinking and of social behaviour should not be underestimated. At a more mundane level the discussion will enable the children to outline what has to be done and to identify sources of information, whether in books or through experimentation.

3 Next should follow selective and controlled reading, and observations and experimentation where appropriate.

4 Further discussion should follow as to how the information should be collected – what notes or recordings are necessary – and how the information should be reported. As the information is reported, discussion will continue about the amount, the emphases, the balance and the presentation of the reportage. Revisions will be made and evaluated by the children and sometimes at the instigation of the teacher.

5 The finished report should be used. The individual child or the members of the group, as the case may be, should be required to read the final draft critically with a view to discussing his or their reactions to the work now that it is finished. This is a chance for the children to appreciate their own work and to learn that it is appreciated by the teacher in that she thinks it worthy of being reread and allows time for this to be done. Other individuals in the class should then be expected to read it.

There should, however, be one point of reservation about throwing open the report for everyone to read. There are some occasions when a child produces an individual topic on something of personal interest. It is merely normal courtesy for the teacher to seek the child's permission before the work is exposed to everyone. Some topics can be used by children to express personal feelings and use intimate information which they may not wish to be made public. In these cases the child's wishes and sensitivity should be respected. This same point can apply to other aspects of writing, stories, poems or letters which contain private, personal or embarrassing information, and it is for the child not the teacher to judge what is private, personal or embarrassing.

Naturally, the emphasis in each of the above five points will vary according to the age and ability of the children. At first children will tend to copy verbatim from books and this will be acceptable, but gradually through juniors two and three they will be weaned away from copying and will learn to paraphrase and to extract and reproduce texts in their own words.

READING EXERCISES IN TEXTUAL UNDERSTANDING AND APPRECIATION

These should be regarded as an adjunct to reading as part of projects and as part of other aspects of the curriculum. If not, they can assume an undue amount of time and importance in the school day that may not be warranted in terms of their effectiveness. However, it is possible to devise some artificially created exercises which, if used with discretion, can prove helpful.

Sequencing
To begin with, sequencing exercises in which a series of statements can be rearranged so that they make a piece of continuous prose or verse can be used effectively to promote thoughtful reading behaviour with all children from the older infants upwards. This can be done as a group activity with great effect, because it will allow children to witness how others are thinking about the possibilities for rearranging the text, and if one remembers that texts of varying complexity can be used it becomes obvious that this can become a taxing exercise, demanding sophisticated reasoning power, if the teacher wishes to plan for the best readers in the upper junior school.

At the outset known texts should be cut up. Nursery rhymes, folk tales or a story or statement which the children have made very recently should be used. For example, the children in the infant classes can be asked to rearrange the following:

| To fetch a pail of water |
| Jack and Jill went up the hill |
| Jill came tumbling after |
| Jack fell down and broke his crown |

or they can be asked to place in sequence a series of pictures depicting a series of easily recognised actions or events, which if arranged in a particular sequence tell a story. Or it could be a series of statements. For example:

1 a child asleep in bed;
2 the child getting up or washing in the bathroom;
3 the child and family at breakfast;
4 the child leaving home for school.

Under each picture there could be a related sentence, or the children could be required to create the statements to go with each illustration, depending upon the abilities of the children. Otherwise the exercise could consist of the sequential arrangement of the statements.

Simple exercises such as these involve quite sophisticated behaviour. First the children have to read statements that stand virtually in isolation. These have to be retained in mind whilst reorganising the thoughts provoked by these discrete statements so that a sequence of thought emerges. Finally, the printed form of the thought pattern has to be arranged in the appropriate sequence. In some cases a child will not be able to resolve the sequence mentally and will have to be trained to resort to trial and error behaviour, rearranging the text and reading the new sequence to see if it sounds right.

Numerous variations of this exercise can be devised. Sometimes the units will be large, such as paragraphs or verses, whilst at other times the units will be short – lines, phrases or sentences. Sometimes, and especially with reasonably competent readers in the junior school, the sequence may be debatable, and there will be much value in discussing the issue in small groups, with reasons having to be given for the various possible arrangements. Initially reading aloud as a self-checking procedure will be encouraged but subsequently silent reading will be required.

Sequencing activities can be related to, and most probably precede, some activities in art and craft. A book admirably suited to this purpose is *101 Things to Make*, by Janet Slingsby (see Further reading). The construction of each item is described in two, three, four or five boxes, each box with an accompanying illustration. The tasks vary in complexity and likewise the instructions vary in detail. Many of these could be transferred onto card and used as sequencing exercises to be completed before or even during the craft activities. This book and others like it should be regarded as an integral part of the junior school's reading development programme. What better experience could children have than following and interpreting the instructions and testing their interpretation against their progress in making the model?

Another publication which students will find useful, this time by the Centre for Reading in the University of Reading, is a booklet of sequencing exercises entitled *Sequencing*. This can be reproduced in unlimited numbers by schools, and is in effect a collection of ready made pieces of apparatus.

Cloze procedure

Another exercise, differing from sequencing in that it is not activity based but nevertheless demanding in terms of mental activity, is the deleted-word exercise known as cloze procedure. The exercise consists of filling gaps, which are sometimes made on a regular period basis, say every seventh word, or sometimes on the basis of a particular type of word, say adjectives or pronouns. The idea is that the reader must use semantic and syntactic cues to decide upon a suitable word to fill the gap. Frequently this involves reading that which precedes the gap and that which follows it in order to ensure that the correct word or an acceptable one is chosen. Naturally, many gaps can be adequately filled by more than one word, so that the reader has to make a choice. This fact alone is a strong feature of this exercise, because if the cloze exercise is done as a group activity then discussion can take place concerning the claims of one or the other word to fill the gap. In this way finer points of meaning can be raised and children will learn how to resolve them.

This exercise can be given individually but then it loses some of its effectiveness.

Reflection upon texts

One of the most important skills of studying is the ability to decide what is important and what is peripheral in a text and to be able to distinguish several levels of importance within any passage or book. To some extent this ability develops naturally out of the reader's interest in some of the things he reads. However, the matter should not be left to chance and the teachers in junior schools should set out a programme to develop the children's ability to reflect upon what they read and to make decisions about its importance. Lunzer and Gardner (1979) pointed to the ability or disposition to reflect upon texts as the most important factor, so far as they could see, in comprehension, and the fact that their study covered secondary school pupils should, needless to say, alert primary school teachers to the need to prepare children for this type of reflection.

It can be done in several ways. In the first place, asking children about what they have read and, in particular, asking them to recall and repeat orally the gist of what they have read is an excellent basis for further development. Secondly, the background reading in preparation for projects, the reading done in connection with modelling in craft work and experimentation in science work and reading mathematical texts in order to resolve mathematical problems adds another dimension to reading. Thirdly, passages can be devised which contain one, two or three main points which have to be extracted and noted by the children. When children have become adept at picking out the main point in a passage, then the two main points and so on can be identified, until a stage is reached where the reader can be expected to distinguish between main and subsidiary points.

Work on these passages should not be a protracted affair. The best effects will be obtained by using them as small group exercises where children learn the pros and cons of this type of work on texts. Individual work can be reserved for follow-up practice and, as such, is a good means of getting a group of children gainfully occupied and off the teacher's hands leaving her free to deal with another group.

A variation of this type of exercise is the task of changing the meaning of a text: a gloomy situation changed into a hopeful one, a sad situation into a cheerful one, an ending changed to alter the outcome of a story. This type of exercise requires the reader 'to stand back from the passage' and to think in abstract terms of an alternative meaning.

However, direct training in literary appreciation is the most potent method of ensuring reflection upon texts. Unfortunately, it is not one that has found favour amongst teachers in primary schools. For years now the external examination boards for secondary schools have shown that those schools which set out to teach appreciation rather than rely upon its natural development tend to get the best results in this type of exercise. Yet this has been regarded as having nothing to do with primary schools, and they have, in the main, made only a half-hearted attempt to instil some form of skill in appreciation in their pupils. Appreciation of literature should begin in the infant school and should be fostered throughout the junior school years.

The Bullock Report (DES, 1975) made a very constructive suggestion connected with the development of appreciation of literature by suggesting that duplicate copies of books should be used, with small groups of children reading the same book simultaneously, followed by discussion amongst the group in the presence of the teacher, who has also read the book. Student teachers should plan and prepare for such discussions in some detail. The objective should be to challenge the children to reflect analytically upon what they have read, especially when the children are in the upper classes of the junior school. There should be an attempt to get them to appreciate the author's use of language, descriptive and narrative powers, delineation of character, and ability to tell a tale with all that is implied in that skill. Yet the teacher should avoid dominating the discussion or allowing it to develop into a question and answer session. The idea should be to set the children thinking and discussing ideas so that they feel themselves more and more involved in the exercise. In the end they should be left with the feeling that there is more to a good book than simply reading it.

Crossword puzzles
If carefully selected, crossword puzzles can be very effective in calling attention to meaning in language and to the study of orthography. Apart from the use of clues to arrive at specific words, the children's minds can be turned to the question of serial probability in the English spelling system, the fact that an initial *t* can only be followed by *h, r,* and *w,* apart from the vowels, that an *l* as the penultimate letter in a word can be followed usually by *e* or by a limited number of consonants, seldom by vowels other than *e,* and that certain strings of consonants stand together in words whilst others do not. Hence we have the opportunity through crossword puzzles for problem solving in a language context. Such behaviour will promote word identification skills and help to establish an approach to spelling which is more experimental than approaches which rely purely upon memorisation. In considering word building from an orthographic point of view, we are adding another dimension to spelling in which the constraints of the spelling system are being actively considered.

COHESION IN TEXTS

Perera (1984), in a very important and enlightening contribution to our understanding of the reading process, shows in the last chapter of her book that many difficulties in reading have their source in the grammatical structure of texts. Having quoted evidence that readers strive to hold a whole clause in the short term memory whilst reading a passage, and having acknowledged that the size of the clause can be critical in that the short term memory store can easily become overloaded and its contents lost, Perera puts forward three hypotheses: 'reading is likely to be harder when the grammatical structure of a sentence is not easy to predict. . ., when a sentence does not divide readily into optimal segments for processing. . ., when a heavy burden is imposed on short term memory.' A style which is uncomplicated, a message that unfolds logically and predictably, and which is presented in reasonably short clauses and sentences is going to ease the reader's task considerably. Yet in any piece of continuous prose of any merit there are going to be connections that have to be made across the boundaries of sentences so that a clear message evolves.

Consider the following passage:

> To find him sitting by the fireside was unexpected to say the least. The wanderer had left home many years ago when I was merely a child, but I had retained over all those years a clear picture of my boyhood hero. Captain Morgan, sailor and pirate, smuggler and murderer was impressive in any light, but by firelight and its inevitable shadows he conveyed a sense of foreboding. Anxiety took over, almost panic and I began to wonder what our reunion would signify: excitement or simply trouble? For I had heard of exploits that wrought havoc in the villages of the Caribbean and of Spain's western seaboard; exploits that could not be thought impossible in other settings!

The reader has to realise that *him* in line 1, *the wanderer* in line 2, *my boyhood hero* in lines 3/4, *Captain Morgan* in line 4 and *he* in line 5 all refer to the same person. Furthermore, *sailor, pirate, smuggler* and *murderer* all have to be related to Captain Morgan; it has to be assumed that *exploits* are those of Captain Morgan; and the ellipsis in the last sentence has to be understood. Furthermore, the nominal repetition of *exploits* refers to exploits similar to those implied in a previous clause, and the conjunction *For* enables a reason to be given for the rising anxiety. If the reader cannot make these connections then he will not understand what he has read even though he may recognise all the words. The result would be confusion of a kind which could have been the basis of Vernon's idea of cognitive confusion (Vernon, 1957).

Hence, anyone who teaches children to read at any stage must be aware of the need to promote understanding of the cohesive ties in texts. How it is done will depend upon the age and reading ability of the child, but the fundamental basis of such teaching must lie in reading to the children so that they become familiar with the connections that are made across the boundaries of sentences and clauses. At first these will be relatively uncomplicated, nominal repetition will become obvious through stress and intonation, pronominal substitution may be clarified by the reader adding the actual noun, and the connection between ideas in the form of conjunctions can be reiterated in another form. The listeners will experience the impact of the links in the form of an understood story. Perera (1984) recommends that reading to children should continue through the junior school and into the secondary school, so that children will become familiar with a full range of grammatical constructions.

In addition, Perera recommends a whole series of activities that will make the child aware of the constitution of texts: what is connected with what, how the links are made, picking out the sequence of ideas, identifying all references to a single thing, and so on. Any teacher wishing to study the nature of comprehension and develop a teaching programme that goes deeper than the simple sequencing exercises that are spreading through the primary schools like wild fire should read Chapter 6 in Perera's book, 'Children's Writing and Reading'. And whilst reading that chapter it should be borne in mind that exercises such as are mentioned are so much more effective if done as a group activity, in the same way as are sequencing and cloze exercises, because the group organisation provides the opportunity for discussion and cooperative study. Problems can be raised and resolved with help, so that the exercises become a problem solving activity rather than a once and for all test.

Group prediction activities

Group prediction activities can be used to stimulate awareness of the possibilities and alternatives that can exist in texts, and it would be in keeping with the thesis of this book if the activities began with the construction of texts.

A group could be challenged to complete sentences such as the following in as many ways as possible in order to achieve a variety of meanings:

Aeroplanes are safe. . . . .
. . . . it is safe. . . . .
To fight is. . . . .; to run away. . . . .
Feeling tired, I. . . . .

From phrases and clauses such as these it would be possible to think of a variety of outcomes, some corresponding and some contrasting with each other. In this way children would learn to think about texts, to devise possible constructions to match their thoughts, and thereby gradually learn what to expect from texts.

Exercises of this kind could become an arid and dull occupation if done by individuals, but if done as a group activity where the challenge is to intervene and build cooperatively, the members of the group will build up the same form of motivation that is achieved when one group of children try to outplay another group of children in a team game, where each is trying to make a fuller contribution than the rest.

A FINAL REMINDER

Whatever you do to improve the children's reading ability will have a greater impact if you are seen to enjoy reading. Therefore, you should let them see you reading and enjoying their books as well as books of your own. Occasionally, stay in the classroom at lunch time to read and insist that no one interrupts your reading. When they see that reading is important to you, then there is a chance that they will come to regard reading as important. Furthermore, at play times and lunch times do not always send children out into the playground (or should we call it the barracks square, for that is what many playgrounds resemble?); with the agreement of the head teacher, let them stay in the classroom to read, or write, or engage in art and craft or play readings, and praise them for being so sensible for wanting to stay indoors and engage in such worthwhile pursuits. Naturally, you will have to make provision for adequate supervision, so that you are covered for the purposes of insurance; and children who require a change of scene should not be forced to stay in.

Also, do allow time in the junior school during lesson periods for personal reading, and allow the children to choose for themselves what they read. Avoid the ridiculous situation found in one junior four class where there were fifty books from the wonderful Puffin series standing on the window sill, yet the children ruefully told a visitor that they expected never to 'get onto those' because they had to complete the full set of 'dull, boring' (their words) readers first. Temptation can be a powerful teaching ploy, but this seemed to be taking things too far!

Further reading

Whether or not you are confronted with teaching children who are finding learning to read difficult, the following book tabulates and discusses difficulties, and is therefore a very useful reminder of the type of difficulties that do arise:

Reason, R. and Boote, R. (1986) *Learning Difficulties in Reading and Writing: a Teacher's Manual.* Windsor: NFER-Nelson.

Those who wish to give further thought to the underlying processes of word recognition should read:

Henderson, L. (1987) Word recognition: a tutorial review; and

Patterson, K. and Coltheart, V. (1987) Phonological processes in reading: a tutorial review;

both papers appear in Coltheart, M. (ed.) (1987) *The Psychology of Reading.* London: Lawrence Erlbaum.

For a more detailed and extensive study:

Henderson, L. (1982) *Orthography and Word Recognition in Reading.* London: Academic Press.

A very useful tabulation and discussion of the sound system in English spelling can be found in the revised edition of:

MacKay, D., Thompson, B. and Schaub, P. (1978) *Breakthrough to Literacy Teacher's Manual.* London: Longman.

Two reports of important research should be read by all who intend to teach children in junior and secondary schools:

Lunzer, E.A. and Gardner, K. (1979) *The Effective Use of Reading*. London: Heinemann Educational for the Schools Council.
Southgate Booth, V., Arnold, H. and Johnson, S. (1981) *Extending Beginning Reading*. London: Heinemann Educational.
Like the majority of research reports of this size, they reflect the ways in which they were designed and must, therefore, be read with care and discrimination. However, both reports have had a significant influence upon attitudes towards the methodology of developing children's reading abilities.

A small but highly suggestive piece of research by Hewitt, G. (1980) and reported in *Educational Review, 32,* 231–44 took the discussion about comprehension a little further. Hewitt questions the validity of the researches of Davis (1972) and Lunzer and Gardner (1979), suggesting that they were based on a false premise, ie that a list of hypothesised skills can be drawn up, tests of these skills constructed, and then by means of factor analysis it can be determined whether comprehension consists of a number of separate skills or a unitary aptitude. Hewitt's objections to this are that the tests used by Lunzer and Gardner did not take into account varying styles of reading behaviour to suit the varying contexts; processes for anwering the questions are not the same as those of typical reading tasks; the psychometric devices used were too blunt in their discrimination amongst the items; it is not possible to know if all the possible skills were covered; and the questions may have been the source of difficulty and not the text. The fundamental question raised by Hewitt is that measures of comprehension such as questions, cloze procedure and recall 'use quantitative means to analyse qualitative processes.' Hewitt suggests a qualitative approach by way of discourse analysis, whereby comprehension is assessed through noting the miscues made in an oral reading, and expecting the pupil to paraphrase the text and then discuss it, including questions, with the teacher.

From reading Hewitt's report it is obvious that prior knowledge, decoding ability and understanding of vocabulary all affect ability to extract meaning. It is not clear what part syntax plays in all this – perhaps in Hewitt's experiment with twelve year olds in a remedial class the poor decoding of words obscured the limitations of the reader's ability to manipulate syntax. An answer might be obtained if the experiment was replicated with average and good readers. However, what did emerge was the propensity to impose the reader's own thoughts and ideas upon the text, and the scope for distortion here was increased by the reader's deficiencies in decoding and in his knowledge of the vocabulary. Hence, we see emerging the controlling factor of word recognition, and knowledge of word meanings is emphasised. The experiment itself is too small and the sample too untypical for the results to be anything other than suggestive. Nevertheless, it is important to acknowledge Hewitt's argument and to be mindful of it when attempting to assess the ability of a person to comprehend a text.

Some useful suggestions for promoting spoken English in the classroom are contained in:
Sansom, C. (1965) *Speech in the Primary School*. London: Black.
Readers should note the date of this book and discriminate accordingly.

For those who would appreciate some guidance in ways of developing an understanding of literature by children the following series will prove informative:
Allan, C., Harkness, S., Love, J., McLullich, H. and Murdoch, H. (1986) *Reading 2000 Book Study Guides*. Edinburgh: Oliver and Boyd.
These cover novels at five levels:

Level One:	*A Gift from Winklesea*, by H. Cresswell.
	The Owl who was Afraid of the Dark, by J. Tomlinson.
Level Two:	*Danny Fox*, by D. Thomson.
	Super Gran, by F. Wilson.
Level Three:	*Charlotte's Web*, by E.B. White.
	Little House on the Prairie, by L.I. Wilder.
Level Four:	*Dragon Slayer*, by R. Sutcliff.
	The Borrowers, by M. Norton.
Level Five:	*Carrie's War*, by N. Bowden.
	The Eighteenth Emergency, by B. Byars.

These do not contain the text of the novels but are a study guide for teachers.

A useful resource for teachers in integrating reading with art and craft is:
Slingsby, J. (1981) *101 Things To Make*. London: Hamlyn.

Helpful resource books published by Usborne for children during the period when they are learning to write are:
Children's Britannica First Steps. General editor Heather Amery.
The First Thousand Words, by Amery and Cartwright.
Picture Word Book (classified by topics such as The Party, The School, Clothes, The Park, The Toyshop, The Garden, The Workshop and The Street).
Children's Word Finder, by Civarci and King, also classified by topics and suitable for lower juniors.

Finally, everyone concerned with the teaching of reading will wish to be familiar with the following important contributions to the organisation of the teaching of reading:
Bennett, J. (1985) *Learning to Read with Picture Books*. Stroud: Thimble Press.

Waterland, L. (1985) *Read With Me: An Apprenticeship Approach to Reading.* Stroud: Thimble Press.

Moon, B. and C. (1986) *Individualised Reading* (18th edition). University of Reading: Reading and Language Information Centre.

Meek, M. (1988) *How Texts Teach What Readers Learn.* Stroud: Thimble Press.

7 Teaching slow learners to read and write

It is not the objective of this chapter to provide a study of the causes and manifestations of difficulties in reading and learning to read. All that has been written already in previous chapters indicates the nature of the skills and behaviours that have to be acquired if learning to read is to take place, and it is in the acquisition of these skills and behaviours wherein the difficulties may lie. Most of these difficulties have been recognised for many years now, and they are encapsulated in the table of typical errors taken from Pumfrey (1976) and reproduced in Appendix 2. This includes substitutions which may or may not make sense, no response because of a failure of recognition or an inability to make a response because of cognitive confusion of some kind, additions to the text which may or may not fit the sense of the text, omissions of words or phrases, repetitions indicating uncertainty, self-corrections, mispronunciations caused by insufficient knowledge or a misinterpretation, disregard for punctuation, and reversal of words or phrases.

Perera (1984) takes us beyond the actual errors of Pumfrey's list and looks for reasons. She contrasts the fact that oral language is universally learned whilst many children find progress in reading extremely difficult, especially after the early stages. She suggests that the sources of difficulty lie within both the reader and the reading process. Readers cannot rely on non-linguistic information, such as the body language of a speaker or the presence of what is the object of the communication. They must rely solely upon the text to obtain the message. Secondly, the language of texts differs in some grammatical constructions and discourse structures from everyday speech and thus the reader may be confused. Thirdly, the reader has to organise the texts in terms of grammatical constitutions, and especially in terms of the composition of phrases, whereas this is done in speech through intonation, spacing and pauses.

The types of difficulties that emerge according to Perera are: those caused by the illegibility of the text, because the printing or writing is badly formed or is obscured by encroaching illustrations, and those caused when the content of the text is unfamiliar to the reader so that in trying to sort out to what the text refers the reader becomes confused.

To these can be added the use of unfamiliar vocabulary, difficulties caused by the grammatical form, and texts that are not clearly organized in such a way as to present the message in a familiar way. Furthermore, Perera concludes that 'if unfamiliar subject matter expressed in technical vocabulary combines with intrinsically demanding sentence structure, then the chances of full comprehension are much reduced.'

This approach by Perera to reading difficulties takes us away from a simple view of testing which looks at each error a child makes when reading as a discrete mistake. It suggests that reading errors can more profitably be examined in the light of the specific text confronting the reader and by taking into account the use the reader is able to make of that text. This suggests that in spite of the fact that discrete word identification tests correlate highly with prose reading tests, such tests do not tell us what difficulties the reader may have when confronted by prose texts.

Miscue analysis

In order to resolve this problem and suggest wherein lies a particular reader's difficulties, Goodman (1969) put forward his ideas on what he called 'miscue analysis'. His suggestion was that errors are not necessarily absolute but are frequently relative to the text and the reader. A misinterpretation on the part of the reader may be the source of subsequent errors. Hence an error, or as Goodman called it a miscue, must be seen within the context of the whole text or passage for it to be evaluated and appreciated.

This raises in our minds the question of whether the error made by the reader is indicative of some element in the text that is unknown to him or whether the error was caused by some other misinterpretation elsewhere in the text. An unfamiliar word may represent the former type of error, whilst the latter must be seen in terms of a larger unit of language than the individual word. Such information would be invaluable to the teacher because it would indicate the type of teaching response that was necessary. In the case of the unfamiliar word, obviously the child has to be taught one way or another to recognise that word in future. If, on the other hand, the reader has allowed himself to be misled by the text or by his train of thought being diverted as a result of a previous error, then the teaching should require that the reader reassesses the text, checks the original error and correspondingly readjusts to the text that follows.

A point of caution here: the original error can itself be a miscue in that it may involve a word that would otherwise be known to the reader had his thoughts not have been upon something else. For example, a reader could come to a text fully expecting it to accord very specifically to his preconceptions of the subject matter, so that he may read a plural where he was expecting a singular noun, or he may read a synonym for the actual word or he may add adjectives where none existed simply because the additional adjective more accurately and adequately expressed his thoughts upon the subject matter. Hence the need for the teacher to be sensitive to the child's true ability and to be wary of jumping to rash conclusions about what the reader can and cannot do. One very important point that Goodman made was that the assessment of a child's miscues should not commence until the child had passed the first paragraph and was well into the text. This enables the reader to adjust his thinking to the text in prospect; it turns the first paragraph into an advance organizer (Ausubel, 1968), thereby laying the foundations for subsequent thoughts on the passage as it is being read.

A muted caveat concerning the validity of miscue analysis is the reservation that it is solely concerned with oral reading and may not represent what happens in silent reading. One cannot be sure of this because we have so little to illuminate the processes involved in silent reading. However, our study of the composition of written language and our understanding of what has to be accomplished in order to interpret it do suggest certain strategies that must be taken by the reader and these do in large measure accord with the idea that miscues whilst reading silently are possible and do take place as was seen in reading the passage *Boys' arrows* in Chapter 1. Hence, it can be asserted that no teacher of reading should be unaware of the concept behind the term 'miscue analysis', namely: that reading should be regarded as a totality in which the various elements interact with one another.

Students on school practice will not have time to carry out a complete miscue analysis, although they may be able to do so on a weekly attachment. Even so, to carry out a full miscue analysis as suggested by Goodman and Burke (1972) is a rather lengthy and complicated process, and there have been suggestions that a restricted analysis could be carried out. This amounts to the teacher using a number of symbols, similar to those used by Pumfrey (see Appendix 2), to mark on a treble-spaced typed copy of the text the miscues made by the reader. The miscues are subsequently tabulated and, on the basis of three readings of different texts, a profile of miscues for the child is drawn up, so that the teacher may make an assessment of the weaknesses and reading behaviour of the reader.

Arnold (1982), closely following Goodman, lists the miscues as: refusal to read a word or phrase; the substitution of one word for another; the omission of a word; the insertion of a word into the text; the reversal of a sequence of words or letters; self-correction of a miscue; an undue pause or hesitation in the reading; and the repetition of a word or phrase already read correctly.

Based on a block graph system whereby each category of miscue has a column, the occurrence of the above miscues as registered on the teacher's marked copy of the text can be transferred to the graph and a clear indication will be obtained of the ratio amongst different miscues. From this profile the teacher will get some idea of where the emphases of her teaching with that child should lie, and in any case a limited analysis of the reader's difficulties will form a more instructive picture of those difficulties than the majority of general tests of reading ability, especially if all that is available to the teacher is a graded word reading test or a sentence completion test.

Any student or teacher wishing to use a modified form of miscue analysis as a diagnostic device should read Arnold (1982), Chapter 4, and should obtain Goodacre's manual *Hearing Children Read* (1979) from the Centre for Reading at the University of Reading.

THE USE OF DIAGNOSIS

Having decided upon diagnosis, one has to hesitate and ask, how should we interpret these errors or miscues in reading? The most striking thing about the list of miscues is that they fall into two categories of mistakes. Taking Arnold's list of miscues, substitution and non-response (refusal) constitute a wrong response to a word in the main, whereas omission, insertion, reversal, self-correction, hesitation and repetition are all concerned with language behaviour rather than with the identification of words. They do not necessarily represent an inability to respond correctly to a word; they are simply an inappropriate form of reading behaviour. Furthermore, even substitution and non-response may not indicate that the reader cannot recognise the word per se; they may simply mean that what the child is thinking, possibly as a result of a misinterpretation in the preceding text, does not tally with what is printed.

This all adds up to the fact that a major concern in our diagnosis is the way in which a reader 'handles' the text, the way in which he uses parts of it, the way he thinks about it and the ways in which he co-ordinates his thinking about the context with his response to the print before him. Only a portion of his miscues are concerned with an inability to identify some words correctly.

Therefore, we are faced with a decision that has to be taken. It concerns the degree to which the reader's problems lie in an inability to identify words, the degree to which they are caused by his ineffectual use of texts, and the degree to which they are caused by particular texts.

For those children who find reading difficult the problem of word identification will be present. Underwood, G. and J. (1986), Francis (1982), Fernald (1943) and many others have found that a deficiency in word recognition skills is a serious problem which distinguished these children from their peers who were better readers. Brierley (1987), discussing brain function and reading, suggests a close relationship between the brain's ability to search for patterns and the child's ability to notice similarities and differences in sounds and in letter formations. Thus in any remedial programme a great deal of attention will have to be given to developing a child's ability to see patterns in letters, to recognise the boundaries within words that are significant for meaning and for pronunciation, and to search in the memory score for a meaning that can be attached to the printed word.

It was the desire to deal with this aspect of remedial reading that was predominant in the thinking of many teachers and writers who were concerned with the remedial teaching of reading and who used games and word identification exercises – such people as Stott (1962) who produced a series of games, thirty items in all, that constituted his *Programmed Reading Kit*. These games were primarily concerned with teaching children to attach sounds and meaning to discrete words. An example of the type of exercise is the one in which children had to assemble three cards, known as 'half moon cards', each with a part of a word printed on it, and with one of the cards containing a cutout semicircle on one side, whilst the other card had a semicircular bulge on the side that was to be placed adjacent to the other card, as illustrated in Figure 7.1.

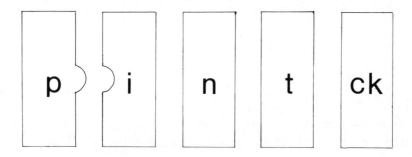

Figure 7.1

This device could be extended to include syllables and common letter strings. Many other exercises similar in intent to these can be found in the *Programmed Reading Kit*, as well as in Hughes (1970, 1972) and in a very useful study of learning difficulties in reading and writing by Reason and Boote (1986).

However, whilst accepting the need to look for patterns in words and to interpret them in terms of sounds, we must also accept that the search for meaning lies at the heart of the matter and this suggests another approach to the problems of word identification. It is the approach that permeates the earlier chapters of this book and seeks to identify words through the text in which they stand. It is an approach which lends itself to the use of additional cues extraneous to those provided by the word itself – semantic and syntactic cues – which when added to those that can be picked up from the word, such as an initial letter sound or a particular segment of the word, make it that much more likely that the child will be able to work out a reasonable response to the word itself.

There are other advantages to this approach. One is that it is a much more meaningful approach to the child in terms of reading. Beard (1987) has criticised the games and exercise approach, such as Stott's, on the grounds that the children learn to play the games and do the exercises but, because of the fragmented nature of the material, it does not necessarily add up to reading. Furthermore, it will be remembered from the discussion of the categories of miscues that many of them are concerned with textual reading rather than word identification, so an approach which practises the child in reading texts will help him to overcome such things as additions, omissions, repetitions, and reversals, as well as lead more naturally into the identification of unfamilar words.

Remedial teaching: three possibilities

If we are serious in our intention to tackle deficiencies in reading or the disinclination of children to read then we must set up a close monitoring system based on observation, within the infant and junior classes of our primary schools, that will detect any lack of normal progress in the reading development of every child and identify those children who in Moseley's terms 'could do better' (Moseley, 1975), and differentiate them from those whose problems are more fundamental and who may fall within the category defined by Brierley (1987) as having specific developmental problems, such as dyslexia, which may have their roots in maturational failures in precise regions of the brain.

Those who 'could do better' could be picked up virtually at the outset of their problem, given extra and more frequent help, and followed more closely so that a spurt in learning would be achieved and maintained. The importance of a type of 'crash' programme, consisting of more sessions than are usually set aside for reading, short in duration and frequent in occurrence – certainly more frequent than once a day – has never been fully appreciated in our schools, although the original SRA Reading Laboratories were intended to be used in this way. Arnold (1982) has pointed out that there is much evidence (Campbell, 1981; Southgate Booth et al., 1981; Maxwell, 1977) that the time allocated to hearing individual children read is minimal, and if this is so for all children then the effect on those who are falling behind must be devastating. Many of the problems that arise in the early stages of reading development are caused by cognitive confusion and lack of system (Vernon, 1971) and by what Cashdan (1969) called a gap in the child's understanding of the totality of reading experience. In other words, these children have difficulty in sorting things out and putting all the bits together.

The suggestions of Vernon and Cashdan lead one to the conclusion that the appropriate methodological approach would be one that helps to bring clarity to the child's thinking by engaging that child in a total language experience. A child does not learn to ride a bicycle by learning separately how to sit, how to balance, how to pedal, how to lean into a turn. Similarly with learning to read, confusion will result if the learning process is fragmented.

A combination of methods that meets these demands, and is one that can be adjusted to all ages of children, even those children who slip through the monitoring system and become known as 'backward readers or very slow learners', can be drawn up from three sources.

I SUPPLEMENTARY HELP THROUGH ADDITIONAL TEXT
CONSTRUCTION

The first source is the methodology proposed in Chapter 5 above, wherein the emphasis is on the construction of texts using *Breakthrough Sentence Makers* and on reading texts with a familiar story or message. Those children identified by the monitoring system as not doing as well as they could should receive additional and more frequent short sessions on these reading activities. These would take place at the optimum time for the benefit of the child and not, as so often is the case, only for the short period when the teacher is freed by the presence of a student on school practice. Those children identified as having a more fundamental problem could, under such a monitoring system, be referred early to experts in these matters so that advice and guidance could be passed back to the teachers.

2   SHARED READING

The second source is an approach that has come to be called 'shared reading' and it complements the above approach. There are two forms of 'shared reading': one proposed by Carol Chomsky (1976) and the other by Meek (1988). Both of these versions could be adapted to any age level provided that suitable texts were chosen and provided that, in the case of the method suggested by Meek, the teacher adopted a suitable personal relationship with the child.

Carol Chomsky describes a method used with eight year old children who were having difficulty in reading. The children were allowed to select short books whose contents were recorded on tape. The books were just a little difficult for the children to read although the subject matter was suited to their chronological age. The children listened to the tapes whilst following as closely as possible the text of the books, and they were encouraged to take part in the reading by joining the taped voice in the first place and gradually taking over the reading of parts which they thought they knew. Chomsky reported growing enthusiasm amongst the children for the task and they were allowed to take the tapes and books home to demonstrate their skill to their parents. At first the children memorised the tapes, but gradually showed an increasing tendency to tackle parts of texts unaided by the tape. Difficult words were recorded on index cards, retained and learnt by the children, and the teacher devised games of find-the-word or constructing in wooden cut-out letters a word taken from the text. There was matching of words and comparisons of words, all associated with the texts and, therefore, all associated with the child's reading behaviour.

There are several very important considerations for learning and for teaching in Chomsky's method. The first is that the child is able to witness reading as a participant by comparing what he sees with what he hears; he is witnessing, so to speak, a reader sorting things out and putting the printed words and phrases together to form a coherent message, and thus he is being helped towards an understanding of the totality of the reading experience (Cashdan, 1969). He is an apprentice reader in the words of Waterland (1985). Secondly, he is being surreptitiously encouraged to memorise things in a meaningful pattern – in this case the story – so that print is being associated with meaning and not the other way round at this stage. Bruner (1960) and Brierley (1987) both emphasise the role of pattern as an aid to memorisation and learning. Thirdly, the teaching that is done additionally to the reading is still within the compass of the reading material, so that even discrete exercises are in this case closely related to the reading matter and to the act of reading. Finally, the actual reading activity under this method can be very private. The child has the support of the tapes and he can use them as a 'face-saver' if he wishes. No one likes to be seen as a failure, and in this method the child can cover failure by asserting that he is listening to the tape. Nevertheless, the teacher can, if she thinks it appropriate, challenge the reader to break away and attempt to read unaided, knowing that the reader can revert back to using the tape if necessary.

Whilst the reading activity can be private in Chomsky's method, it can also be a group method, whereby two or more readers listen to the tape and enjoy the story together and eventually take it in turns to attempt to read unassisted by the tape. Furthermore, the exercises and word-learning activities could be planned on a group interaction basis.

Meek's approach is much more intimate between adult and child – an advantage and a disadvantage for reasons that are obvious to anyone who is sensitive to the relationship between teacher and child, and who is familiar with the large classes that are found in so many urban primary schools in Britain. Basically, the approach is concerned with more than attempting to read a book and memorise words. In fact, it can more accurately be described as an introduction into the study of a book. The teacher and the learner talk together about the book – everything about the book: the cover, the orientation, the author, the title, the illustrations, the characters and events and the story as it emerges. The emphasis is on participation and discussion between teacher and child, and the child is allowed to initiate ideas on every aspect concerning the book, just as would be done between a sensitive parent and child.

As the discussion proceeds and as the pages are turned the teacher helps with the text, but the child is encouraged by implication, involvement and attitude to participate in the evolving story by anticipating the text, expressing views on what is or should be happening, and being encouraged to notice aspects of the orthography and draw unfettered comparisons between words, or ideas or actions. The intention must be enjoyment of the book so that the child will want to 'read' it again and again. Meek read *Rosie's Walk* with Ben five times altogether before he was encouraged to 'read' it himself. All in all it was an enjoyable experience from which he learnt much about the totality of reading, about books, about print, about interacting with texts and about the structure of words.

As the child progresses from picture books, through illustrated story books, nursery rhymes and folk tales to novels, the emphasis is always on talking about the book, enjoying its tale, understanding its message, its place in the scheme of things. It is in fact a process of getting all one can from a book and not merely decoding the print. To understand this approach fully and to enjoy Meek's enthusiasm for books and for children, students should read her book, *How Texts Teach What Readers Learn*, and refer to *Rosie's Walk* by Pat Hutchins, a Puffin Book, and the other children's books that Meek mentions (page 41).

Some teachers whose schools have converted totally to the approaches of Waterland and Meek have expressed some apprehension about the efficacy of such a method, used on its own with large classes of children. The answer to this argument surely is that as the method has so much to commend it, especially in that it introduces children to a fuller understanding of texts and books of all kinds, it would be desirable to use it at least alongside other methods in order to reap the advantages offered. Young beginners and slow starters alike can gain so much in understanding the nature of reading from such an approach, provided that the books selected for use are age-related in their contents. *Rosie's Walk* would not be suitable for junior school children.

3   FERNALD'S METHOD

Finally, the third source from which we can draw in our construction of a methodology to help those who do not find reading easy is one that was inaugurated in a clinic in Los Angeles in 1922 by Fernald (see Fernald, 1943). As an approach, it is closely associated with the approach described in Chapter 5 above in that it involves the reader in the construction of his own texts. However, the methodology is one that many would think more appropriate for older children, although not all would agree.

In devising the method Fernald proceeded from the assumption that children who were failing to learn to read effectively needed remotivating and thereby needed a new approach; what they did not require was to be subjected to a methodology that had already failed them. This is understandable because no one likes to be reminded of failure. Everybody enjoys success, and according to Fernald what slow or failing readers required was to be convinced that they could succeed. Her first step, therefore, was concerned with *remotivation*.

This was done by proving to the child that he could learn to spell and to recognise any word he wished, and the method she adopted was based primarily upon a kinaesthetic approach, through the sense of movement, although the other senses of sight, sound and touch were also incorporated within the method.

The process of remotivation can best be illustrated and emphasised by describing how this was done by the writer (Roberts, 1960, 1961) when teaching a class of thirty-seven slow learning ten year old children, seventeen of whom had reading ages below six years on the Schonell Graded Word Test (Schonell, 1945, 1975). When I boasted that I knew of a secret method by which I could guarantee to teach anyone to spell any word, members of the class wickedly suggested that I might display my secret powers by using the accepted 'genius' of the class – a boy called Michael who could just about manage to recognize the words *egg* and *bun* on the Schonell list, giving him a dubious reading age of 5.2 years. Michael who came from a family of non-readers thought he was about to emigrate with his family to Australia, so he chose the word *emigrate*. (Any Australians reading this will be relieved to know that their officials are mindful of Australia's better interests and Michael stayed with us long enough to prove the efficacy of Fernald's method.)

After he had selected the word *emigrate*, I told him that if he traced the word with his forefinger 50 times he would then be able to write it without copying. The thought of such a task daunted Michael but delighted the rest of the class, who proceeded to urge him on as he traced with his forefinger the word written on the blackboard, saying as he did so /em/,/i:/,/greit/. Naturally, after six tracings Michael thought his arm was about to drop off, but the urging of the others was relentless and he managed a further four or five tracings. Then came the crunch; Michael was convinced by the ache in his arm that he knew how to write the word correctly without copying, and of course he failed, much to the delight of rest of the class. Fortunately, I was able to use that to spur him on to prove them wrong by telling him that he hadn't given himself a fair chance; after all, I had said fifty times was necessary! So he set off again with a more determined and confident air, and after another dozen tracings and many sighs, huffs and puffs he succeeded in writing the word without copying. The effect was electrifying: Michael was jubilant, performing a primitive war dance before the blackboard, and the remainder of the class, after momentary astonishment, were convinced that spelling was after all 'kids' stuff'! Perhaps I should recommend young teachers to confine this remotivation to an interaction between the teacher and children individually and privately; on the other hand it might be argued that nothing ventured, nothing gained. All I can say is, make sure you succeed and do not go into any teaching halfheartedly.

Now the method which Fernald suggested to follow the remotivation period, which incidentally will not always be as short and effective as it was with Michael's help, included the children electing to write a story or other form of prose message, asking for words that they thought they could not spell, tracing them until they could be written without copying, and then including them in their written text.

Fernald suggested that the words should be written by the teacher on small index cards and subsequently stored in a personal box file by each child. When I used this method I wrote the requested words on the back of the sheet of paper containing the child's original story and the child had to write that word for storage in a personal dictionary under the title of the story in which they were to appear. Fernald's way had the advantage of teaching alphabetical order, and it caused the children to look closely at the letter sequences in order to place the words correctly in the box file. My way had the advantage of causing the child to write the word a third time – once to test whether he knew the word, then to include it in his story and, finally, to store it in his personal dictionary note book. It also had the advantage with very slow learners that they seemed more able to retrieve the words through remembering the context or story in which they had used them.

The stories completed, the teacher takes the original and copies it for the child, either writing it in a clear 'unjoined' handwriting or typing it onto a jumbo typewriter. The child is then asked to read aloud the fair copy and afterwards to learn any words that were spelled incorrectly on the original. These had been noted in red on the back of his original script. Gradually, the child builds up a book or folder of things that he has written, and he can read these to friends in his class or exchange books and read the stories written by others. This can involve an enormous amount of reading, far more than these children would submit themselves to if confined to the published reading schemes, and it provides the children with an excellent excuse to stay in at play times and at dinner times during the cold winter months.

There are many advantages in Fernald's methodology. First, and by no means least, as can be imagined Michael had never looked at one word for so long in all his school life before his confrontation with the word *emigrate*. Children using the tracing and vocalisation method have concentration forced upon them, but in a natural way. Second, the teacher in saying the parts of the word as she writes it and expecting the child to say those parts as he traces the complete word indicates to the child the boundaries within the word that are significant for the pronunciation of that word, a practice advocated by Bryant and Bradley (1985). Third, the words are ones selected by the child within a context that is meaningful and of interest to him.

Thus the child who previously has been confused by the task of learning to read is shown how to look at words, how to split them up, and is required to use a multi-sensory learning technique, whereby he is using his kinaesthetic, visual, auditory and tactile senses to retain what he has been shown. This is a far cry from the notion that having told a child to learn something our task as a teacher is finished. Furthermore, the storage of words in the box or book files and the retention of the original scripts with the words written on the rear side provided an excellent basis for spelling lessons. Children in the class referred to above were given a period every week when they revised words previously learned. Spot checks were made, and all members of the class knew that one error entailed revision through tracing–vocalisation–writing of that word, whereas two errors out of a spot check on four words meant revising the whole collection again. Subsequently, small groups of children were drawn together to study further and in greater depth the features of some of the words they had in their collections.

These are all important attributes of this approach, but they are not its only strengths. Earlier in this chapter it was stated that cognitive confusion may lie at the heart of reading failure, and by implication anything that clarifies the issue will be beneficial. Part of the difficulty facing anyone learning to read is to find out how to look at words, seeing the composition of the significant elements and learning how to remember those words. So far it has been demonstrated how Fernald's method helps the learner in this aspect of reading. However, the implications of all that has been written so far in this book are that word identification is not the only factor that may cause difficulty.

Perera (1984), in discussing reading difficulty at sentence level points to the difficulty of storing too many elements from a text, a difficulty that is present in all aspects of processing information (Miller, 1956). According to Miller, only seven bits or separate pieces of information, such as words, plus or minus two, can be retained in the short-term memory before some kind of chunking has to take place, with the newly formed chunk becoming in its turn a bit in a fresh build up. Perera suggests that the clause is an important unit which readers strive to hold in the short term memory, which is another way of saying that the reader has to extract the general meaning from a clause and place it with the general meaning extracted from other clauses to build up the overall meaning of the text. If the reader is the one who is originating the ideas that form the text, then this processing difficulty has a different form. The writer under Fernald's method has himself formulated the ideas behind the text and has constructed the clauses that contribute to that text. These ideas are in his head when he comes to read what he has written and has been copied out for him by the teacher. Hence the difficulty of processing the perceptual input of the text is reduced, and indeed he is learning from the very fact that he is doing what he can already do with familiar texts.

A further difficulty in reading indentified by Perera concerns global discourse organisation. A reader is helped if he knows what is coming. Usually, that information is gleaned from the texts, and the earlier in the text the better for the reader. Through writing their own stories for reading matter, the children following Fernald's approach have already primed themselves before they even start to read the text. Furthermore, they will not find the structure bewildering, and they will be aware of the cohesive elements within the text because it is their story and they know the story frame.

These are all very important considerations where reading difficulties are concerned. Obviously, a reader has to come to terms with them, but it is the argument here that it is better if the reader can learn to cope with them through using them with supports rather than through unaided confrontation with them. Fernald's method offers that support. It puts the child in the position of knowing what is coming in the text, because he has formulated the ideas conveyed by the text and he has done it in ways that are manageable so far as he is concerned. For example, one ten year old child in the class mentioned above after a visit to the circus wrote, '*Yesterday I went to the circus and it was good and it was good and it was good*'. When he came to read what he had written he had no trouble whatsoever because it expressed his feelings and thoughts precisely. Furthermore, he had learned to spell and recognise all the words in that sentence – no mean feat for a child with a reading age under six years. The reading lesson had turned into a writing, spelling and problem solving exercise. It is at this point that reading and writing interact forming a total language experience consisting of text construction (thinking, writing and spelling) and text interpretation (reading).

A COMBINATION OF METHODS

No one can lay down exactly what procedures a teacher should use with children who are finding reading and writing difficult. The important thing for the teacher is to be aware of the difficulties presented by the complexities of these tasks, difficulties presented by the texts, difficulties presented by the child – his lack of information and his lack of acquired behaviours. Having made herself aware of the difficulties and having assessed to what extent they exist in her children, she must then adopt a flexible approach calling upon any or all of the methods so far mentioned. Much will depend upon the age of the children as well as upon their reading ability. Until recent years schools were looking for an ideal method and many tended to revert to a mechanistic approach through a restricted form of phonics. This cannot be regarded as satisfactory.

For those children who 'could do better' it is unsafe to rely upon one approach or a single methodology. A combination of approaches and methodologies is required so that children can see the issues clarified, they can understand the associations that are made in meaningful settings, they can obtain practice in making those associations and clarifying their meanings, and they can do this through the uses of all their senses.

Children who can read, but not very well

Fernald suggested a way of helping children who read with difficulty. It was this: they should scan the page to be read picking out any words that they did not recognise. These would be learned by her tracing–vocalisation–writing without copying technique, the words being stored in a box file for future reference. I found this identification of unfamiliar words prior to reading very difficult to establish, so I opted for an easier approach. The reader was encouraged to make an exploratory study of the book to establish the gist of its contents. This was easier with nonfiction than with fiction, although in the case of the latter, the title and the fly leaf, which sometimes carried a synopsis, were indications of the type of story contained in the book. The children were encouraged to ask one another about the books in the hope of establishing book talk in the classroom. Then they were encouraged to read the book silently but ask for any words that were unfamiliar. These words had to be written by the child on his book marker which may run to two or three strips of paper stapled together – and the reader continued with his silent reading. At an appropriate place in the book – the end of a chapter or section – the child had to learn the words by the tracing–vocalisation–writing without copying technique. At the end of the book the child was tested on his ability to read the words on his book marker and then to spell them. The same sanctions were enforced as with the checks made on words used in their stories: two mistakes and they did the lot again. Weekly spelling checks took the children back over all previously learned words, so that the effect was cumulative. More and more words were learned and there was weekly reinforcement, and the more they learnt the easier it became, so that eventually there was a noticeable drop in the tracing that was done; the children would begin to rely upon looking intently at the words making an active, conscious effort to memorise them and then writing them, without copying of course.

Significant increases in reading ability were registered amongst all the children in the class of slow learners mentioned above, some increasing their reading ages as measured on the Schonell Graded Word Reading Test by upwards of two years. It is difficult not to imagine even more startling increases had I used the combination of methods that I am now advocating.

Further reading
For those who wish to study some of the research that has been carried out in connection with difficulties in reading:
Vernon, M.D. (1971) *Reading and Its Difficulties*. Cambridge: Cambridge University Press.
Moseley, D. (1975) *Special Provision for Reading*. Slough: NFER.
Young, P. and Tyre, C. (1983) *Dyslexia or Illiteracy*. Milton Keynes: Open University Press.
Beard, R. (1987) *Developing Reading 3–13*. London: Hodder and Stoughton.

Those wishing to use miscue analysis as a form of reading test should read:
Goodman, Y.M. and Burke, C.L. (1972) *Reading Miscue Inventory*. New York: Macmillan.

On the other hand, those wishing to use it as an integral part of their teaching programme for diagnostic and teaching purposes should refer to:
Davies, J.A. (1980) *A Developmental Study of Children's Reading Miscues*. MEd. Thesis. University of Manchester.
Arnold, H. (1982) *Listening to Children Reading*. London: Hodder and Stoughton.
Burke, E. (1976) *The Development of Reading Strategies Among Primary School Children*. Doctoral thesis. University of Manchester.

and for a summary of various ways of tabulating the results of a miscue analysis read:
Beard, R. (1987) *Developing Reading 3–13*. London: Hodder and Stoughton.
Goodacre, E. (1979) *Hearing Children Read*. Reading: University Centre for Reading.

A useful collection of assessment texts is contained in:
Arnold, H. (1984) *Making Sense of It: Graded Passages for Miscue Analysis*. London: Hodder and Stoughton.

For those who wish to widen their knowledge of the treatment of disabilities in reading there are three very useful sources:
Reid, J.F. and Donaldson, H. (1977) *Reading: Problems and Practices.* London: Ward Lock Educational,
containing particularly informative papers by Merritt, who raises the question of reading neurosis, and by Cotterell, who suggests a formidable range of exercises and teaching ploys to meet a vast range of difficulties.
Clay, M.M. (1982) *The Early Detection of Reading Difficulties: A Diagnostic Survey with Recovery Procedures.* Tadworth, Surrey: Heinemann.
Reason, R. and Boote, R. (1986) *Learning Difficulties in Reading and Writing: A Teacher's Manual.* Windsor: NFER-Nelson.

Anyone wishing to look more closely at the part played by tracing in the learning process and especially in relation to learning to read should consult:
Hulme, C. (1981) *Reading Retardation and Multi-Sensory Teaching.* London: Routledge and Kegan Paul.

There are many references to the work of Bradley and Bryant which students of reading will find interesting and informative.

An introduction to the problematic concept of dyslexia can be obtained from the following:
Vernon, M.D. (1971) *Reading and Its Difficulties.* Cambridge: Cambridge University Press.
Miles, T.R. (1971) More on dyslexia, Ingram, T.T.S. (1971) Specific learning difficulties in childhood: a medical point of view; and Naidoo, S. (1971) Specific developmental dyslexia,
three papers which form part of a symposium on reading disability in the *British Journal of Educational Psychology, 41*(1).
Pavlidis, G.T., and Miles, T.R. (eds) (1981) *Dyslexia Research and Its Application to Education.* London: Wiley.

8 The development of writing

Before one can develop children's abilities as writers it is important to be aware of what writing involves. Essentially it is the composition of a message – a train of thought – and its translation into written symbols. Other details are involved but these are the two major elements that must be kept clearly in mind. Their nature will change as the skill of the writer develops, and they will vary according to the substance of the writing. This change of nature is especially so in the case of the translation into written symbolic form. At first the writer will be concerned with the message, then with the details of producing the correct symbols – letter formation and spelling – and finally, with the form and style of the writing so that it matches the substance of the message and expresses most effectively the thought patterns of the writer.

Hence, throughout the junior school there must be a sustained effort to improve and develop children's abilities to compose messages, and there must be a parallel drive to improve the quality of expression as displayed in the written texts.

Personal narrative writing

The type of writing that seems to come naturally to young children is personal narrative. In this they tell their stories – what is happening to them, what they did or what they are going to do – they write about people they know, and they write about characters that inhabit their real and their imaginary worlds. This type of writing frequently finds expression in the once ubiquitous News that was a feature, and still is, of so many primary schools. During the early stages this personal narrative is quite close to normal children's speech, but it is the task of the junior school teacher to extend the range of structures used in this writing, so that noun and verb phrases can be employed with increasing effect, verb tenses can be controlled, and more complex constructions and as yet unfamiliar structures used. Children must be weaned away from compound sentences with their plethora of *ands* and *thens*: '*I went to the shops and I bought some sweets then I came back and I went to bed.*' In their place must emerge an ability to use connectives more sparingly and appositely, a process that can be aided by the teacher amending the child's writing in the presence of the child, cancelling and altering the connectives as appropriate, and then reading out the altered text to the child and asking the child to read it, so that he becomes familiar with the sound of the revised style through hearing it read to him, and from his reading, 'gets the feel of it'. Obviously, this alteration of text should not be done in a condemnatory manner; it should conform to the study approach advocated throughout this book, introducing the child to the ways in which you as his teacher would write his story and allowing him to experience the revised style.

From this type of teacher intervention the child will learn the efficacy of short sentences, and he will witness the emergence of complex sentences with a variety of subordinate and embedded clauses. Perera (1984) states that 'At the age of eight, there is rather more subordination in samples of children's speech than there is in comparable samples of writing; by ten, the relationship is reversed, with about a third more subordinate clauses in written language; by seventeen, the difference between the two modes is even greater'. This is a very interesting trend, and it is one that deserves a little attention. How does it come about? The implication could be that it happens naturally, developing from the experiences children gain from the books they read. And so it may, but one would be more certain of its optimum development if the teachers of eight to eleven year olds set out to develop consciously this trend. They could do it through amending children's written work, altering the structure to show the possibilities of using subordinate clauses effectively. Likewise, the attention of children could be drawn to this aspect of grammatical structure in a very natural way during the group construction of texts on an overhead projector. Children would be made aware of the skills that they were developing and they could be encouraged to look for the use of complex sentence formations in the books they were reading. This is far removed from the old style grammar lessons, because it is done in the context of an activity – constructing or reading a text – that is itself interesting, and the grammar aspect can be introduced as merely enlightening and enhancing the activity. The objective is not the identification of the grammatical structure but its use for other purposes.

As children see alterations made to their written work when amended by the teacher, as they participate in the group construction of texts and as their advanced reading ability enables them to concentrate more easily and readily on the language of their books, they will come to see that what they write must have form and cohesion. At first their texts will frequently end abruptly having no adequate conclusion. Perera presumes that the young writers tire, and decide to finish almost in a flash: '*Then I went home and told my mother*' seems to have been the salvation of many a struggling writer! Also their texts will frequently lack cohesion, in that the parts of those texts will not hang together. There will be no clearly discernable gist emerging from the text and the various cohesive ties – reference, substitution and ellipsis – will not sustain a degree of cohesion sufficient to convey that gist.

The following account of a school trip was written by a child for a student teacher:

> Yesterday our teacher took us on a school trip to the museum. It was boring. They took us all round the town and we arrived late. There were mummies and lots of old spears. They looked very dangerous. They said we must keep quiet in the museum.

The student in discussion with the child suggested alterations so that the final draft was:

> Our teacher took us on a school trip to the museum yesterday. The journey was boring, because they took us all round town and we arrived late. In the museum there were mummies and lots of old spears. Some of the spears looked very dangerous. The attendants told us to keep quiet in the museum.

The revised passage has clearer cohesive ties, but the more important point about this exercise was that it provided another step towards the acquisition of the writer's craft, such as the clarification of issues and the establishment of a clear pathway for the reader. Furthermore, the skill of the work done by the student teacher lay in basically accepting the style and organisation used by the child, so that the end product still related closely to the child's original draft whilst taking the child a little further along the road to skilled writing.

This action by the teacher was not discouraging to the child in any way; in fact, the child was very pleased with the result and still regarded it as his own. Teachers should not hesitate to give help. All too often in the past, teachers were discouraged from any critical assessment of children's writing in the belief that criticism would be inhibiting. Art teachers went through a similar phase when it was thought inhibiting to tell a child that the donkey's tail shouldn't be placed as though it was coming out of its mouth! But how are children to learn if they are not shown what is correct or what is desirable or even preferable? Children's writing that lacks cohesion should be corrected, again not in any derogatory manner, but simply as a helpful suggestion. They may not be able to act upon the advice always, but at least they should be given the chance, and in any case, it is through experiencing change that they will eventually change and adapt. Kress (1982) in another context, but to do with form in writing, says that children learn much to do with written language by osmosis. We should not underestimate the power of osmosis in the learning of young children, but we should not rely upon it happening willy nilly. It can only occur if the experiences are provided.

Children in the upper infants and first year of the junior school will move from the production of clauses as the basis of their writing to sentence patterns. This process is helped considerably by teachers inserting capitals and full stops as the children write, so that they see how it should be done. For two reasons this craft approach is far more effective than taking in their work and marking it. The first reason is that if it is done whilst the child is 'on task', the amendments, additions and alterations will be meaningful to what that child is doing there and then. He will see the teacher's suggestions in terms of his own cognitive processes and what he is trying to write, so that gradually he will fully appreciate these suggestions as improvements. On many occasions when children are told by the teacher what should be done they accept it because it is the teacher saying it, but they do not appreciate its significance. They must see it as an improvement for themselves.

The second reason is that marking of any description after the work has been completed and handed in becomes increasingly remote from the task itself in the eyes of children. In the meantime, between writing their text and receiving it back marked, they will have passed on to other thoughts and activities, and to revert back to earlier thoughts and get back into the spirit of the particular piece of writing would be well nigh impossible for young children. The effect of the marking would be diminished because of its lack of immediacy and the inability of the children to benefit from such an academic and abstract exercise.

STRUCTURE

From time to time teachers and those who write about the promotion of written language have suggested that the various types of writing – narrative, descriptive, scientific, technical and historical – frequently conform to a characteristic structure (Hoey, 1979 and Davies, Greene and Lunzer, 1980), and that personal narratives often consist of a setting, followed by a sequence of events or actions and ending with a conclusion. Certainly, children need to acquire an ability to approximate as closely as possible towards these goals by the time they reach the end of their primary schooling. However, young teachers should give the development of such powers some thought. To have imposed a conclusion in the above passage concerning the visit to a museum would have been unnecessary and unwise. The objective was that the children should relate their reactions to the school trip, not that they should draw conclusions of any kind. The intention of the exercise was not the production of an essay but a statement about an event. Naturally, there will be other occasions where a conclusion of some kind would be appropriate; it will depend upon the topic and the objective for writing. Needless to say, there should be training in writing essays which have a beginning, a middle and an end, but it cannot be imposed universally or too early in the development of a child as a writer.

Applebee (1978) has argued that very young children are aware of the necessary elements of a story frame, defined by Perera (1984) as being more than the links between successive events and having an 'overall shape which holds together the characters, the time and place of the action, the development of the plot, the outcome, and so on' – 'a global organisation of structure'. This frame, schema or 'story grammar' as it is sometimes called, consists of: setting, character(s), theme, episode(s), outcome, evaluation, or equivalent terms, although Perera points out that not all of these will necessarily be included. Glenn and Stein (1980) found that fifty-two per cent of their sample of kindergarten children, sixty-nine per cent of nine year olds and seventy-six per cent of eleven year olds could orally produce stories with an episodic structure, which was acceptable in meeting the requirements suggested by many who have produced models of stories.

Stein and Trabasso (1982) give a slightly elaborated example of a simple story frame or schema (see Appendix 5) which may be used as a pointer for primary school teachers in their assessment of children's narrative writing. It suggests a model upon which some English teaching could be based. Use was made of the model by a student (Anita Jones) during a primary school practice where she discussed the model and the example provided by Stein and Trabasso with a group of children. She then worked with the group on the production of a story which conformed to the model. The following was the result:

SETTING:
Captain Miller of British Airways flew on the Manchester to New York route. He was based in Manchester.
INITIATING EVENT:
On one trip, halfway across the Atlantic, he saw a huge electric storm directly in front of him.
INTERNAL RESPONSE:
The dangers of this type of storm were well-known and Captain Miller realised that he must change course.
ATTEMPT:
He asked for a new course to take him in a southerly direction in order to fly round the storm.
CONSEQUENCE:
This took him further south than he intended and he began to realise that he was running out of petrol.
REACTION:
His only chance was to head for the Azores.

The children then saw this as a challenge and they began to produce pieces of writing based on this simple pattern. The advantages gained from this were not simply confined to the production of pieces of writing; the activity very effectively ensured that the children were aware of structure and its use in writing. Thus they were experiencing writing as a craft; something that conformed to a pattern; something that could be shaped consciously by them.

Obviously, to stress the use of this model relentlessly would be inhibiting and would have the undesirable tendency to cast the children's writing in a rigid, imposed frame. Nevertheless, its periodic and judicious use will serve to remind children of the need for structure, and consequently, the need to learn to plan before writing – a point that will be taken up later in reference to the work of Bereiter and Scardamalia.

Similarly, in the case of scientific reports, there will be the aim that children in the upper junior school will be able to describe logically the sequence or progression of an experiment, report the results clearly and, where appropriate, draw conclusions. This will be achieved in the same manner as was the case with personal narrative, whereby children are shown what is required and subsequently have their attempts altered by their teachers at the time of writing. Some will question how this can be done with a class of 35 children, and the answer is that it cannot be done if all are writing their reports simultaneously. The solution is obvious and unchallengeable: only a small group of six should be engaged on this type of work when it is the intention of the teacher to teach – in this case to teach the children to write scientific reports.

Impersonal non-narrative writing

Impersonal non-chronologically ordered writing seems to present children with greater difficulties than does chronological personal narrative. This type of writing is concerned with ideas, objects, phenomena, explanations and arguments (Perera, 1984). It is concerned with the organisation of ideas and arguments, and as such entails a more abstract view of writing. Obviously, if it is concerned with relating the sequential steps in a scientific experiment, the child has an outline which he can visualise from the scientific activities and which he can use as a guide to his writing. Even so, many adults do not find it easy to convey an accurate description of an experiment verbally. Thus we can see a pressing need to engage children in the oral organisation of their thoughts before they write. Then, with their ideas clarified, they will be more adequately prepared for the task of expressing those ideas in writing. Finally, the teacher should go over what is written with the child, so that together they can determine whether or not the text adequately conveys the intended message.

Perera (1984) reports research by Kroll and Wells showing that when nine year old children were asked to write a story and to compile written instructions for a game they had played there was a significantly higher occurrence of subordinate clauses in the latter. Similarly, when a student (Graham Melrose) working under my supervision required children to devise through oral discussion competitive games to be played in physical education lessons and then to write out the descriptions of these games, an increase in subordination compared with their personal narrative stories was detected. These two instances suggest the importance of devising activities that will have a propensity to produce the kind of writing that is required. In these cases it is the production of more complex sentences that is achieved through the requirement of written instructions.

As an additional contribution to teaching children to produce non-narrative writing of a descriptive, scientific, technical or historical genre, sequencing activities as described in Chapter 6 will be invaluable. They present children with all the subsections of a text, which they have to sort out into a sequence, and in doing so they gain familiarity with the way in which such writing is presented. Here again we can appreciate the value of integrating activities, such as speech, writing, reading and the manipulation of texts. All have their contribution to make to the development of a writer.

The contribution of reading should not be seen only in terms of sequencing activities. Children need to read scientific, technical, historical and geographical texts throughout their period in primary schools. How else can they familiarise themselves with the ways in which such texts are presented? Just as they learn how to produce personal narrative writing partly by osmosis when reading novels and short stories by accredited authors, so they will learn much about technical writing by osmosis when reading technical reports. Furthermore, there is no reason why we should not deliberately and pointedly prepare them for such writing by giving them the opportunities to read examples immediately prior to engaging upon the activities in hand.

Hence a science experiment carried out by children can be placed in a sequence of short lessons thus:

1 Children read reports of similar experiments to the one envisaged.
2 Children carry out the experiment accompanied by oral discussion of what they are doing or trying to do.
3 Children discuss with the teacher how they will report the experiment and formulate their report orally as a group composition and construction.
4 Children write their reports individually, supervised and helped by the teacher.
5 Teacher and child critically review the report written by that child and make any necessary amendments.

The fifth and final point should not be regarded as an unwarranted burden for the teacher. After all, many teachers love to boast that they hear every child in the class read aloud every day, so why not hear what every child has written read aloud, if not every day, then fairly frequently?

Finally, a further point to remember in all this is that in personal narrative the writer is writing about himself and about familiar people and things; he is telling his story and, by implication, he has a reader. This is not so implicit in non-personal, non-chronologically ordered writing and, therefore, it is up to the teacher to keep constantly in front of the child the idea that his writing will be read; they will read it together, it will be retained in a science folder or the like, it will be kept for reference, it will be read as part of a wall display (displays are not merely to cover the empty wall spaces), or it will be produced for visitors to see. (How many teachers act as visitors to other classes to enjoy the work produced by that class?) In this way, the writer will gain a sense of purpose as he will be writing to some purpose. Hartog and Langdon (1907) drew attention to the futility of writing without a specific purpose in mind, and Vygotsky (1962) reminded us that the problems posed by the lack of an interlocutor meant that the writer did not get the virtually simultaneous feedback that a speaker receives. Hence the need for a recipient or purpose, real or implied, and the advantage of teacher and child reviewing a written text, either at the time of writing or immediately afterwards. The passage in Figure 8.1 was written by Siân, aged eleven years, whilst looking out of her house on a winter's day.

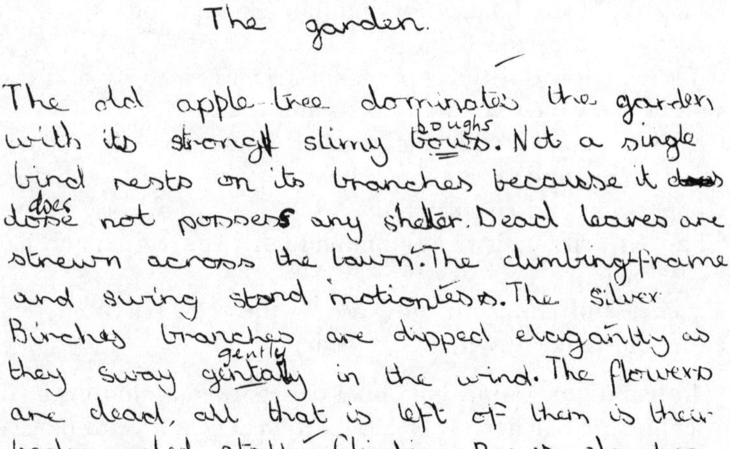

The garden.

The old apple-tree dominates the garden with its strong slimy boughs. Not a single bird rests on its branches because it does not possess any shelter. Dead leaves are strewn across the lawn. The climbing-frame and swing stand motionless. The silver Birches branches are dipped elegantly as they sway gently in the wind. The flowers are dead, all that is left of them is their bedraggled stalks. Climbing Roses clamber over the small archway. There is a rose patch that has been neglected. Brambles meander round the gnarled rose stems. Birds chatter and flutter about their adventure playground. They swoop down on all the unfortunate worms. There is a slug's silver trail that glitters up the crooked path. The slug sits and sulks at the end of the trail. A wet piece of newspaper lies on the grass. The house watches the garden but that too is rejected. The owners have left.

Figure 8.1

Immediately after the completion of this piece of writing one of her parents went over the passage with her, responding to the quality of the expression and indicating with ticks points for approval. In the case of one particularly noteworthy sentence a spelling mistake was deliberately ignored so that the sense of elation about the quality of the language would not be marred. Thus the immediacy of the reaction to the child's effort plus the whole-hearted approval offered by the adult added to the child's sense of achievement and maintained a sense of elation that should be the result of all pieces of work well done. Furthermore, the fact that particular parts were selected for comment heightened the awareness of the writer to the formations that she had used.

Further, it must be remembered that the recipient may in some cases, of course, be the writer himself in that he is writing in order to retain some information or to satisfy himself – writing can be an enjoyable and exhilarating experience!

PERERA'S FRAMEWORK OF TYPES OF WRITING

For reasons of simplicity and in order to emphasise the range covered by writing, this discussion has dealt with the extremes of a simple matrix proposed by Perera (1984). She offers this as a replacement for that suggested by Britton et al. (1975), in which they proposed transactional and poetic writing emerging from a basis of expressive writing. Perera's matrix, whereby children's earliest writing is chronologically ordered and is closely personal, is one that teachers will recognise easily. This early stage relates events to the writer and his intimates. Children's writing then progresses through less personal writing to impersonal writing, with a gradual development of non-chronologically ordered subject matter of a kind that is at first closely related to the writer but then develops gradually into distinctly impersonal writing. The writer will expand through comparison, contrast, evaluation and explanation, in an increasingly logical way, upon relationships that are not personal but are concerned with objects, ideas, arguments and theories and explanations.

Speech and discourse development

The emphasis that is given above to small group discussions and to teacher–child interaction through speech has a specific part to play in the child's development. The kind of spoken language that the teacher uses will be determined by the activities and the purposes upon which it is based. This language will be used as a model by the child, and it will be practised in the discussions with other children, not always in the pure form of the teacher but in varying degrees of approximation to it. Phillips (1985) in discussing discourse development, of which he gives five styles – hypothetical (*what about?*, *how about?*, *if*); experiential (*I remember, once*); argumentational (*Yes but, Yes well*); operational (use of pointing words, *this, that, these, those*); and expositional (initiated by *where, who, what, when* questions) – suggests that group discussions amongst ten to twelve year olds should be based on practical activities such as mathematical problems and scientific and CDT experiments. These discussions should begin with a planning stage *away from* the materials that will be used. The activity would then take place, followed by further discussion away from the activity. A second activity, modified following the second discussion, would follow and this would be followed by a final report-back stage.

The interesting point here is the discussion *away from* the materials and the activity, which forces the children to formulate their speech in the abstract. Furthermore, Phillips suggests that in the junior school, with older children, it is important for the teacher to withdraw from these discussions in order that the children may 'discover for themselves, as they were able to when they were younger, which strategies are most appropriate for a particular educational discourse.' Otherwise, with the teacher leading the discussions and the children impelled to 'get it right', they will not get the practice they need.

An effective way of promoting discussion is to set upper juniors the task of writing story books for infants. First they must read a selection of literature used in infant classes, and a number of themes should be extracted to form the basis for groups writing to those themes. Each group should then set about compiling a story and producing a book. This must be a joint effort by the group, resulting in one story in one book. Naturally, to achieve this there will have to be considerable and continuous discussion. The story will have to be outlined, written, refined through further discussion and, at the same time, discussion of the format and presentation will be necessary. Every child within each group must be encouraged to participate fully in the discussions and decisions of his group. The teacher must not hesitate to suggest that improvements could be made either to the story or to its presentation in book form. This in itself will stimulate and ensure discussion, but a watching brief should be kept by the teacher to see that these matters are discussed and that the group does not simply leave it to its cleverest member to redraft or draw the improvements that are necessary. Finally, having tried their stories out on the infants, the discussion groups should reconvene to assess orally the degree of success achieved. A decision will be taken on possible improvements and, if deemed necessary, the cycle of discussion and drafting can continue.

Writing books for younger children has frequently been used as part of a writing development programme, and because it has been regarded as an individual activity it has not always produced the desired development. The essential ingredient that is proposed here is that drafting and critical reappraisal are essential. No child can produce his best under the severe constraints of writing for a specific audience 'at the drop of a hat'. The product has to be worked at, considered, discussed, tried, reassessed and reproduced, and it is suggested that writing as a group with interspersed and accompanying discussion is the surest way of achieving this goal. It is also the most effective way of ensuring that children develop the several discourse styles illustrated by Phillips (1985).

SPOKEN AND WRITTEN LANGUAGE AS PART OF LANGUAGE DEVELOPMENT

This aspect of speech development is not one that new entrants to teaching will find prominently mentioned in primary school syllabi, nor will teachers be found to be consciously developing it in their classrooms. All too often teachers will be satisfied with the undifferentiated group talk that accompanies the performance of tasks – something that is not to be despised, but neither should we think that we are doing something positive to develop the children's powers over spoken language if that is as far as the promotion of speech goes. If, however, we wish to develop their powers of argument, their powers to present a case, their power to reflect upon ideas and evaluate them, in other words, to take their use of speech beyond the narrative and descriptive, then we must follow the advice of Phillips and set up situations that require children to argue, to present a point of view whilst heeding other points of view, to reflect and to evaluate what is to be done. Group projects should not consist simply of the collection and regurgitation of information; they should require the children to argue for certain procedures, to consider the actions that are necessary, to allocate tasks on a rational basis, to consider reproduction of information and material and to decide upon the optimum layout. The teacher's role should lie simply in challenging the group to talk about all these aspects, and she should not be concerned primarily with their solution. Obviously, the eventual solution must be considered important, otherwise the levels of expectation of the children will be lowered, but whilst the project is in progress and the report or story is in the making, the essence of the activity must be the thinking that goes into it and the language that accompanies, illuminates and contributes to that thinking.

The production of class newspapers provides fertile ground for development of this kind. Frequently, they represent an undifferentiated activity so far as speech goes because they are written and produced as a supposedly class activity, but on an individual basis. There are little discussion and reflection, and hardly any decisions that have to be made on a communal basis. Usually, the pushiest or the brightest child makes the decisions – in fact that child does most of the thinking and in some cases has been known to do all the work. However, if the production of the newspaper – or it could be an interest journal – were to be organised on the basis of groups within the class being responsible for specific sections, such as school news, interests, sport, letters to the editor, and so on, then the teacher could lay down some structure for discussion. For example, what sport and games are to be included in the appropriate section, what views and whose should be presented, are those views fair, could they be presented more adequately or more effectively, could the format be improved? It would be up to the teacher to challenge the decisions and answers to those questions. A final challenge would come from the children themselves when they reviewed the finished project and evaluated it in terms of effectiveness, interest, design and quality.

Science and CDT experiments, as well as art and craft, lend themselves equally well for the development of spoken language provided that they are seen as problems to be solved and not simply processes to follow. There must lie in the problems a question of uncertainty. Too often children have their paints mixed for them and seldom are they challenged to produce the appropriate mixture or to attain the desired outcome from their application of paint. Too often in primary science children are shown what they are going to do before they are given a chance to experiment. This challenges neither thought nor language, and it may be the reason that primary science is undervalued by many secondary science teachers. Again the teacher should set the problem to be solved and suggest a structure for the talk amongst the group that will attempt to solve the problem. This will not be easy for the teacher who is not scientifically minded, and it forms a strong argument for specialist advice amongst the teaching staff of every primary school. It should alert ambitious young graduates to the use they could make of their degree subjects, or good A level achievement, by applying their specialised form of study to the needs of the primary stage, and to thinking not in terms of knowledge but in terms of the thinking and language involved in the activities. A body of knowledge is only useful in that it can be used for some purpose, and the argument here is that it can be most appropriately used as a basis for learning how to think, how to speak and how to write, both in general terms and in specific ways that are opposite to the subject matter.

Finally, we must heed the warning given by Phillips (1985) against structuring being 'equated with teacher prescription of ways of talking. This would be to ignore what we know about children's competence in 'doing it themselves'.' We should be concerned to guide them as to what should be discussed rather than tell them how to discuss things. Out of this, over a period of time and with much practice, the children will develop a disposition for quickly adopting the appropriate genre of discourse for the task in hand. This process will form the basis upon which children will build a parallel disposition for adopting the appropriate genre or mode of writing. The two developments must be regarded as part of the whole process of language development, both spoken and written. To try to develop writing in isolation and as a separate activity from speech is to try to promote a lopsided programme –

one which can produce only a shadow of what is possible when both aspects of language are promoted simultaneously and in unison. The five discourse styles – hypothetical, experiential, argumentational, operational, expositional – described by Phillips can be seen as contributing to the five major genres or modes of writing – narrative, descriptive, scientific, technical and historical – proposed by Kress (1982), in that practice in both speech and writing sensitises children to the demands of both through comparison and contrast by osmosis.

Kress (1982) reminds us that a young child's written language lags behind the writing of adults in syntax and also behind that child's own speech. How far behind depends upon the child's exposure to written language through reading, the composition of his family's speech (this may or may not be close to the composition of writing), and the type of teaching that the child gets (whether or not the differences between speech and writing are illuminated for him by the teacher). Hence, any emphasis that teachers give to speech as an integral part of the curriculum and to arousing the children's awareness of the form of their speech will obviously help them in the construction of their writing. They will begin to feel the possibilities, maybe imperceptibly at first, of approximating more closely to the form of written language used by adults in books written for children.

The writer took part in an experiment in the schools of Coventry many years ago when school dinners were arranged on a 'family' basis with six or eight children and a teacher sitting together and sharing out the food from tureens. I think the idea was to reduce waste by encouraging children to take only as much as they needed, and in this the scheme was an instant success. However, its educational, not to mention its social, successes were equally impressive, apart from a few instances where teachers were unaware of its possibilities. The small groups engaged in discussions about the division of food, its nature, its value, individual likes and dislikes, and from this supportive platform talk developed along miscellaneous lines. Frequently, this bore some relation to what the children had been writing or were about to write, and so clearly contributed in substance to that writing as demonstrated by remarks such as, 'I know what I can say in my story/description/ explanation', 'Do you think I could write. . .?', and other such statements that indicated that the children were searching, subconsciously when the discussion began, for help in formulating their written work.

The important thing about all this was that the children were placed in a situation, informal in atmosphere but nevertheless with constraints, that encouraged them to engage in rational, sensible and profitable discussion. To this they responded by making the most of the situation for themselves. The teacher wanted a restful lunch, and so if she had any sense she did not make the decisions about the apportionment of food – she expected the children to make those decisions – and neither did she treat the dinner time as she would a discussion session in the classroom. This placed the initiative with the children; they discussed matters that were engaging their thoughts rather than the teacher's, and thus the language sprung from their thoughts rather than being imposed upon them by the teacher. Yet the teacher participated in the discussions, and the more effectively she played the part of participant rather than leader, the more effective her role as providing a language model became. Children experienced new possibilities in the use of language which they had the opportunity of emulating at least.

Just one point of caution! Do not rely solely upon speech to produce the desired developments in written language. Perera (1984) in contrasting the grammatical patterns of writing has referred by way of example to the general use of elliptical answers in speech, giving 'the cow' as the oral answer to the question 'which animal provides our daily pint of milk?', and to the tendency amongst children to use this elliptical pattern likewise in their written language. She goes on to suggest that there will be occasions when the teacher will want to insist on complete sentences in the answers given and will wish to explain the necessity for using a different pattern in writing from that used in speech. It is this last point that is so important in our teaching, because it is through comparing and contrasting writing with speech that we sensitise children to the requirements of written language. Throughout our consideration of the teaching of reading we saw the power of comparison and contrast in learning – learning the shape of a letter by comparing it with other letters, looking at words that have some points of similarity, and so on – and so it is with learning to write: what we say can be compared with how it is written; the order in which we write about an experimental sequence can be compared with our oral recall of the experimental sequence. Speech can form the basis for comparison, but in order to appreciate fully the comparable points, the child must have been exposed to written language through good literature and through well written impersonal non-narrative writing, and must be developing a sensitivity to structure and form.

LINGUISTIC FORM, COGNITIVE STRUCTURE AND CONTENT

Reference has been made in many places above to the idea of associating children's writing with their activities. This accords with the view of Kress (1982) that linguistic form reveals cognitive structure and content, a view that leads on to his acceptance of Halliday's stance which 'sees the child as an active participant, a "constructor" of language, acting in response to the demands of a varied environment, including the language of the social group in which the child grows up.' The intervening stages between childhood writing and adulthood writing are then regarded 'as a response by the child to its perceived needs in relation to a given environment'. This points inevitably to the importance of provision: provision of a variety of writing situations, provision of encouragement to experiment, and provision in the form of feedback as a response to the child's efforts, but all within the accepted notion that the provision is to make possible and to sustain development and not simply to match the achievements of the skilled adult writer. Thus it is vitally important for teachers to understand the developments that occur as children pass through the junior school, and to this end they should regard as required study the relevant sections of the books by Perera (1984) and Kress (1982) referred to in the further reading section at the end of this chapter. In particular they should acquaint themselves with the arguments of Kress*, in which he puts forward his two models of causality: the powers theory which proposes that one thing causes another and this is mirrored in language where there is embedding and subordinating syntax, and the regularity theory of causality expressed in a chaining syntax which leaves the cohesive ties implied but not explicit. As examples he gives Text 27(a) as the form expressing the powers theory.

* Kress, G. *Learning to write*, Routledge and Kegan Paul

Text 27(a)
Yesterday while we were playing Red Rover Jody and
Stephen collided, and therefore Jody's ear began to
bleed, impairing her hearing. With the intention of
restoring her hearing, the teacher told Jody to clean her
ear. In an attempt to prevent another accident, the
teacher said that we could not play the game any more,
so as a result we chose another.

and Text 27 as the form written by a nine year old child, albeit not
the best of nine year old writers, as illustrating the regularity
theory:

Text 27
Red Rover
Yesterday when we played Red Rover Jody and Stephen
smashed into each other and (a) Jody had a blood ear
and she couldn't hear (wer)(w) very well (and). then she
had to go and clean her ear.
Then the (we) the(er) teacher said we can't play it
again and then we played a nother game.

Kress argues that the essential consideration is not that the
'corrected' version, 27(a), is how a skilled adult writer would write,
but whether or not the child's version, 27, expresses adequately the
needs of the writer. Provided that one sees this in terms of
development that can be aided and enhanced, then it seems to be
an invaluable contribution to the argument of the present writer
that learning to write (as with learning to read) is to be seen as a
gradual progress of experimentation towards a goal – that of
sophisticated writing (and reading) – that cannot be seen or
appreciated in its totality by the child; furthermore that it is the
teacher's task to guide the child towards that goal, taking care to
regard syntactical inadequacies, miscues, spelling mistakes and
other deviations from adult behaviour in these matters not as errors
to be corrected, but as indications of the child's way of using the
language skills at his command to express his cognitive processes.
The final chapter of Kress (1982) gives added substance to the
discussion of marking children's work by seeing it in terms of
experimentation rather than in terms of right and wrong.
    A careful approach to Kress is vital, because there could be a

temptation to interpret his illustrations of children's writing as an argument for accepting the child's speech and writing and not making any effort to help the child draw comparisons between his own language and that of others. Such an argument would lead inevitably to disregarding the influence of good literature, fine art and architecture on children and to adopting defeatist attitudes towards the potentialities of teaching.

Composing written texts

At the beginning of this chapter it was stated that the child begins with a concern for the message, and from that will develop a concern for the symbolic representation and organisation of that message. For the purposes of teachers I have reversed that order. Up to this point, the major concern has been to look at linguistic development, with the implication that teachers must first consider the linguistic capabilities of children as they develop so that they will be in a position to give realistic help and set realistic tasks and standards. In many schools and training institutions emphasis has lain chiefly on the motivational aspects of getting children to write and too little attention has been given to teaching them how to compose and write. In approaching the topic in the sequence used in this chapter, I hope I have helped to rectify this idea by showing that there is much for children to learn about writing and much for the teacher to do in addition to concentrating upon motivating the children and then simply marking spelling mistakes, adding a few full stops and capital letters and writing 'good', 'well tried', or 'poor work' at the bottom of the children's work.

Turning now to the composition of texts, there are two considerations for the teacher to comply with. First, the child must have something to compose – a 'tale to tell', a report of some event or activity, an argument to make, or a message to communicate – and secondly, children must be shown how to compose a written text.

Naturally the first consideration – the motivational aspect – will predominate in the top infants and the first year junior classes. There the objective will be to inculcate a burning desire to write and, in so doing, to communicate. Writing will not be done simply to put something on paper that can be put up on the wall display, so high that no child will persevere in reading it! Writing will be done so that it can be read, usually by the writer and by other people as well as by the teacher. Thus time should be allocated for this purpose; emphasis should be placed on the writer rereading what has been written and others should be encouraged to read it. Referring to teachers who have had success in the most unlikely schools in Harlem, Kohl (1977) writes, 'If there is anything common to our work it is our concern to listen to what the children have to say and the ability to respond to it as honestly as possible, no matter how painful it may be to our teaching pride and preconceptions.' The gist of his argument is that it is important to set writing tasks that are meaningful to the children. This is crucial when asking them to write personal narrative. To foist upon children unmeaningful topics or topics to which they cannot relate can be disastrous, as was shown by Donaldson (1978) to be the case with some of Piaget's experiments.

TOPICS THAT EVOKE EMOTION AND FEELINGS

Thought and consideration should be given to the topics chosen for writing. Naturally some things will be immediately stimulating: the birth of puppies or kittens, the death of the hamster, an accident, a birthday party, the prospect of a school trip, game or other event, Bonfire Night, or vandalism in school and so on. Langdon (1961), teaching a class of scholastically uninterested teenagers, noticed their exuberance and vibrance in discussion outside the classroom, which contrasted sharply with their lethargic attitude to classroom work. This suggested the need to inculcate feeling – genuine emotional feeling – into their writing, and Mrs Langdon took advantage of April Fool's day to begin an experiment. Thinking of tricks, she remembered the universal horror struck by the imaginary spider, so on entering the classroom, giving out pencils and paper, she began, 'Look. There's a spider on the wall, a huge one. Quick – write down the first thing which comes into your head about it. Now – as quickly as you can.' She continued, 'Make it brief and snappy – don't stop to think just write what *you* feel.' Then followed, 'Start on the next line, and say something about its body. Describe it as *you* see it,' and she continued, 'Another new line and write three adjectives about its legs,' then, 'Now write of its web . . .' No mention of poetry was made, so that the children were not constrained to rhyme or length and metre. The results were beyond all expectations.

I have quoted this experiment in full to illustrate three things. First, even the least promising children can be motivated if what they are asked to write about involves their emotions and feelings. Second, the choice of subject matter is crucial; and third, the guidance and 'props' that are provided have a telling effect on what is produced. Although Langdon used this approach with secondary aged children, I have used it, as have many of my students, in junior schools with children of all abilities. Adaptations have been made and sometimes it has been thought necessary to insert suggestive comments, questions and views with the request for each line. For example, several students have used a class visit to the swimming baths as the basis for writing of this kind. Before the visit the children were asked to take particular note of the dressing room as they entered, of their feelings when stepping into the cold footbath, the atmosphere of the bath as they entered, their feelings as they stood on the side of the bath preparing to jump into the water, the sensation of going under the water, and their reactions to their emergence from the depths. During the visit these things were all raised by the student teacher and the oral reactions of the children were sought. On returning to the classroom each point in the above sequence was recalled by the teacher and the children wrote accordingly.

This adaptation, whilst losing something of the spontaneity of reactions to Langdon's imaginary spider, did have certain advantages in making the children write about something personal to them but outside their immediate situation. The pre-visit discussion sensitised them to events normally taken for granted, just as we adults may not really appreciate spring with all its vitality and colour in Britain. The incidental oral discussion during the visit intensified the feelings and having to write after the event was an exercise in recall and abstract organisation.

Other topics used have been: sitting alone in a dark bedroom, listening; walking through a wood, lost; catching an escaping budgerigar; preparing for modelling wet, cold natural clay taken straight from the earth.

An exercise closely akin to that of Langdon was devised by a student teacher – Maggie Allan – for use with a second year junior class of eight to nine year olds. She distributed the following work sheet:

Around the School

Different places have different atmospheres. Choose three places around the school and write about your feelings when you are in those places.

Library, playground, classroom, headteacher's room, area, hall at lunchtime, hall during Assembly, the boiler house, the lavatories.

Think what you can see, hear, smell, feel, and discuss this with children who have chosen the same places as you.

Some evocative words to help you:

Smelly, musty, friendly, anxious, whispering, frightening, gloomy, draughty, exciting, hungry, ravenous, noisy, fun, daunting, colourful, cheerful, depressing, nervous, shuffling, clean, cosy, bright, relieved, cramped, comfortable, dull, clattering, chattering, quiet, tired, worried.

When you have written your first draft read it to yourself, make any alterations that you think are necessary, and then read it to a friend.

When you have listened to what other children have written, re-read silently what you have written and see if you can make any improvements.

This proved to be a very successful exercise. Many of the texts were highly evocative, and it was noticeable that children did not restrict themselves to the list of evocative words. Indeed these seemed to stimulate trains of thought which in turn produced evocative phrases and sentences.

THE USE OF ENGLISH EXERCISES

Not all the work in English will be concerned with the initial composition and construction of texts. Sometimes the teacher will wish to engage the children in tasks that require a reaction to written texts and will involve answering questions, and sometimes that work will have the intention of exercising or implanting specific language skills. For these purposes there are some reasonably good text books on the market. Two such sets of books are the books making up the *Worlds in Words* series and *Expression*

Books 1–6, the former compiled by a group of Scottish teachers and the latter by Sybil Marshall, a former primary school head teacher. Both of these sets of books require the children to read, process, organise and produce reactions in speech or writing to poems, prose, pictures and events.

An example is the study of words connected with a theme on the moon in one of the books in the *Worlds in Words* series. The child is required to read the poem 'Silver' by Walter De la Mare:

> Slowly, silently, now the moon
> Walks the night in her silver shoon;
> This way, and that, she peers, and sees
> Silver fruit upon silver trees;
> One by one the casements catch
> Her beams beneath the silvery thatch;
> Couched in his kennel, like a log,
> With paws of silver sleeps the dog;
> From their shadowy cote the white breasts peep
> Of doves in a silver-feathered sleep;
> A harvest mouse goes scampering by,
> With silver claws, and silver eye;
> And moveless fish in the water gleam,
> By silver reeds in a silver stream.

It is considered in Assignment 23, which in turn follows a series of six assignments dealing with the moon and preparing the child for the assignment that he is about to do.

> Is moonlight different from any other kind of light? Find Walter De la Mare's poem 'Silver', in the Source Section. Read it aloud, when you can, several times. Why has he used the word 'silver' so often? Why do you think he has deliberately chosen so many words with an 's' sound? To Walter de la Mare, moonlight is silver. It turns everything it touches to silver. What do you think? Is it 'dead' light? Is it warm or cold? Eerie – or cheerful? What effect does it have on buildings? On water? On trees? On faces? Do some shapes take on a new look in moonlight?
>
> Now in your personal book, write about a moonlit scene – in town, in the country or at sea. Try to describe

the effect of the moonlight on the things it touches.
Describe, if you can, its effect on your mood. What night
sounds can you hear? Are there any movements?

As it stands this assignment is for the individual working alone, but
it is obvious that it could be made even more effective if, after
allowing individual children to sort out their own responses to the
questions that are posed, the teacher organised some form of group
discussion in order to heighten and sensitise the children's
awareness of the words of the poem. In this way reading, writing,
speech and thinking all play prominent parts.

Naturally, this type of work can be adapted to any age from
junior one upwards, but in this particular example it is aimed
specifically at nine to eleven year old children. However, its
effective use will be determined by previous experience in relating
words to situations and transposing these words into print, and in
the discussion of texts with adults, beginning with story time in the
home. Indeed, the essential point about this type of activity lies in
the fact that it is based upon a completely different conception of
the development of reading and writing skills from that approach
which relies on the type of arid exercise which would confront the
child with a number of isolated sentences containing the word *silver*.
In the case of the poem, the child is being involved in an
experience, whereas in the case of isolated sentences he is
performing a mechanical exercise. It is the degree of involvement
which determines the depths of the child's awareness of the usage of
particular words, and no child can become really involved in a set
of sentences which are unrelated and which do not engage him in a
developing sequence of thought.

In other assignments in this series children are asked to compare
texts written for different purposes. One passage describes a boy's
feelings in a rather frightening situation. Then follows this
assignment:

Good writers always choose their words very carefully to
make the strongest possible effect on the reader. Read the
story *The Golden Seal* on page 18. What words does the
writer use and what actions does he describe in the first
two paragraphs to show how terrified Eric was when he
entered the hut? How do Eric's feelings change as the
story goes on?

> Write a paragraph of your own describing a boy standing on a rock in the sea, where he has been trapped by the incoming tide. Think very hard about the words you use to show how he is feeling.

This involves both the interpretation of language and the use of this example in the further creation of language. The child is not being asked merely to write, but he is being directed towards the use of language for a specific purpose and in a particular manner.

A third example of the activities in *Worlds in Words* is an exercise in which two lists of words have to be paired off and then placed in two connected sentences in each case, thus making two-sentence stories which can subsequently be converted into single complex sentences by adding a comma and conjunction. Again this assignment is part of a series of other assignments, all connected by a theme, so that the child is not suddenly confronted by something strange. It is also a good example of how to introduce children to punctuation in a way that makes sense to them, especially if rereading the combined clauses is encouraged. For further guidance about teaching children to punctuate, see pages 131 to 137 in Beard (1984), *Children's Writing in the Primary School*.

The important thing about these three forms of exercise – the study of a text, the comparison of texts, and the specific use of language derived from a source of information – is that each is an experience which stimulates a sequence of thoughts, and does not present the child with a static isolated statement as does the old fashioned sentence-type exercise. Needless to say, the impact of each activity can be increased by the involvement and intervention of the teacher.

I have chosen all three types of activity from the *Worlds in Words* series; equally, I could have chosen similar activities from the *Expression* series or from other modern approaches to the teaching of English. The important thing is that the activities should be engaging, interesting and should be the culmination of a supportive build up of information and familiarity. The old fashioned isolated exercise just is not worth its place in the English syllabus.

SHOWING CHILDREN HOW TO COMPOSE

Mention was made earlier of the fact that different patterns and structures are used in written language from those normally used in speech, and the use of the Sentence Maker from *Breakthrough to Literacy* was one way in which this could begin to be done; the teacher in the junior school needs to continue to show children how to compose texts but she will use other means than the Sentence Maker.

In the first place children need to be introduced to, and trained in, the idea of constructing a logical sequence of ideas. Practice can begin with a sequence of pictures, few in number in each sequence, such as can be found in the collection of sequencing exercises produced by the Centre for Reading in the University of Reading, and continue with pictures taken from children's picture books, ultimately reaching a full sequence of approximately a hundred pictures. Long sequences can be found, for example, in a series of picture books written by R. Briggs, published by Puffin, carrying the titles, *The Snowman, Father Christmas, Jim and the Beanstalk*. Naturally the author's and publisher's permission would have to be obtained to use the books in this way. Parallel with activities concerned with the arrangement of illustrations in sequence will be the sequencing of sentences and larger chunks of text, to be accompanied by teacher-led discussions and eventually by small-group discussions without the teacher. Again the sequencing booklet from the University of Reading will be invaluable as an initial source.

Much of this work will be concerned with personal narrative, but it is important to introduce eventually impersonal non-chronologically ordered writing. This will be dealt with in a similar manner but using appropriate texts. Slingsby's book *101 Things To Make* (1981) was mentioned earlier, and two other books which spring to mind as suitable for suggesting segments for sequencing are by Morris, entitled *Advanced Paper Aircraft Construction Mark I* and *Mark II* (1984). These books contain step by step instructions and accompanying diagrams. Again permission would have to be obtained from the publishers (Cornstalk Publishing at 16 Golden Square, London, W1R 4BN) if it was intended to use the actual wording and diagrams from the books; on the other hand these texts can be used as suggestive models for the production of the student's own materials. The importance of getting things in the proper order can be seen clearly from these books, and by basing the work of arranging a sequence on the construction of a familiar article or on a familiar and known process, this goal is kept clearly in the child's mind – something that does not necessarily come easily to children when composing (Bereiter and Scardamalia, 1985).

Another device that helps to constrain the writer and virtually forces him into keeping to a goal related text is to present him with carefully designed titles which pose a framework and set a problem. Some such titles that have been used are:

A wet day but a good day.
A difficult time but a happy time.
A frightening experience but a worthwhile one.
A good deed but one which hurt.

The use of these titles with middle and upper juniors can be very encouraging and produce surprising results if placed in the context of discussion and interaction within the group.

Bereiter and Scardamalia (1985) found memory search a cause for concern in composing, but found that brainstorming sessions with the teacher taking the initiative were very productive. Where there was no such cuing by the teacher or an external source, the children did little searching. The only thing that was found helpful was to get children to list isolated words that occurred to them concerned with the topic.

This suggests that children have difficulty in organising a text and, basing our response to this difficulty on the principle that as teachers we should take the least resistant approach and present the child with as few problems as possible, we should look to literature to help.

AWARENESS OF FORM AND STYLE IN LITERATURE

Already it has been noted that hearing and reading literature inculcates patterns of language; now, it is suggested that literature can be used to suggest themes. In other words short stories and extracts from children's literature can be used as exemplars which the children can use, and in doing so they will begin to see how stories are composed. The children's stories of Oscar Wilde, folk tales and traditional stories, and any of the collections of short stories to be found in the Puffin series are useful sources. Extracts of anything up to three or four pages can be taken from adventure stories, travel tales, mysteries and so on, so long as they have a simple unitary theme. For example, the meeting with a gorilla, lions hunting, and animals approaching the water hole are three extracts from Alan Moorehead's *No Room in the Ark* that I have used in various ways with upper juniors. The meeting with a gorilla was rewritten; the children hear the story up to the point of the meeting and then had to add their own ending to the episode. In the case of lions hunting, the children were required to lead up to the kill but could decide whether or not the victim escaped. The value of all this is that there is the basis of a theme already composed which the children may copy or upon which they may improvise. The fact that they may choose the latter course adds interest for those who are going to read the outcome, whilst the fact that they are allowed to keep strictly to the theme if they wish is of great help to children in the early stages of learning to compose.

Through literature the child will have experienced the power of captivating opening sentences:

> This is a fierce bad Rabbit; look at his savage whiskers, and his claws and his turned-up-tail. (Beatrix Potter: *The Story of a Fierce Bad Rabbit)*

> Frou was a little forsaken hare. (Lida: *Frou the Hare*)

> If you went too near the edge of the chalk-pit the ground would give way. Barney had been told this often enough. (C.S. King: *Stig of the Dump*)

And of course, there is the incomparable opening sequence to *The Iron Man* by Ted Hughes. In each instance these sentences captivate and alert the senses of the listener or reader.

Other openings do more than captivate; they set the scene or open up a story vista:

> Once upon a time there was an old cat, called Mrs. Tabitha Twitchit, who was an anxious parent. She used to lose her kittens continually, and whenever they were lost they were always in mischief. (Beatrix Potter: *The Tale of Samuel Whiskers*)

> Mrs. Frisby, the head of a family of field mice, lived in an
> underground house in the vegetable garden of a farmer
> named Mr. Fitzgibbon. It was a winter house, such as
> some field mice move to when food becomes too scarce,
> and the living too hard in the woods and pastures. In the
> soft earth of a bean, potato, pea and asparagus patch
> there is plenty of food left over for mice after the human
> crop has been gathered. (R.C. O'Brien: *Mrs. Frisby and
> the Rats of NIMH*)

Similarly, children will gain the experience of different kinds of
endings, such as the just but constrained retribution that befalls the
Fierce Bad Rabbit:

> And it sees the bad rabbit tearing past – without any tail
> or whiskers.

There is the incredible but highly consistent ending to the story of
Ferdinand, the bull who refused to fight the matador and was
returned to sit under his favourite cork tree (Munro Leaf: *The Story
of Ferdinand*); and the uniquely comforting ending for the field mice
after the excitements and perplexities of the story of the rats of
NIMH:

> The sun had set. They went into the house and lay down
> on the soft moss Mrs. Frisby had placed on the floor of
> their room under the roots. Outside, the brook swam
> quietly through the woods, and up above them the wind
> blew through the newly opened leaves of the big oak tree.
> They went to sleep.

Furthermore, from these and from comparable books children will
experience the inner development of stories. For example, Beatrix
Potter's masterpiece as a story, according to Graham Greene, was
The Tale of Samuel Whiskers. Every step in the story is illuminated by
references to the setting, by diversionary comments which add to
the reader's sensitivity by giving additional information, and by a
series of highly captivating events that heighten and hold the
reader's interest. Pere Castor's Wild Animal Books, translated by
Rose Fyleman, of which *Frou: the Hare* written by Lida is one, all
contain a serious study of the appropriate animal through the
seasons, its nature, its habitat, its food, its fears and its life cycle.

From these two examples alone there is much for the aspiring writer to learn.

How stories should begin, develop and end cannot be explained, for every story differs and writers differ in their ability and in their disposition for the use of language. What the teacher can do is, in the first place, make adequate provision for children to experience these things through hearing and reading good literature, and in the second place, call attention to them so that the experience is identified and the children made consciously aware of it. Sometimes this can be most effectively achieved by the teacher purposefully altering the beginning, the ending or even the contents of a story, after the children have read the authentic version, in order to allow comparisons to be made and for the skill of the genuine author to be appreciated. This form of negative alteration should be practised only with the older children in the junior classes, because although it can achieve significant results, it can cause confusion if carried to excess or if it is misunderstood.

Other more direct actions can be taken in addition to expecting the children to learn from the example of literature, but both approaches should be considered necessary. Any direct action should be done either as a group exercise in composing or as an individual response to work that has already been written.

(Incidentally, the reader will have noticed that many of the sentences quoted above are long and complex and we are reminded of the necessity of familiarity with such writing if children are to develop their own skills.)

DIRECT TEACHING OF COMPOSITION

An example of teaching a group to compose would begin with a topic such as 'Trees', and the children would engage in a brainstorming session suggesting words that spring to mind related to trees. For example, *large, wide, big branches, broad leaves, notches, holes.* These would be written by the teacher on an overhead projector or blackboard. Then the teacher and children would engage in converting these words into sentences and then considering whether to join them. The result could be variations on '*The tree is large and wide. It has big branches and it has broad leaves. There are notches. I can see a hole in the trunk.*' This would then be converted to '*The tree is large and wide with big branches and broad leaves. There are*

notches in the trunk, and I can see a hole on the right hand side.' One can see
the intervention of the teacher in this, and it could become a
tedious and uninspiring exercise. However, this need not be so if it
is completed within a very short time, certainly no more than six or
seven minutes at the most, and if the teacher ensures the children's
participation in making the suggestions. The objective is for the
children to see how they can build up a text around basic ideas, and
how with some help their composition can be developed into
something that sounds and reads much better than their original
attempt. If this type of activity is combined with group enjoyment
and appreciation of good literature, with sometimes the teacher
reading and sometimes a member of the group, and always
followed by some appreciative discussion of what has been read or
heard, then the children will develop their powers of critical
awareness and appreciation. Far too often it is hoped that children
will develop these powers and nothing is done to promote that
development; the above types of activity are intended to ensure
development.

Similar exercises, both group and individual, can be formulated
from the old fashioned telegram, whereby a truncated message is
expanded so that the details are added. For younger children, more
constrained messages such as *'Sun hot, ice cream melting, get saucer'*;
whilst for older children so much more can be implied and so much
more left to the imagination in telegrams, such as *'Broken down,
delayed. Hope to get a train arriving midnight.'* The basis of a story is
given, and the expansion can be done either by the children
working in groups but completing individually their own interpretations, or in the earlier stages the whole thing can be done as a
group activity with one common text emerging.

Yet another variation on this idea is to give an outline in phrases
connected with a known sequence of actions such as

Going home from school
Clear away. Go to cloakroom. Put on coats. Walk with
friends. Cross the main road. Under the bridge. Across
the park. Into our street. My dog is waiting for me.

Children then read this, decide whether or not it is readable and
discuss what needs to be done to make it sound more acceptable.
Individually the children produce what they think should be the
text and read their solutions to one another. This type of activity

not only makes them think out a solution, it makes them take note of what others have written and, what is so important, adopt a critical stance. Decisions have to be made concerning the most appropriate adaptations of the original. Hence children are made conscious of the craft of writing in relation to the art of writing.

DIFFICULTIES IN COMPOSING

Bereiter and Scardamalia (1985) report the findings of a series of experiments that were concerned with the difficulties that children face when attempting to compose written texts. The difficulties they list are those of goal-directed planning, where the deficiency is not so much what to write but how to write it convincingly; the difficulty in writing other than narrative forms; the difficulty of sustained production when there is no interlocutor as in oral conversation to urge the writer on; the limitations children experience in a memory search, manifested in children's complaints that they cannot think of anything to write; and, finally, the lack of depth in any attempt at revision by children.

Early in their research work they were attracted by the arguments that the difficulties of learning to write were caused by the heavy information processing load of such a complex task and by the difficulties of writing anything other than simple narrative. Subsequently, they have come to believe that 'learning to compose . . . involves massive up-grading of a discourse production system', no longer dependent on inputs from a conversational partner, 'so that it can function autonomously in a goal-oriented manner'.

During their researches they noted that children possessed an 'impressive facility in adapting to and finding ways around these limitations'. In order to produce a discourse more appropriately suited to written text than to conversational speech they tended to use a strategy which the researchers termed 'knowledge telling' and they describe this strategy as turning any writing assignment into a topic and proceeding to tell what is known about that topic. This strategy, which is generally suited to narrative writing, helps the hold to formulate discourse, as it eliminates the need for detailed or more abstract planning, and it helps the child to see a relatively clear and uncomplicated pathway through the topic. In other words 'knowledge telling' strategy simplifies the task of composing by helping the child as a writer to relate simply and straightforwardly to his immediate knowledge and preoccupations.

However, this strategy, whilst enabling children to produce a simple written discourse, circumventing by its very simplicity the difficulties identified by Bereiter and Scardamalia, is adequate neither for the production of a more sophisticated narrative form nor for the more exacting demands of non-narrative expository writing, which involve careful planning, preparation and deployment of arguments, organisation of material, adjustment to audience and appreciation of effect. It provides for 'a minimally adequate response' and can be 'appreciated as a way children manage to cope with a task that is initially too complex for them. It could thus take its place among the many other simplifications that children . . . subsequently outgrow . . . But school practices, in turn, appear to be finely adapted to the knowledge telling strategy and thus (unwittingly, of course) support its perpetuation.' So say Bereiter and Scardamalia, but is this rather depressing outcome of research in North America congruent with the advances made in recent years in the techniques of teaching children to write in British schools?

Many teachers in Britain will recognise the difficulties which have been identified, and they will readily recall practices which go some way, at least, towards the mitigation of those difficulties. Some of these practices are mentioned by Bereiter and Scardamalia: group discussions before writing, teacher–pupil discussions (pompously referred to as conferences in North America), oral rehearsals, group brainstorming sessions to produce ideas, the compilation of a list of discrete words related to a topic, and the provision of feedback and guidance in revision. But the thing that is missing from this list, and it is something about which Bereiter and Scardamalia show some hesitation, although it could effect the massive up-grading of the child's discourse production system that is essential if the child is to develop the full potential of a skilled writer, is the part that could be played by the teacher whilst the child is engaged in writing. During a 'master class' in music the maestro does not hesitate to intervene during the performance; he does not wait until it is complete before helping the student to realise a better or more appropriate interpretation of the music. This example has been adopted in some British primary and American elementary schools and it has every chance of improving the situation found by Bereiter and Scardamalia in the following way. By intervening during the actual writing process, just as the maestro does in a master class, the teacher can approximate to the role of interlocutor, and in so doing she can help to sustain production, prod the child's memory, and provide vocabulary; but more importantly, she can help the child to develop discourse schemata – ie the mental structures that guide the writer in structuring and organising his composition. Sustained help of this kind over a period of time can only be assumed to be cumulative. The child will gradually imbibe the ways of a writer from participating with a skilled writer – the teacher – in the production process. In the early years, up to the age of approximately eight, the teacher will play a predominant role, but this will begin to diminish as the child develops the ability to plan, organise and develop his thoughts. The child will become gradually more and more independent and cease to rely in his writing upon a 'what next?' approach. Although there is always something of this approach in all writing, the difference is that the skilled writer has a general plan and any traces of a 'what next?' strategy are minimal, especially in non-narrative writing.

The whole approach in this book to the development of writing is intended to resolve or at least to alleviate in some degree the difficulties that have been identified by Bereiter and Scardamalia.

The descriptions in Figure 8.2 and Figure 8.3 were written by Jonathan at nine years nine months and ten years one month respectively and give some indication of the support given by 'knowledge telling'. In each case Jonathan was encouraged to think over the events in which he had participated. For less able writers more time would have to be given to recalling orally what had happened before they were ready to write. Both the pieces of writing indicate the value of having a basic theme and a familiar sequence of events to follow.

earlier   every   Royle   Jonathan 9⁹ yrs.

I was very excited when my father said
we could go to the match between City
and Juventus. When the night came I was very
excited. It was raining and cold. We had to
have tea erleyer because the match started
at 7.30 pm. We left home at 6.15 pm
First we went to John Harward's house
to take him to the game. On the motorway
you could see blue and white scarves hanging
out of car windows. When we got to
the pitch everyonee was shouting. I only saw
3 Juventus fans. When the teams came out
evrey one was shouting. Juventus kicked
off and held the ball for about a minute then
Rolye got it and passed to Tuert who
shot and hit the cross bar. Sometimes I
thought that Juventus were going to score.
The Kippakx stand were always waveing
their scarves. Just before half-time Barnes
took a corner and Royle kicked it
up in the air and kidd back-headed it
in to the net. The City fans went
mad, they shouted and waved their scarves.
I did the same but I was still shouting aj after the rest of the people had
stopped. In the second half nogh not much
happened. The best part of the second half
was when Tuert hit the bar. At full
time it was. 1-0 to City.

Figure 8.2

Walking home   in the Rain

puddle
splash
worried
relieved
echoing.

a quarter to four

At 3.45pm Mr. Anderson let us out of school.
There was a mad dash to get our coats on and
go home it was like a cattle sp stamped. Luckily
I was the first one out so I would not get
pushed in to the mud. As I came to where
Someone had wrote UTD on the wall I stopped
and wondered who could have done it. Then
I ran my fastest up on to Ramiles Avenue. stopped
to see if mummy had come to collect me. but
she had not. When I got half way down Ramiles
it was pouring with rain. I could hear
it on my hood, it was like hundreds of cap
guns going off at once. I ran on till I came
to the church then I had to cross all the
grass. The grass was very muddy to cross. My
shoes were drenched and the wetness had made
my socks wet too and I felt very cold.
The grass looked as if it was silver and the drops
of rain on the tips of the grass looked like
perls. When I got to the crossing lady I said
to myself "She must be very wet and cold." And
she looked it too. I ran all the way up Temple
Drive then I turned round to see if I could see
mummy's car but in vain. Luckily there was
no one in the passage because when there is people
push you in the bushes. As I walk over the
brige I saw that the path in front of me

was covered in mud so I had to cross it by going
round the edge. Finally I came to the road
corner which I had to cross. A car spun round the
at a great speed, the car itself sounded like
Concorde. As I walked along the pavement I
had to jump over all the puddles because all
of them were so deep. Franly Finally I arrived got home
but when I rang the door bell there was
no answer so I rang again but there was

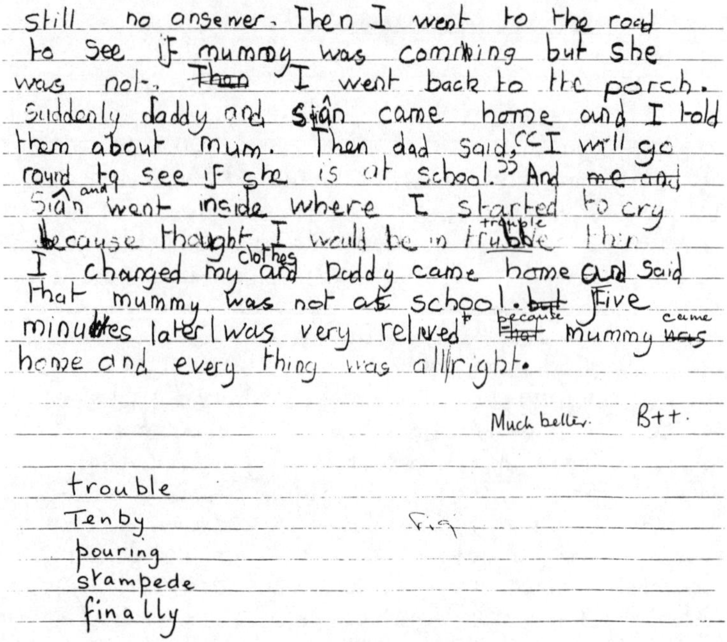

Still no answewer. Then I went to the road
to see if mummy was combbing but she
was not. Then I went back to the porch.
Suddenly daddy and Siân came home and I told
them about mum. Then dad said, "I will go
round to see if she is at school." And me and
Siân went inside where I started to cry
because thought I will be in trouble thr
I changed my clothes and Daddy came home and said
that mummy was not at school. but Five
minutes later I was very relieved because mummy came
home and every thing was all right.

                              Much better.   B+ +.

trouble
Tenby   Fig
pouring
stampede
finally

Figure 8.3

Jonathan's task in both cases was to produce narrative; on pages 227–231 will be found examples of writing of a different kind where the writers could not rely upon a train of known events. In the exercise which centred upon *Alone on an Island* on page 229 the teacher provided a model so that the pupils had the opportunity to improvise within a given framework; 'The Garden' on page 192 required expansion upon an observation; whilst 'A Night Catch for an Owl' on page 227 required the creation of a theme plus exposition upon parts of that theme.

However, it would be foolish to assume that writing of the calibre quoted above was achieved without practice and, especially in the case of 'The Garden' and 'A Night Catch for an Owl', without a long period of induction into the processes of writing. Herein lies a response to the problem posed by Bereiter and Scardamalia. Familiarity with the language of poetry and of books and an apprenticeship in writing enable children to begin to make the 'massive up-grading of a discourse production system' of which they wrote.

POETRY

I have been concerned to show the important contribution made to a child's developing ability to write by reading good literature and by hearing good literature read aloud by his teachers and by his peers. This link between reading and writing is equally pronounced where poetry is concerned, and especially between hearing poetry read aloud, reading it aloud oneself and trying to compose and write poetry.

It is perhaps symptomatic of the approach to poetry in our primary schools that I felt constrained to include poetry in a chapter on writing rather than in a chapter on reading. Generally, too little concerning the reading and appreciation of poetry is done in our schools, possibly because many teachers themselves do not read much poetry. Another explanation may be that the teaching of poetry fell into disrepute because it was, in the first third of this century, treated in a formal stylised manner, which had a tendency to kill enjoyment of the poem. Thus the opportunities given for reading and studying poetry seem to be few and far between, yet students are encouraged to get the children to write in poetic form – an improbable task on such an inadequate basis of reading and poetic experiences.

This inadequate provision for the study of poetry is a pity because there is much to be gained from its study; much can be learned about the use of language to convey meaning and to create feeling; much can be learned about the use of words and the power of words; and much can be learned about the various patterns of language and the alternatives and opportunities open to the writer.

However, these aspects of a poem cannot be studied purely as an academic exercise, as linguistic devices apart from their effects upon the reader. They can only be appreciated within the context of the nature and purpose of the poem in which they appear, and their effects will be constrained by the effect on the reader of reading the poem. Thus the study of poetry can only be done within its appreciation, and this can in turn only be done with the necessary degree of intimacy through a small group where the full reactions and the maximum interactions of each reader or listener can be given full rein.

Note that I am referring to the overt study of poetry, in which the teacher has certain objectives in mind such as the use of language, the arousal or conveying of feeling, the study of word usage, the balance of language and the effects of particular poetic devices. Any one or several of these could be in the teacher's programme. However, the study of poetry has another aspect, namely where it is appreciated personally and individually by the pupil. This aspect should be encouraged, but it will only have general success if it is part of a school programme that regards poetry as an important part of the children's reading, and if the child has also experienced interactive group discussions about poems of all types.

I discovered the strength of children's desire to enjoy poetry in an unexpected place. As a young teacher of a fourth year junior class of very slow learners at Wood End Junior School in Coventry, and faced in those days with the gargantuan task every Friday afternoon of working out total and average attendance for the week, I set aside Friday afternoon before play as a children's choice period. They could do what they chose apart from reading comics (an activity reserved for wet and cold playtimes and lunch breaks), playing cards or joining dots to acquire squares. The choices were: continuing with ongoing art and craft work, dramatic play in small groups, reading, writing in a personal and private notebook, or completing some other aspect of the curriculum work. The only proviso was that they should require as little of my attention as possible. I was amazed at the selections of work made by these children. Frequently poetry was chosen as reading matter, and I noticed an irresistible urge for the children to read to me snippets from the poems that they appreciated – usually a welcome break for me from the rigours of calculating average attendance!

POETRY AS AN ASPECT OF LEARNING TO WRITE

Just as we saw the advantages of showing the early readers the nature of the task by engaging them in their construction of texts, so the children in the junior school and even the top class of the infant school in some cases will acquire a more sensitive understanding of the powers of poetry by using it to attempt to express their own feelings and to describe their own reactions. Hence, the objective will not be to produce poets as such, even in the sense that our objective will be to produce children who can write clearly and effectively before they leave the primary school. It will be to allow children to experience the act of writing in some ways that are poetic. What they produce may be predominantly prose but may in parts approximate to the poetic, or even achieve it. This approximation to poetic writing should not be regarded as failure to write poetry, but rather it should be valued as an emerging awareness of the use and power of poetic form in writing.

References made earlier to children's general development from phrase to clause to sentence in compositions suggest that there is a natural basis for the composition of written language that has poetic elements within it.

The composition in Figure 8.4 on 'The Snow' was produced by Siân, aged seven and a quarter, was then written out for her, not to show her what she should have done, but merely as an alternative way of arranging what she had written.

Figure 8.4

The Snow
The snow is falling so gently and white
It is fun for the children;
They make snowballs and snowmen
It's freezing cold;
Icicles hang from roof-tops high
And little glass balls with leaves inside
Hang from the bushes.
The wind blows so harshly on our faces;
People wrap up warm
And go sledging.
It's fun.

You dash down slopes so fast
And sometimes you land flat on your face.
It's cold and icy
And it hurts so painfully
It makes you cry.

No emphasis was placed on this rewritten form. In fact it was simply used in the hope of demonstrating the importance attached to what she had done by giving time to copying it out. Nevertheless, it was seen as a contribution to her growing awareness of poetic conventions.

It is important to see this not in terms of poetry but in terms of language sensitively used to convey meaning and feeling on the part of the writer. Thus we should not be concerned with lines or with rhyming, although Bryant and Bradley (1985) have demonstrated children's appreciation of rhyming and alliteration; we should be concerned with the expression of an idea succinctly written. This will appear most likely in the first place as a phrase, later in clausal form, and eventually it will be sentence based.

Poetic writing should be seen also as contributing to the development of non-chronologically ordered text. Scenes can be described, as in the above poem 'The Snow' and elements in that scene can be expanded upon, ideas can be launched and explored and arguments can be made. Hence in practising writing that takes on a poetic form, having read poetry of a similar kind, the child will be moving towards writing that is both non-chronologically ordered and impersonal. Writing of this kind is a natural outcome of poetic writing, although much that is poetic is also personal. In fact, all types of writing can be found in poetry, but it is the contemplative postures that are naturally encouraged in writing poetry which are so conducive to non-chronologically ordered writing.

In many schools poetry writing seems to crop up virtually haphazardly, simply when the teacher thinks of it, and the result, as might be expected, often leaves a lot to be desired.

Poetry should be seen as something to be introduced to the children over the whole of their school lives, just as they are introduced to prose through good literature and through practice in its use to express thought and communication. As we read books to children, have children read for themselves, both fiction and non-fiction, and frequently use these as the bases or as exemplars for the children in their writing, so we should read and have them read poetry throughout their primary school years.

From their reading of poetry should emerge discussion. Children should be encouraged to select their reading to match their mood, and poetry should be used to capture or create a mood. As children's attention is drawn to various types of poetry, so they will gradually become aware of patterns of poetry, just as Wells suggested they would become aware of the patterns of language through stories and oral language. Benton and Fox (1985) described the enjoyment gained by three children taking the speaking parts of two cows and the presenter in the poem 'Cows' by James Reeves. As the objective was the presentation of this act to the class, the children felt the urge to practise intonation and different ways of speaking the lines in order to achieve the best possible effect in front of their fellow pupils. It is easy to imagine the feeling for the language that would develop in this activity. It is noteworthy also that such a seemingly simple activity can involve reading sensitively, discussing the use and effect of language, appraising critically the application of voice to text, appreciating the value of rehearsal in effecting change and acquiring the habit of committing text to memory.

The object of all this activity in the eyes of the children was to please others and enjoy doing so. This desire on the part of children to share their enjoyment with others should be encouraged continually whilst at the same time emphasising the need to pay one's audience the compliment of careful preparation. Children should be encouraged to prepare meticulously their reading of a poem to a friend or to a group, or even occasionally to the whole class. It can then be seen as a gift to one's friends, but it will have the distinct scholastic advantage of ensuring that the reader really studies the text and experiments with its most appropriate interpretation.

In all this it must be kept clearly in mind that poetry is to be appreciated and, in order to appreciate it fully, it must be read aloud, discussed intimately and not studied formally. As awareness grows, selections from the exemplars set by poetry will be made imperceptibly and used in the child's own compositions. These will not necessarily be regarded as poetry or given the title of poetry; they will be seen primarily as written work that just happens to have some of the attributes of poetry, because as Martin (1966) warned, 'it is themes in children's writing that are important, and if, at this age, they try to treat their themes as games and use rhymes and marked rhythms and stanza-forms, they destroy the symbolic themes which are the mainspring of their writing. Their control of language is not good enough to incorporate what they really want to say into formal patterns, so the rhymes take control and produce, on the whole, trivial writing in which the sound dictates the sense.' However, Martin does find a mitigating circumstance in some of the less effective approaches by teachers to poetry writing, in that the child 'is usually free to write a poem as one pleases' and goes on, 'most teachers will not 'correct' poems in the way they feel it necessary to correct prose, so writing a poem gives a sense of freedom from the rules of language, and such a sense is the starting-point of creative uses of language. Furthermore, poems are usually short and intense in feeling, and they are more like talk than is most prose, so in all these ways they are particularly appropriate to young and immature writers.'

To quote this reliance by Martin on the seemingly inefficient practice of some teachers is done solely to emphasise that we should not place impediments to the production of written expression of thought by imposing constraints for which the children are not yet ready. Only with increasing experience of and immersion in the various forms of expression can poetry eventually emerge. The following poem was written at the age of eleven and a half years by Siân, who had read a great deal of poetry. The influence of those experiences is obvious in the controlled use of language, and the use

of a situation charged with emotion enables the writer to use her
ability to create atmosphere through poignant imagery (Figure 8.5).

A night catch for
an owl.

Twittering birds circle around his motionless
head.

His downy feathers ripple in the soothing
breeze.

A dark veil descends and shrouds the earth.
The mellow moon shines dimly,
The Sparse branches reach out to puncture it
The still form of the owl is silhouetted
against the velvet black sky.
His ears are alert,
His sparkling eyes dart about,
Searching for his prey.
The night hides the petrified mice as
they search for food.
Down in the under-growth he hears a
rustling.
Into a clearing comes a fat, young
mouse in a grey coat.
The owl swoops down gracefully.
His threatening claws are outstretched
As mercilessly he lands.
Thrusting his claws into the young flesh

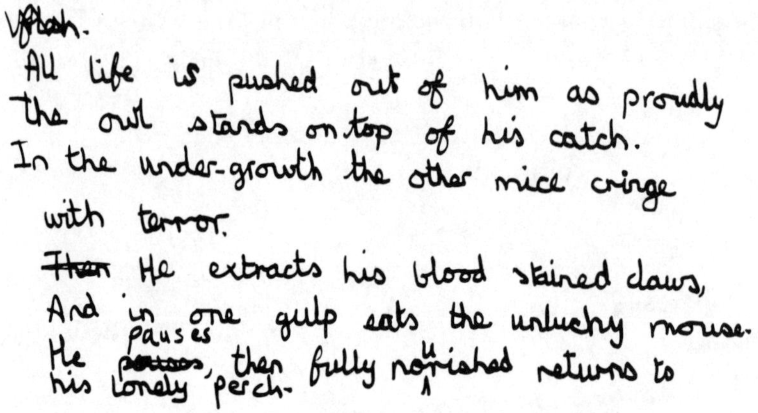

Figure 8.5

AIDS TO WRITING POETRY

Brownjohn in two books (1980 and 1982) discusses various ways of helping children to use poetic forms, which students will find thought provoking. In this book the value of nursery rhymes was acknowledged in the early stages in learning to read and with the almost universal interest in jingles, together with the fact that jingles are memorable and seem to imprint themselves upon children's minds, it is easy to acknowledge the propensity that children possess for imitation. Graham Melrose, practising with fourth year junior school children, presented the following poem as a model story with no mention of poetry.

Alone on an Island, by Alice

Alone on an island
Except for the things I hear.
Listening
To the seagulls screaming
The sea roaring on the rocks
The howling of wild dogs.
Looking
For people

For people long gone
Gazing along the endless beach
Searching the endless blue of the sea.
Smelling
The scent of seaweed drying
And the burning wood of the fire
Thinking
And dreaming alone
Of faraway places
And people
One day they will return for me.

The children were required to read it, Graham read it to the class, and a discussion followed that concentrated upon the theme and not the actual poem. Graham read the poem aloud once more and the children were asked to read it yet again for themselves. Finally, they were asked 'to write about being alone on an island' – the word poetry was not used. Figures 8.6, 8.7 and 8.8 are representative of what was produced by the children.

Alone on a Island

On the Island
I was on my own,
Listening for people long gone
Listening to the sea roaring
with the wind
Listening to the Parrots
talking to each other and the
boars get grunting
Listening to the leaves rushling
and the twigs snaping with the

to branches
looking for people
Looking for ships and airplains flying
over.
Smelling the sent of the flowers and
the salt from the sea
Smelling wood burning in the fire
Thinking of my faimly long gone
thinkeing that my faimly miat come
back to keep me comperny to take
me back with them.

Figure 8.6

On my own

Alone on an island.
listening for the sea suishing.
listening for the wild dogs hounding.
Im listening to the Rocks.
I am all alone.
looking for people.
Im looking for animals.
look arand for people.
I was waiking for some one to come for
me.
No boat or aeroplane's came.
I Culd smell the Salt out o the sea.
I was thinking if any one wuud
come.
I was alone on an island.

Figure 8.7

Alone on an island

I was alone on an island,
I was listening
and thinking,
The sea was roaring
the wind was howling
and seagulls screeching.

Then the rain came,
It was dark now
even more frightening,
Good it was
morning.

Figure 8.8

The first poem (Figure 8.6) is sensitive, imaginative and captures the feeling; the second poem (Figure 8.7) is a reasonable attempt to capture the mood; whilst the third poem (Figure 8.8) shows unimaginative attention to the model and illustrates the price that may be paid in terms of creativity if attention is directed too closely to form rather than content. However, the value of the whole exercise was that for some it drew attention to form whilst for others, better prepared to take advantage of the activity, it presented an opportunity to relate feeling to form. Unfortunately, there was not sufficient practice time left for the student to enquire into the background experiences with poetry of these children. A guess would be that they differed considerably, but it is not only experience of poetry that is a factor. Depth of experience of literary form and sensitivity to experience are also potent factors, plus a facility to think and to use language flexibly and appositely.

Experience can be extensive, but if sensitivity and ability is lacking then the child cannot benefit fully from that experience.

A teaching pattern

Hesketh (1966) gives an interesting insight into writing poetry and relates how her poem, 'Prayer for Sun', 'grew from a long-drawn-out experience'. Jilly Cooper, a journalist, told an interviewer of the effort she put into writing short essays for the Sunday Times – I think it averaged out at ten hours per essay – and Harold Riley, the Salford painter, spoke of the importance of knowledge of and sensitivity to the background to his painting of Salford. Yet children are frequently expected to compose and write a story in the space of a double lesson – two hours to cobble together a text, when skilled professionals require time for thought, time for planning, time for writing and time for 'polishing'!

A pattern which I found useful in making space for these complex activities, and one which could be adopted to the production of prose or poetry and could be used with either a small group or with a class of children, was one suggested by Whitehead's consideration of a learning cycle (Whitehead, 1955). He suggested that there should be a cyclic process in learning with three stages: romance – the arousal of interest and involvement; precision – where there is attention to the details of learning; and generalisation – where what has been learned is applied or used in some way. This pattern is particularly appropriate in the case of learning to write, because within its framework all aspects of the writing process can be encompassed, and it provides the teacher with a simple but adaptable model which ensures coverage of every aspect.

In establishing a pattern for teaching we should ensure that every child gets a substantial basis from which to proceed. Simon (1985) has expressed concern about the 'pedagogic romanticism' of the Plowden Report (DES/1967), with its emphasis on dealing with each child as an isolated learner, and he argues the case for starting from what children have in common, establishing general principles of teaching, and then proceeding 'to determine what modifications of practice are necessary to meet specific individual needs . . . It may well be that these include the use of co-operative group work as well as individualised activities – but these are carefully designed and structured in relation to the achievement of overall objectives.' Mind you, this was always accepted as a general pattern within the schools; only the full-blooded child-centred approach theorists really tried to cope with spontaneous activity for every child.

However, Simon's paper serves to remind us of the importance for teachers of a clear pedagogy, and the one suggested by Whitehead's cyclic learning process seems appropriate for many aspects of the curriculum, and especially for teaching children to produce many forms of written English. Perera (1984) has pointed out that writing can be a lonely process, frequently done in isolation and lacking immediate feedback. The pattern that I am going to suggest is particularly useful in helping children to feel a common sense of purpose and it provides opportunities for feedback whilst they are engaged in the composing and writing processes.

The stage of romance

Beginning with the stage of romance, it is essential that the writer should be sufficiently motivated to want to write. Playing a record, showing a film or picture or simply giving a title is not sufficient. There has to be a sustained effort to create a desire to write, to see a need to write and to discuss the possibility of writing in such a way as to get the children ego-involved in the process.

This means that the children have to understand and appreciate the context in which they are going to use language. We cannot presume that they will switch their thoughts and concentration readily from preoccupation with the demands of mathematics or from the stupor and the frequent boredom of school assembly to an engrossment in the joys of writing. They must be prepared for each transition. To illustrate the point about context and understanding, the following incident occurred centring round the simple concept of strike action. It happened on a visit as External Examiner to a student practising with nine year olds in a Birkdale (Southport) primary school.

External Examiner, to a boy who was not writing when he should have been:	*Are you on strike?*
Boy, looking perplexed:	*What?*
External Examiner:	*Are you on strike?*
Boy:	*What did you say?*

External Examiner:	*Are you on strike?*
Boy, still looking perplexed:	*Strike?*
External Examiner:	*Yes*
Boy:	*What?*
External Examiner:	*Aren't you working?*
Boy, with understanding spreading	
across his face:	*Oh! Hah Hah! That's a good one.* (Beginning hurriedly to write.)

It can only be assumed that it did not occur to this well-heeled boy from Southport that the word 'strike' would be mentioned, and certainly not by a be-suited visitor to his school!

So children must be prepared carefully and sometimes at length for what they are going to do. Do not expect them to switch easily into a new line of thought. The motivational preparation can prove crucial, and may make all the difference between writing that is done with commitment and understanding and writing that is not.

Naturally, in preparing children for writing the object is not merely for the teacher to raise issues and make suggestions. It is to get the children involved in thinking about what they will write. Thus their involvement and interaction are essential, even at this point in the proceedings. For this, discussion is necessary; whereas listening to the teacher, which may be necessary, is just not enough to ensure engagement in the building up of ideas – themes, modes of expression, vocabulary – that will constitute the process of composing.

There are a number of ways of guiding the child towards the expression of his thoughts and ideas. Most of them can be pitched at any level of complexity to suit the age and ability of the children. A series of pictures linked by a common theme can be used as the basis for a story. The teacher could discuss the pictures with the children, and the children could then give their own oral versions of the story before writing it on paper. Similarly, a few evocative words which are loosely connected, or two or three poignant sentences, can be used, and with the use of technical aids it would be possible to use a series of sounds – for example, screeching tyres followed by a crashing noise – in the same way.

As the child acquires greater skill in the interpretation of pictures, there can be variations in the use of pictures as stimuli for writing of a different kind. The use of series of pictures, which impose severe constraints upon the stories that can be interpreted from them, will gradually give way to series which contain a very loose theme, so that the children will have greater freedom to inject their own interpretations into the story or information deduced from the set of pictures. Hence the writer will pass from matching his language to a closely prescribed situation, to a different and more complex form of activity in which he has virtually to create the situation. This implies a far greater degree of imaginative behaviour: the creation of ideas and their expression in written language.

Similar forms of imaginative writing will emerge when the children are given a picture to interpret which contains an action which is insufficient to stand alone and which is part of a more complex action, or any picture which can be regarded as the beginning or the culmination of a story.

An even greater degree of abstraction of the child's thought from what he actually sees before him can be achieved by expecting him to construct a past or a future for any unusual or old object. Or, at an even higher level of abstraction, the child may be asked to create an existence, past, present or future, for an abstract form, such as part of a branch or root of a tree, a bent piece of metal, or a piece of shaped pottery or Plasticine, which is unrecognisable in its functional form.

Teachers using pictures in the lower junior school should make sure that the children can interpret them with relative ease, and that the parts of the picture that are irrelevant to the story do not distract the children from the main theme. Furthermore, it is imperative that there should be discussion, either with or without the teacher, before the children begin to write.

One of the easiest ways of introducing a topic for imaginative or certain types of descriptive writing is by means of a story, read or told by the teacher, or told by a child if he has a special experience to communicate. The object of the exercise will be for the children eventually to retell the story in their own way or to make up a similar story.

The teacher should spend some time, before she ever begins to employ this method, in emphasising to the children that the story they will hear will only serve as a model or a repository of ideas. They must not feel in any way compelled to follow the story in their own writing. They can, if they wish, develop a totally different story from ideas they have gained through listening to the teacher reading the story.

The teacher's story should be short and uncomplicated. The overall plan should be clear and simple, and contain, if possible, certain highly interesting and noticeable or memorable parts. There is some evidence (Gates et al., 1931) to show that children prefer stories which contain a series of climaxes, spread throughout the stories. These significant parts should be recalled and discussed immediately after the story, and they should be referred to at opportune moments throughout the whole exercise of writing.

It would be unwise to attempt to stipulate the stories, or the type of stories that should be used for this introductory purpose. Children's interests vary from week to week and from day to day. However, it will be clear to most people that the stories selected should be written by authors who possess a good literary style. Short passages can be taken from books, as was mentioned earlier.

During the discussion, which should usually follow the story, the children should be encouraged to express opinions about various aspects of the story and to formulate a way of communicating their feelings to others. This type of discussion will fulfil several purposes: it will give the children a chance to wallow in the enjoyable or effective parts of the story, by recalling those parts which have appealed to them; it affords the children an opportunity to clarify their ideas and to begin to plan their own written contribution; it allows the teacher and the children to identify ways in which the story is made interesting and effective; it allows the children to gather ideas and ways of expressing their own thoughts from one another and from the teacher; and it forms an early tentative introduction to the appreciation and evaluation of style.

The stage of precision
As the discussion proceeds, the stage of precision is reached, and this involves preparation in greater detail by discussing words, phrases and ideas used in the story. This is helpful to the children in two ways. It suggests words and phrases and ideas that the children may themselves use in writing, but it also has a deeper significance. It ensures that the children become accustomed to the search for exactitude in the meanings of phrases and sentences, and that they acquire the habit of probing the meaning of any piece of written work that they come across. They will also begin to be more

selective and discriminating in their use of words, phrases, clauses and sentences.

This type of language training is far more thorough and satisfactory than the type of vocabulary training which merely introduces children to words without giving them insight into word usage. The teacher should encourage the children to jot down, in a personal notebook, any phrases they can think of that will be apposite to the story they are about to write, so that they will not forget them before they need to use them, and in the hope that they may treasure them for future use. This part of the whole exercise is particularly useful for those children whose ability to express ideas in writing is weak. They can pick up the suggestions of other children and use them as their own.

The precision stage will also include some discussion of the various ways in which such a story can be retold, how it can be altered to appeal to individual children, or how its total effect can be changed. Again the level of the discussion will depend upon the intentions of the teacher, the ability of the children, and their familiarity with this method of working. Teachers cannot hope to get the best out of any method at the first trial or on every occasion.

All this discussion is a vital part of the whole process. It shows children how to prepare for written work through the selection of words, the construction of phrases and sentences that are apposite to the writer's purpose and the planning of a story. These highly skilled forms of behaviour cannot be learnt instinctively, and the teacher should attempt to give children frames of reference within which they can work effectively.

This part of the work should not be rushed and crushed into the first ten minutes of a period allocated to written English. If it is done thoroughly, without losing either some of the romance of the story or the excitement of gaining technical knowledge (ie the technical aspects of writing) it will be the period in which the child is taught most and in which he learns the basic skills that contribute to the composition of continuous prose. The discussion of word usage can become engrossing to the child if he is interested in the story or topic and if he is keen to use the words in his own story. Searching for suitable words, phrases and language patterns can become as interesting as seeking the solution to a problem or solving a mystery.

Finally, before the children begin to write, the teacher should ask them to recall either to her, to their partners, or to themselves, whichever is most appropriate, their plan of the story. This should take only a few moments, and it should not intrude too much upon the child's thoughts.

As they begin to write, the children should be aware of several important facts. The original copy of their story will be a rough draft, and later there will be opportunities to alter the original draft. This is important because some children find it inhibiting if they know that they cannot alter a statement once it is written down. Also the teacher will wish to inculcate the habit of trying an idea in writing and then attempting to improve the way in which that idea has been expressed. They should know that correct spelling, although desirable, is not essential at this stage. It is content that matters here, and spelling will be dealt with in more detail later. Finally, the children should be reminded that they can refer to the display, which the teacher will have made, of the words and phrases discussed at the beginning of the precision stage. They may also have made their own notes of these, to which they can refer. By doing this, they will not have to divert their thoughts from the general gist of the story, because this is not an appropriate time to learn words. If they cannot find a suitable word the teacher will help – but the learning of the word should come later.

The stage of generalisation
Having clarified the plan, the children begin to write. This is mainly a period of generalisation, in that the writer is using the skills that he has learnt, both immediately and over a longer period. However, it may in some instances revert to a precision stage, when the child is trying a construction that is entirely new to him.

Whilst the children are writing, the teacher should be constantly assessing their progress. Where necessary, either with individual children or with groups of children, she should offer help in the form of suggestions, ideas, appropriate words or ways of expressing particular ideas. Sometimes she may feel that it would help to recapitulate the original story or recall specific parts of it. She should always be ready to help the child who has stopped writing and who is beginning to gaze round in a dream-like manner. In these ways the teacher acts as spur and aid. It would be unrealistic not to expect some flagging in concentration when faced with the difficult task of writing, but frequently a word from the teacher is all that is required to help the child to bring his mind back to the task. On the other hand there may be times when some children rush heedlessly on, not stopping to consider the content of what they are writing. These children may be impulsive children, or children who are going through an impulsive stage (sometimes children who have had a feckless upbringing and teachers who have not been able to compensate for this neglect), and it will be necessary for the teacher to select opportune moments to suggest that they should reconsider what they are writing and proceed with a little more care.

A new cycle
With the end of the first draft of the story, there starts a fresh cycle, beginning with romance; the excitement that children are going to hear one another's stories. Several children are allowed to read out their stories, and there is some discussion. It is the teacher's task here to select those points which are noteworthy and to give them emphasis: an unusual or effective phrase, an aptly used word, an interesting point, a well formed style of expression.

This short period of romance is followed by precision. The children try to improve their own work. They can add ideas picked up from the readings and comments, they can alter parts of their story, and they should be encouraged to reselect words and phrases that are more effective than those they have used. Adults and professional writers use ideas gained from other people, they 'borrow' words, and they alter and correct their original drafts, so why not children? If the teacher establishes this as common practice, the children will acquire the habit of reassessing and improving their work, and this can be far more productive than the old way, whereby the teacher made the corrections and the children merely looked at them. Some students will find themselves practising alongside teachers who will tell them that children do not like revising what they have written. This merely indicates an attitude to writing that has been inculcated by the school, and it is one that needs changing as soon as possible.

When this task has been completed – and it may involve additional periods of discussion, reading and further improvement – the children then turn to spelling. An adequate supply of suitable dictionaries, appropriately chosen to suit the age and ability of the children, should be available. The children should look up any words they think they may have spelt incorrectly, and they should be encouraged to discuss spelling with the teacher. She may also initiate word study within the meaningful context of the story.

This period of emphasis on spelling will vary in length according to the occasion, but in any case, it need not be too long, because when the stories are read by the teacher, she may select spelling mistakes for further work. If need be, no word which has been mispelt need be ignored, and the spelling instruction that follows will be more effective because the words have a significance for the child.

When the tasks of writing and improvement have been carried out, we come to the final period of generalisation in which the work is written out neatly and prepared for presentation. The amount of time spent on this will vary. Not all work needs to be meticulously presented. Occasionally it is enough to say, 'Well that was fun, we'll leave it at that.'

On the other hand, the presentation of work is an important part of the development of competence in written English. Children should be encouraged to share their stories with others, and time should be allotted for children to read their own stories or those of other children. Usually this should be a personal matter arranged among the children, so that they can fulfil their purpose in writing and communicate the joys of story writing to one another (Hartog and Langdon, 1907).

By treating every stage and substage in the composition of a piece of writing separately, it is possible to allow the children to concentrate upon each part of the process. When they are dealing with content they are not searching hopelessly for words to express their ideas, and when they are checking their spelling they are not worrying about content, although in each case the one is carried out in the context of the other. Improvements in content are not stifled by the need for neatness. An ordered pattern of working is introduced, and the danger of confusion and bewilderment is avoided.

This is extremely important at the primary stage. It gives the children a feeling of security from which they can become adventuresome. And within the ordered pattern the children are shown that it is possible by conscious effort to raise their standards of writing.

Many teachers will wonder how much time should be allocated

to this cyclic process in writing. The answer must surely be that it will vary according to the needs of the children and the objectives of the teaching. However, in general terms, it is not envisaged that the above process should be cramped into a single session of one or two hours. It may take up the greater part of a day, or it may be spread over a week, with other activities intervening. This is not unreasonable when one considers that professional writers or poets would seldom, if ever, complete a short story or a poem, from the origination of the idea to the final draft, in one hour or even in one day.

Naturally, the optimum benefits will be derived from this pattern of learning – the cyclic process – if it is done with small groups of say, six, children at a time. This will allow a much greater degree of involvement by the children, and it will intensify the whole process – greater involvement and concentration of discussion, greater personal help from the teacher and the greater togetherness of a small group. Repetition of the process by the teacher taking one group at a time is a small price to pay for the benefits of small group teaching.

Writing for personal reward

This approach described above may form the basis of our teaching of written expression, but it should not be the only method used. Interspersed with these lessons should be a variety of different approaches, especially those where the children are allowed to choose their own individual stories, and where writing arises out of all types of activity. For example, the normal activities of a lively classroom – drama, gymnastic activities, dance, movement, games (the description of an exciting movement) and craft work (describing a process or noting one's reactions to an artistic experience) – can stimulate the child to write. Sometimes the writing will take place immediately, and it will stand as it is written. At other times there will be a form of the cyclic process, in that the romance stage of the event or action will be followed by discussion, guidance and suggestions from the teacher, and this will be followed by the writing, the presentation and reading of the work. The writing that emerges will vary in length and form. Sometimes its form will be prose and sometimes poetry.

Now the teacher cannot know when some part of an activity has had a particular impact on a child, and so she is not always in a position to suggest that writing should follow. Therefore, in order that opportunities for writing based on deep or vivid personal experiences will not be missed, it is essential that every teacher in the junior classes should consciously attempt to inculcate the habit of turning to writing as a natural outlet for feelings, thoughts and reactions to experiences.

An example of a case where the teacher cannot know the impact of an event upon a child is when at the baths the children are told to jump into the water. Some will be so excited by the overall experience of the visit to the baths that one small incident amongst many others will pass almost unnoticed, whereas for others, the actual jump into the water will be a profound emotional experience. If, later, they find the opportunity to release this experience in written form, the writing will reflect the depth of their feeling, as well as helping to relieve any tensions that may have developed from the experience.

INCULCATING THE HABIT OF WRITING

How can the teacher inculcate this habit of writing in order to express deep feelings? It will be a difficult task for one teacher in a school to accomplish; only in a concerted effort by all the teachers, throughout the years, will it be possible to achieve a natural and willing response from the children. The first step is the establishment of the habit of discussing most events and experiences in small groups. When the teacher joins these discussions, she should resist the temptation to rush the children into saying something about their reactions before they are ready. Furthermore, some children will not wish to expose their thoughts to a random group of fellow pupils; they may only be prepared to discuss the matter with a close friend or with the teacher.

From a general atmosphere of oral discussion and the self-examination of feelings and thoughts, it is an easier step to the expression of these thoughts in written form than it is for children who do not have the habit of intimate discussion in school amongst friends. After the discussion, it is the teacher's task to remind the children tentatively, without necessarily pressing them, that they could communicate their thoughts to a friend – or record them for personal retention only – in writing.

With frequent suggestions that they should write out their thoughts, the children will gradually acquire the desired habit of using writing as an extension of an experience, either to relieve emotion or to dwell further upon that experience. Encouragement by the teacher before the writing takes place, and appreciation by her after it has been completed, are probably the strongest contributions a teacher can make to the establishment of this habit.

LOOKING AT CHILDREN'S WRITING

It is imperative that the writing that children are asked to do should be in a realistic vein. Children do not write angry letters to adult newspapers nor to employers; children find it difficult to write with feeling or even sensitivity about something that is remote – in order to do so they must become involved in pre-writing thought and they must undergo a period of motivation; children do not find it easy to review a book – most adults find it difficult to do so; and children do not seem to find it natural to illuminate stories by using technical knowledge or scientific knowledge, yet it is this type of illustration that enhances the impact of a story. Hence, it is important to have in mind some of these constraints when planning writing activities for primary school children.

Letters to a newspaper should be confined to the class or school newspaper and should be concerned with matters that preoccupy children, such as what is right, just and fair for them in their home or school environment. The expression of strong feelings should be based on feelings strongly felt and not simply on reactions that are expected of the writer. Writing showing intensity of feeling should be discussed and evaluated within the group, and in this sense reviewing can be matched to actual reactions and not to ones that have to be assumed. Furthermore, in this way reviewing a text can be confined to a limited topic or subject matter. In the case of a novel, reviewing might take the form of reactions to an event or action in the book, or to a personal response to a specific happening.

Whenever possible children should receive indirect training in the form of the discussion of texts that they have to read. With teacher participation and guidance they will explore the various ways of reacting to different texts, and they will begin to adopt or formulate their own particular forms of reaction. Nold (1981) pointed to the inability of children to revise their work unassisted, whereas Graves (1979) has shown the response to guidance and encouragement in revising texts.

A discussion took place between a teacher and a girl aged ten (third year junior) about the use of the stocks in the Middle Ages. The girl then wrote the following story.

No escape

I was walking in the cobled stone streets when some rich nobelman pointed at me and said, 'There she is the pick-pocket, quick grab her'. It just so happened that two police men were strolling down the street and they heard what the man had said and they were rushing at me I was far to scared so I just stood gazing at them. They grabed my arm and started to pull me to the stocks I strugled to get free but the more I strugled the firmer the grip grew on my arm. They told the town cryer to tell the people that there would be a person in round about a quarter of an hour. The town cryer went of crying, 'Here all about it, here all about it there'll be someone in the stocks in a quarter of an hour.' In the end I stopped struggling and alowd them to drag me to the ever dreaded stocks. When I got there people began to shout, 'Pick-pocket', and, 'we'ave got lovely surpprises for you.' Even the birds seemed to be saying pick-pocket, pick-pocket. I started to kick the police men. I was furious I started swearing and suddenly, going still and then to jurk out of their hands. Eventually they got me over the stocks they were open and seemed to be waiting to swallow me up. They put my neck on the neck hole and my hands in their special hole. I tried to escape but the wooden bar went down I tried to lift it with my neck but the clamps had been put on. I was as helpless as a newly born baby. People started throughing bad apples and bananas they came from every direction. I tried to hide my face with my hands but I could not reach. There was a stench of rotten fruits, which made me feel sick. My neck started to ache with the wieght of the top part of the stock, my hands fell limply from my wrists. After a bit I began to feel rather dazed after being hit so many times by the rotten fruit. At last people began to go home talking excitedly about what had happened. I thought that there would be no escape from the stocks but in the end the police men let me go and they said, 'Let that be a warning', and I ran of into the slum part of town to try to rid of the gastly smell.

The writer was then asked to reread her story and to make oral suggestions of ways in which the story could be improved. These are the points made by her:

I could have described my terror at being led to the stocks.

I could have spent more time being in the stocks, and I could have described what I could have done to the people who were throwing things at me.

I could have described the feel of the texture of rotten food as it hit my skin.

Then I could have expressed my relief at being let out of the stocks.

I could have put an extra paragraph at the end saying how long it took me to get rid of the stench of the rotten food.

Spelling mistakes were dealt with as follows:

a a small number were selected for discussion, for example:

hear   – reference was made to the *ear* and the shape of an ear being roughly similar to an *a*, so that the child would have these points of reference in future.

allowed   – referred to word *allow*, and addition of *-ed* because it had happened.

off   – attention drawn to the difference in pronunciation between *off* and *of*.

b the other spelling mistakes were merely mentioned and the child learnt the correct versions off by heart.

Finally, grammatical mistakes were looked for and teacher and child discussed the reason for changing 'they were rushing' to 'they rushed'.

Discussions such as those described above can be followed by the group or individuals re-constructing the text and comparing what they produce with the original in terms of effectiveness, feeling, sensitivity, strength of argument and structure, as appropriate to the particular type of text, although this extended activity may not always be appropriate.

Inexperienced teachers will be interested in Newman's framework for looking at children's writing (Newman, 1984):

1 Intention — decisions on topic, audience and content to be included.

2 Organisation — conventions followed in layout, organisation and ordering of the contents.

3 Experimentation — experiments with various types of language and conventions. For example, the use of metaphors, using representations of and approximations to spelling. Is there an element of risk-taking which is part of experimentation?

4 Orchestration — sorting out intentions, organising the writing and experimenting all combined simultaneously.

With this framework in mind, the teacher retains clear objectives and is continually reminded that the aim is not 'patchy' writing – it is a balanced presentation, which cannot always be achieved, but which is something at which to aim. Furthermore, with such a framework in mind it will serve as a reminder that there are other things than spelling mistakes to look for in the written work of children. A disturbing situation uncovered by the Assessment of Performance Unit (Department of Education and Science) was the fact that children tended to regard neatness, spelling and punctuation as important, whilst ignoring such aspects of writing as form, style, cohesion, organisation, audience and general appropriateness.

The development of these wider aspects of written work are the underlying theme in the writing workshops of Graves (1983). In these he establishes a 'process' which covers everything from start to completion of the piece of writing: 'rehearsal, spelling, forming letters, rereading, voicing, selecting information, crossing out, editing, drawing, rehearsing, revising, reorganising'. These elements vary in proportion according to the ability of the writer and the specific task in hand. Basically they are concerned with preparation, production, development involving revision and presentation. However, it is these elements which create the significant and crucial difference between teaching children to write and merely providing them with the facilities for writing.

In primary schools in Britain it can be claimed that generally insufficient attention has been given to the complete process of writing. Recently, the Children's Writing Project has helped to rectify this in some schools. However, there is room for much progress. An interesting feature of the work of Graves (1983) is the emphasis given to working at a piece of written work, and his suggestion that crossing out and revision are essential aspects of the work is one that should be taken very seriously and developed as part of the teaching of written English. This aspect was also referred to earlier in the discussion of the cyclic process and was part of the work done by me in a Coventry junior school (Roberts, 1965). Whereas I encouraged the use of erasers as well as crossing out, Graves thinks that crossing out has a more positive effect than erasing in promoting revision. Crossing out seems to be replicated on the word processor, and it may be that the use of word processors would further encourage revision and alteration. The impermanent nature of the writing on a screen and the ease with which alterations can be made may act as an additional spur to revision.

These elaborate approaches to teaching children to write will be applied in the upper part of the junior school, but varying degrees of approximation to these approaches will emerge in the lower junior classes, especially if done in small groups where 'showing how' will be the norm rather than 'telling what to do' (Graves, 1983). There will be preparation and production, but with less emphasis on revision, redrafting and, in many cases, presentation. In the early stages of writing the children are so totally engaged in the physical task of writing, that they should only be asked to revise and redraft when they are fluent writers (Perera, 1984), and even then there is a need to proceed with care in order to avoid overwhelming the children.

Nevertheless, there should always be room for some discussion between teacher and child about the way in which that child has expressed its ideas in written form. M. Grand speaking to Doctor

Rieux in *The Plague* by Albert Camus says, 'I grant you it's easy enough to choose between a *but* and an *and*. It's a bit more difficult to decide between *and* and *then*. But definitely the hardest thing may be to know whether one should put an *and* or leave it out.' It is only by raising these matters at opportune moments whilst meaning is reverberating in the writer's mind, comparing what is written to what is intended, that they can begin to be resolved. Thus children must be trained to reflect upon what they write as they write and not too long after the writing has taken place. Towards the end of the junior school the term 'writing workshop' should indicate working on the text as it emerges and adjusting it to approximate more and more closely to the meaning that is intended. Thus the application or use of grammar will be acquired and refined through experience of what is acceptable in terms of the needs of the writer to communicate and of the reader to understand.

Spelling

It is important to regard spelling as part of development in writing and not as a separate subject to be treated in isolation.

The following text was written by Siân, aged seven years and seven months, and it presents clear evidence that she is in the process of acquiring a spelling system. *Misrbel* is an attempt to relate spelling closely to sound, and it is clearly very close to the way in which we would pronounce the word *miserable*. However, she is led astray in overemphasising the phonic elements in *people's*,

a windy rainy day

It's a misrbel rainy day
The wind is tossing the
Trees and levaes about
I like to see the
Streekes of rain drops
Runing and racing down

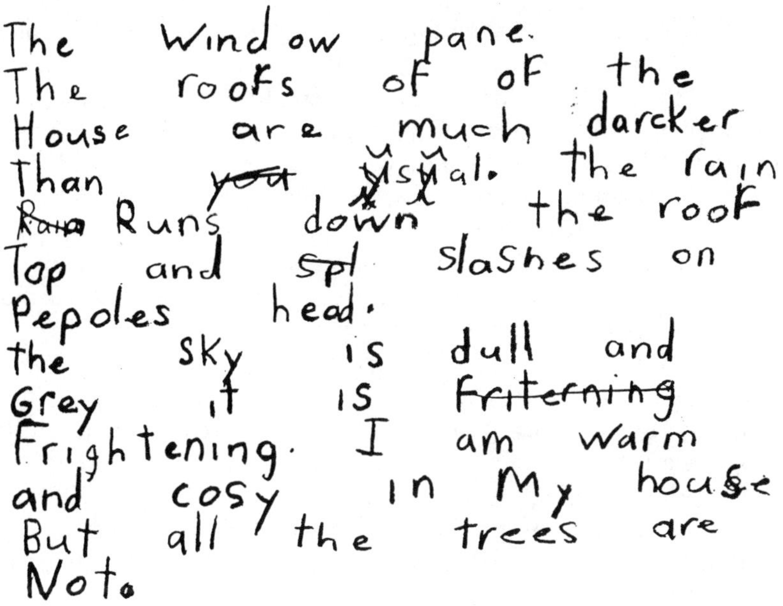

The Window pane.
The roofs of of the
House are much darcker
Than you visual. the rain
Rain Runs down the roof
Top and spl slashes on
Pepoles head.
the sky is dull and
Grey it is Fritening
Frightening. I am warm
and cosy in My house
But all the trees are
Not.

Figure 8.9

possibly because she was hazily aware that the word *people* has an unusual digraph. *Levaes*, on the other hand, indicates clearly an emerging awareness of the need to attend to the spelling pattern as well as to the sound pattern; how else could one explain the appearance of the *a*? *Streekes* contains what Herriot (1971) calls virtuous errors. The writer is aware of the sound of the digraph *ee* and is also aware that one way of forming the plural is by adding *-es*. Similarly in the word *darcker*, the writer is familiar with the *ck* digraph. In these three instances of virtuous errors it is a matter of acquiring a knowledge of when to use these formulations and when to use alternative constructions. Knowledge of this kind can be acquired either through laborious drill in which the spelling of specific words is repeated frequently and with increasing danger of boredom, or it can be encompassed within a developing propensity to see words in their context and to relate them closely to that context. The difference between *beech* and *beach* is remembered, eventually, in relation to the context of these words. This is not always so straightforward, but it is unquestionably more interesting to learn to spell words in relation to their use in a language context than it is to learn them as isolated symbols, especially if the teacher discusses spelling with the child from the stand point of developing ability rather than from that of a 'right or wrong' position. Children at the stage of Siân in the above text will profit from comparisons and contrasts provided by the teacher. For example, the contrast between *street* and *streak* can easily be taken into consideration by a child who is already familiar with the digraph *ee*. Comparisons and contrasts are the essence of learning to spell at this stage. Only later when children may have more or less given up the quest for correct spelling will more radical measures be necessary.

There are two things that we must keep clearly in mind. In the first place it is the spelling system and not the sound system that carries the meaning in written English (Chomsky, 1970) and, therefore, as meaning-predominating words can best be appreciated in a text, their meaning will be emphasised and meaning and spelling will be related in the minds of children. In the second place, the learner is more likely to be involved voluntarily in learning to spell words that he needs to use for a specific purpose. Hence, the words that a child learns to spell should be drawn from what he has written or from what he has read. They should not be given as words unconnected from the basic activities of reading or writing.

There are some forms of spelling disability that are so severe that it is impossible for the nonspecialist teacher to do much about them. These are usually grouped under the title of dyslexia, about which there is still controversy. To deal with this issue requires a special study of the work of Miles (1971), Ingram (1971), Pavlidis and Miles (1981) amongst others. However, there is plenty of evidence that some severely retarded spellers can make substantial progress if given suitable help, especially in the middle and upper junior classes. Fernald's (1943) work with teenagers in America and that of Roberts (1960) with upper juniors in Britain showed that children who were virtually non-spellers at ten years of age or later could gain a fair knowledge of the spelling of words that were used regularly in the stories that they wrote.

CAUSES OF WEAKNESS IN SPELLING

Excluding spelling difficulties that are congenitally based, the usual causes of weakness in spelling are: an insufficient store of basic spelling patterns; an inability to call up what is known or has been partially learned and apply it; an inadequate grasp of the nature of words – their various elements such as letters, blends, syllables and letter strings of various kinds; an inadequate familiarity with the serial probability of letters in words; and an inadequate degree of application to learning. From this list it is obvious that awareness of spelling patterns is the crucial basic factor. This is not to be confused with the rules of spelling which are too complex for children to learn as rules and apply anyway. In order to spell, one has to be able to build up a word from a visual representation of the word in mind. That is not to say that the sound pattern does not help; it does, but often only in a suggestive way, and the speller has to be aware of the need sometimes to deviate from the actual sounds of the word. Thus he has to have a growing familiarity with words as seen, he has to be aware of the sound pattern which he must translate into written symbolic form, and in this translation he will be guided by his knowledge of the letters and groups of letters that represent certain sounds, he will be guided by his awareness of serial probability in the letter constituents of words, and he will be prompted by his knowledge of the meaning of the word and the associations he can draw between that word and other forms of that word, for example *hear* and *heard, sign* and *signal, medic* and *medicine, nation* and *national* (the relationships of these words is indicated by their spelling and not by their sound).

BACKGROUND TO GOOD SPELLING

Attention should always centre upon words that have meaning for each child. That is, they must be words that the child needs to use in his work, either as part of his writing or as part of his reading. The latter is equally important because so much depends upon building up a visual picture of words and, provided the child is confronted with that word within a context that is interesting to him, the more varied the situations involving the confrontation the better.

Whenever words are considered, there should be overt and

deliberate comparisons drawn with words of associated meaning, or if not that, then words of similar construction. For example, *where, there, here,* or *position, caution, station.* In the former, the three words carry a reference to place, whilst in the latter the letter string *-tion* is a common construction that has to be learned simply through familiarity. The former can be appreciated in terms of meaning, whereas the latter cannot. Thus we have here a good illustration of the need for the learner to acquire a 'set for diversity' (Harlow, 1949), and it is up to the teacher to create the necessary flexibility in approach which encourages children to explore alternative solutions, whilst being mindful that many letter strings are invariable. In some instances phonic analysis will give the answer, as in such phonically regular words as *cat, catch, battle,* whilst in the word *beautiful* it will give only a partial answer: the second half of the word is phonically regular whereas in the first half only the *b* and the *u* give anything like a phonic cue. The *b* is of course virtually invariable, but *u* can at best be a pointer, assuming that the learner is sufficiently flexible to experiment with its two basic sounds of /u/ and /u:/, as in *mut* and *mute*. For words containing the digraph *ea* the learner is left with numerous alternatives: as in *idea, beautiful, bean, ideal, ocean, feast, feather, fear,* and in many other words where there are almost imperceptible variations of sound caused by the interference of the preceding or following consonant sounds. Hence, the teacher's task is to establish the habit of looking at the word and its parts, drawing comparisons with known words, looking for semantic connections (*heard–hear–ear*), phonic connections (*caution, station, position*), or phonic pointers (*beautiful, scissors*), and making a conscious effort to remember the appropriate spelling.

Children must become familiar with cases in which the final letter of words is doubled, such as *twin, twinned; shin, shinned; bid, bidding;* and in long words with stress at the end of the word: *refer, referring; occur, occurred.* These can be contrasted with *twine, twining; shine, shining; bide, biding; tune, tuning; fine, fined;* and longer words with initial stress, such as *open, opened; enter, entered.* The final *l* preceded by a vowel is always doubled – *travel, traveller; cancel, cancelled* – except before *ish, -ism* and *-ist* (*devilish, capitalism, capitalist*) and where the *l*, as with other consonants, is preceded by a digraph – *appealing, concealing, howling, conceited, repeated, sleeping, dealing, feeling, swooping.*

For the distinction between *-able* and *-ible*, it is useful to remember that *-able* occurs more frequently than *-ible*, and as someone suggested, 'able is probable while ible is only possible', but this can only be a pointer and therefore, not a great help except perhaps to remind the teacher to see that children learn individual words of this kind thoroughly.

In the case of *-ise or -ize*, it is possible to be more assertive in pointing out that four words always end in *ize: assize, size, prize* and *capsize,* whilst the choice of *-ice* or *-ise* can be demonstrated by drawing comparisons between the following four instances:

the advice   the practice
to advise   to practise

The sound distinction between *advice* and *advise* will help to resolve the difference between *practice* and *practise.*

There are certain polysyllabic words in common use which middle and upper juniors need to remember, because of the question of which letters are doubled, and perhaps this can be made easier by showing them in a categorised formation, thus:

1:1	1:2	2:1	2:2
haphazard	necessary	appearance	accommodation
	harassed	innocent	embarrassed
		accurate	
		occasion	
		anniversary	
		corridor	

These words need to be committed to memory and to this end are best learned in relation to a visual pattern in which they are laid out.

The rule '*i* before *e* except after *c*' makes it necessary for children to learn the exceptions: *feint, seize, weight, height, heir, reign, feign, rein* and *reindeer.*

In order to meet these requirements, it is not enough for the teacher to tell the children to learn certain words; neither is the old familiar practice of requiring a child to write out newly encountered words three or six times sufficient (it is uncanny how widespread was the choice of three or six!). The complexity of the task of learning to spell, which it must be remembered is not a finite accomplishment for the complete speller is a rarity, demands a more sophisticated and all-embracing, foolproof methodology for the child, and variations in the strategies which teachers employ towards different categories of spelling problems are necessary.

The nearest approach to an all-embracing technique for learning to spell is that suggested by Fernald (1943). This, you will recall, teaches children to spell words that they require for their reading or writing. The teacher writes the word in large script on a card, and shows the child how to look at the word by splitting it up into pronounceable units through articulation, whilst at the same time tracing the word with the forefinger. This tracing–vocalisation procedure is repeated until the child thinks that he can write the word without copying. The child writes the word, checks it and stores it for future reference.

As a technique, Fernald's procedure is excellent. It enforces visual impressing of the word with attention to its parts, it involves activity rather than simply requiring the learner to look at the word, which avoids a passive attitude by the learner, it shows the learner something of the ways in which words are constructed, and it provides the learner with a simple but all-embracing procedure to follow. However, all this is not sufficient in itself. Following a procedure such as the one suggested by Fernald must not be allowed to become simply a mechanistic response on the part of the pupil. It must be accompanied by mental involvement as well as physical involvement, and this means that the learner must be made aware of the significance of what is being done. This can only be achieved through comment and discussion initiated by the teacher. For example, in beginning the procedure for learning the word *pencil*, the teacher might comment that the word can be pronounced, or sounded, in two parts, /pen/, /sil/; the child imitates and then traces and vocalises; then the teacher asks the learner to listen for the sound of the first letter as he sounds the first of the two units, /pen/; similarly with the sound of the first letter in the second unit /sil/, but in this case pursuing the matter further by noting that the letter c in this case is not as in /k ae t/ but more akin to the s in /s æ t/. By these comments and any ensuing discussion between teacher and learner, the latter will experience a growing awareness of the vagaries of English spelling.

These procedures should ensure the initial learning of words accompanied by a growing awareness of English spelling, but the matter must not be allowed to stop there. The teacher must ensure that there is a conscious effort by the learner to remember what has been learned. The child must be required to return to the word after a very short interval and subsequently at frequent intervals, so that his memory of the word is refreshed and his learning reinforced.

The words that a child learns to spell should be stored in a personal box file of index cards, which is kept on the child's desk or table and is thus readily accessible for reference when the child is writing. However, this will not be the source to which the child is referred when revision of spelling is taking place. To do so would be to take words out of their context, and in order to avoid this impediment to learning, the source to which they are referred should be the original drafts of the writing in which the spelling difficulties were encountered and the book-marker slips on which unfamiliar words, subsequently learned, were written. By this procedure the children would at least be reminded of the context in which the words were encountered. If these sessions of spelling revision are held weekly the cumulative effect will enable the child to revise more and more words and to do so with increasing ease and effect.

Finally, the teacher must devise ways of displaying words in such a way that the children can, in referring to them, draw comparisons between words and categories of words, as indicated above in the case of doubling certain letters within words.

Punctuation

Like the ability to spell, the ability to punctuate is something that has to be given time to develop, but is something that needs attention. Punctuation is something that is noticed by children when reading, but which needs explaining in the context of what is read in order for the children to become aware of its purpose. As they acquire this awareness, they must then proceed to attempt to use the simpler forms of punctuation as their writing develops. The full stop and capital letter which arise first in a child's writing are not the easiest of concepts, for the simple reason that it is not easy to talk about them in terms other than as the beginning and end of a sentence, and the concept of a sentence is by no means an easily identifiable entity, especially for the very young learner of six or seven years of age.

This approach to punctuation led Cazden et al. (1985) to see the acquisition of an ability to punctuate as a developmental process which begins with the learner having punctuation, in particular the full stop, pointed out on numerous occasions when engaged in reading activities, and later being shown typical places where it occurs, but without explanation, for the simple reason that children cannot understand the necessary concepts of phrase, clause and sentence. These concepts will take time to impinge upon their awareness, and only towards the upper end of the junior school will they be able to identify them with any degree of skill. In the meantime, they will become gradually sensitised to the written form of a statement, a question, and possibly a phrase and clause, in the same way as they recognise dogginess – that is, by having dogs pointed out to them, not explained (Smith, 1982).

As children proceed through the later stages of the primary school they benefit in their ideas of punctuation from their participation in the group composition of texts that was referred to above. They will notice where the teacher punctuates; they will be involved in discussion as to where to punctuate; they will have their own compositions punctuated by the teacher; and, at appropriate times, they will be given short and specially constructed texts to punctuate – not the long passages requiring every kind of punctuation that are a more appropriate activity for the more able children in secondary schools. It is important to establish and reinforce an ability to use the simpler forms of punctuation first of all – the full stop, the capital letter, the comma, the question mark and speech marks.

A skeletal reminder for teachers

1 Before asking children to write you must ascertain the degree to which it is necessary to establish a theme:
  a it must be of interest to each child personally, otherwise its effect upon their writing will be diminished. Adults can think abstractly and can more readily adjust their writing to the reader's interests. This is not so with younger children, hence their writing must be more distinctly personal and its theme

more clearly delineated.

b children are going to think more egocentrically, and in order to provide them with models that stretch their thoughts outwards they must be intimately acquainted with stories that are read to them (Wells, 1987).

c teachers must devise ways of stimulating children's thoughts upon a theme. Infants will write 'as the story emerges' whilst juniors must progress to 'planning a story before writing'. Provision cannot be prescribed; it is something that will vary with the nature of the topic, the individual child and the teacher. All that can be said is that the teacher must rely upon a background sensitivity to that which provokes thinking in children, and the more intimate the interaction between teacher and child, the more effective the stimulation.

2 The theme must be developed:

a the story of Alaminta, discussed earlier, illustrates the influence of previously heard stories, but additionally children in the infant school must be engaged in conversation about the actual elements within the story or message that they are attempting to write, so that each child will gradually grasp the notion that his thoughts can be expanded. Furthermore, these young children should hear the teacher read aloud the stories of their classmates, so that they will come to realise that their theme can be written in a form that differs from the one they have adopted.

b juniors with their expanding background familiarity with stories can profit from more explicit reference to the expansion of a theme – comparisons can be drawn between the writings of classmates, noting through specific reference various ways in which the theme has been expanded, and discussion between teacher and child can be concerned with ways of elaborating upon the elements of the story. Juniors, and in particular upper juniors, can be challenged to elaborate upon a theme or upon certain elements within a theme, and the discussion between teacher and child can become more abstract and academic in its nature.

3 Re-drafting and refining what has been written:

a all of us can lapse into the acceptance of writing as it emerges, and even when we reread silently what we have written there

258   Teaching children to read and write

is a tendency not to identify points that require improvement. One remedy is to reread aloud what has been written. This frequently illuminates errors, unclear statements or missed opportunities to expand and elaborate particular points. Therefore, it is suggested that from the earliest stages children should be encouraged to acquire the habit of rereading what they have written and to reread aloud whenever they feel the necessity or are being pressed to redraft material.

b teachers should establish an expectancy for redrafting, for expansion, for refinement, for pruning, as the case may be. This will automatically propel the child beyond an acceptance of 'the story as it emerges' towards planning a story before and during writing and subsequently redrafting on the basis of re-forming the original plans.

c teachers should remember that children are resilient and will not wilt in the face of correction or suggested alteration. Their initial attempts at writing should not be regarded as original masterpieces but as first steps towards a reasonable piece of writing. To condemn such initial attempts and submit them to a cold analysis would be folly in the extreme, but to study them with the child and to attempt to improve upon the naturally imperfect seems to be sensible and necessary.

4 Exemplars from children's literature can be used with juniors to illustrate form:
   a the use of captivating openings;
   b the use of openings that set the scene;
   c the use of factual information to illustrate a story;
   d the inner development of a story;
   e the importance of apposite endings;
   f and finally, juniors should begin to study the various uses that can be made of illustrations: to repeat the text, to elaborate upon the text, to go beyond the text, and to anticipate the text. The last point is well illustrated by the drawing that follows the actual shot from the hunter's gun in *The Fierce Bad Rabbit*. Munro Leaf in *The Story of Ferdinand the Bull* uses drawings in all the ways mentioned and has produced a book that is well worth studying with ten to twelve year olds who are about to write stories for younger children.

A checklist for children's writing

So that teachers may keep a clear, if simple, record of each child's progress in written English, the following checklist is offered. It covers the various aspects of written English that have been referred to in this and preceeding chapters and it records prowess in the simple terms of above average (A), average (B), and below average (C). This list should be used in conjunction with the framework for looking at children's writing suggested by Newman (1984) and referred to earlier in this chapter. If used over the span of the primary school period it will show progress in the child's ability to write.

A B C

1 A facility in various types of writing,
  a personal narrative:
  b impersonal, non-chronologically ordered:
  c descriptive:
  d expansive:
  e poetic:

2 Ability to develop a theme,
  a thematic continuity in which new information is not allowed to subsume that which is known:
  b thematic variety, where extensive repetition of vocabulary is avoided but the theme maintained:
  c end-focus, where meaning is clear and unconfusing:

3 Development from utterance to text,
  a as indicated by a progression from a phrase or clausal structure to the use of sentences:
  b by the introduction of paragraphs:

4 Grammatical development,
  a phrase structure:
  b clause structure:

5 Ability to use connectives, avoiding compound

A   B   C

and producing complex sentences:

6 Ability to achieve cohesion,
  a global or overall cohesion:
  b local cohesion between sentences:
  c use of ellipsis:
  d avoiding undue repetition of the name of the subject

7 Ability to use appropriate tenses,
  a present tense:
  b past tense:
  c future tense:

8 Ability to use number correctly:

9 Ability to use features more appropriate to written than to spoken language, such as longer subject noun phrases, more noun phrases and fewer pronouns and pro-forms:

10 Ability to punctuate,
  a full stop:
  b capital letter at beginning of sentence:
  c comma:
  d speech marks:
  e question mark:
  f use of initial capital letters for real nouns:
  g apostrophe:

11 Ability to overcome spelling difficulties created by,
  a phonic irregularities:
  b doubling or not doubling of letters:
  c adding *-ible* or *-able*:
  d adding *-ise* or *-ize*:
  e adding *-ice* or *-ise*:
  f silent letters:
  g digraphs:
  h discriminating use of phonic analysis:

A B C

12 Ability to redraft where necessary what has
been written:

13 Sense of audience, appropriateness of 'tone' or
type of writing:

14 Vocabulary,
a width:
b degree of sophistication in usage:

15 Legibility,
a of handwriting:
b of layout:

Points 1 to 6 are dealt with in some detail in Chapter 5 of Perera's
book, *Children's Writing and Reading* (1984). Students should study
that chapter closely before taking up a post in a primary school.

Attainment targets and levels, key stage 2 (7–11 year olds)

Requirements relating to key stage 2 will not be introduced until
the autumn of 1990 and the draft Orders will not be published by
the Secretary of State until nearer the time. As with key stage 1
Orders it is likely that those for key stage 2 will be based upon the
recommendations contained in the National Curriculum Council
Report, *English 5–11*, (1989). Therefore, there will be a reasonable
amount of time for the teachers of junior classes to prepare for the
introduction of the National Curriculum in English and as part of
that preparation they should study the Council's report.

As for key stage 1, there are again the same five targets, but with
two levels, 4 and 5, for this key stage. These attainment levels are
summarised below.

At level 4 in speaking and listening children should participate
more fully as a speaker and listener in a group activity; contribute
to its planning and implementation and be able to draw conclusions from it; recall in detail an event or something learned;
question and respond to questions with increasing confidence;
make oral presentations to the class; give explanations concerning
actions or the resolution of problems; tell or retell stories to convey

elements of character, motive and feeling in a structured way; and show the beginnings of sensitivity to vocabulary and audience. Children at this level should become more discriminating in their reading whilst increasing its range; they should be able to read aloud with increasing effect; develop preferences which they should express in group discussion; turn readily to print for information and make effective use of information books; reflect upon what they read and discuss aspects of books and poems with their peers; and they should begin to use various reading strategies. In their writing children should produce stories which have a clear structure, are written in Standard English where appropriate and begin to show a differentiation in use between written and spoken English, with non-chronological writing being organised in a logical way. Punctuation, paragraphing and layout should develop and children should show progress in the organisation, drafting, revising and redrafting in response to discussion. Spelling should encompass the main patterns of English, including the main prefixes and suffixes, whilst handwriting should show increasing fluency in a cursive style.

At level 5 children should have developed powers of detailed oral descriptions, be able to contribute constructively and effectively in discussion or debate, express opinions using supporting information and use Standard English, dialects and other forms of English discriminatingly. Furthermore, they should be able to plan and present with others a dramatic scene or a play. Children should experience growing sophistication and discrimination in their reading with an ability to articulate their tastes, preferences and powers of interpretation to others. From texts they should be able to infer, deduce, predict, compare and evaluate, and they should be able to use referencing skills and be familiar with the various devices that contribute to the layout and design of books. Writing should show a high degree of sophistication in the child: an ability to write effectively for a range of purposes, using stylistic effects, economical constructions, and an ability in redrafting to match text to audience and purpose. Greater depths of feeling will be expressed. There should be an increasing ability to spell correctly words of increasing complexity and words where the spelling reflects meaning, as in sign and signature. Handwriting should be clear and legible in both printed and cursive styles.

As with draft Orders at key stage 1 so at key stage 2 in the

Council's report there are programmes of study to accompany these levels of attainment. These too, or a version very similar to them, will appear eventually on the statute book. These programmes are suggestive and general in form although obligatory, which leaves scope for interpretation by teachers. Hence the opportunities for teachers with flair and imagination are still there, and with the introduction of more science, design and technology into the primary curriculum with all that implies for group work and its accompanying oral discussion, experimental working and reporting both orally and in writing, and the use of information books, there will be increasing scope for the development of a richer curriculum in English than has ever existed in primary schools before.

Further reading
In order to gain an understanding of the development of the ability of children to write and to be able to appreciate fully the teaching techniques that have been suggested in the foregoing chapter, it is essential to study the relevant sections of the following three books:
Perera, K. (1984) *Children's Writing and Reading*. Oxford: Blackwell.
Kress, G. (1982) *Learning to Write*. London: Routledge and Kegan Paul.
Kroll, B.M. and Wells, C.G. (eds) (1983) *Explorations in the Development of Writing*. Chichester, N.J.: John Wiley.

Poetry
Styles, M. and Triggs, P. (eds) (1988) *Poetry 0–16: A Books For Keeps Guide*. London: Books For Keeps (1, Effingham Road, Lee, London SE12 8NZ).
An inspirational guide for teachers and an excellent source of references. No staffroom should be without it!
Benton, M. and Fox, G. (1985) *Teaching Literature: Nine to Fourteen*. Oxford. Oxford University Press,
contains a basic list of poetry written for children and will prove useful as an introduction to the study of literature.
Two books by Brownjohn, S.: (1980) *Does it Have to Rhyme?* and (1982) *What Rhymes with 'Secret'?*. London: Hodder and Stoughton.
Both contain many suggestions for dealing with poetry in primary schools.
Wade, B. (ed.) (1985) *Talking to Some Purpose*. Birmingham: University of Birmingham Faculty of Education,
contains much that is relevant to primary school teachers, and a chapter by Maggie Moore discusses the interaction between poetry reading, talk and the composition of poetry.
Heaney, S. and Hughes, T. (1982) *The Rattle Bag*. London: Faber and

264 Teaching children to read and write

Faber,
contains a good range of poetry for children, as does
Reeves, J. (ed.) (1958) *A Golden Land*. Harmondsworth: Puffin.
Also included are short stores and rhymes.
McGough, R. (ed.) (1987) *The Kingfisher Book of Comic Verse*. London:
    Kingfisher,
contains a wide selection of comic verse for junior school children.

Spelling
Little if anything that has been written on spelling surpasses in usefulness
to the teacher the procedures outlined in:
Fernald, G.M. (1943) *Remedial Techniques in Basic School Subjects*. New York:
    McGraw-Hill.
Other useful books on ways to teach spelling are:
Peters, M.L. (1967) *Spelling: Caught or Taught?* London: Routledge and
    Kegan Paul.
Torbe, M. (1985) *Teaching Spelling*. London: Ward Lock Educational.
Todd, J. (1982) *Learning to Spell*. Oxford: Blackwell,
which outlines a developmental theme.

For those who wish to read reports of some of the main researches into
spelling:
Frith, U. (ed.) (1980) *Cognitive Processes in Spelling*. London: Academic
    Press.
A concise statement of the basic principles of spelling is to be found in:
Stubbs, M. (1980) *Language and Literacy*. London: Routledge and Kegan
Paul. Chapter 3.

Some books for use in the classroom
Lane, S.M. and Kemp, M. (1974) *A Language Development Programme for
Primary Schools*. (In four stages: Books 1–4) London: Blackie.
These books provide a programme for work throughout the junior school
and they can act as a source of interesting ideas. Other sources are to be
found in:
The Primary Language Programme, Books 1–7. London: Heinemann,
which cover the years seven to twelve. The programme is divided into
thirty-five units, each unit having an extract by an accredited children's
writer, followed by work connected with reading, writing and the study of
language. Alongside this can be placed:
How Will It End? 1 to 7. London: Heinemann.
A collection of group prediction exercises and *Reasons for Writing* – a
comprehensive writing programme for seven to eleven year olds (London:
Simm).

Another English series that can profitably be used as a guide for teachers is the *On target* series, published by Macmillan. This is offered as a basic course in English and takes a very useful comprehensive approach, covering grammar, spelling and suggesting a clear programme with plenty of scope for writing.

Blackwell's *Poetry Cards* form a useful resource for lesson preparation in that each card contains three to six poems plus topics to discuss and questions to answer.

McGough, R. (ed.) (1987) *The Kingfisher Book of Comic Verse*. London: Kingfisher,
is an excellent source book for the junior classroom.

Two invaluable sources of ideas for the teacher are the *Worlds in Words* series published by Holmes McDougall of Edinburgh, and the *Expression* series written by Sybil Marshall and published by Rupert Hart-Davis.

McCall, P. and Palmer, S. (1986) *Presenting Poetry*. Edinburgh: Oliver and Boyd,
a series of four poetry books which can be used as teaching material. The teaching material in each book is in ten or eleven units containing three or four poems linked either by a common theme, a common form or which are the work of a particular poet. Each book contains suggestions concerning teaching, discussions and follow up work.

Pemberton, G. (1976) *Write About*, and (1978) *Write About Two*. Exeter: A. Wheaton,
are two sets of picture cards backed with a writing task. These form a useful resource in the form of workcards.

General
For new entrants to the teaching profession wishing to gain some idea of the quality that can be achieved at various age levels in children's writing, reference back to Clegg's work in the West Riding of Yorkshire can still point the way:
Clegg, A.G. (1964) *The Excitement of Writing*. London: Chatto and Windus.

Another book from a more optimistic past that still has much to offer in the form of advice to teachers is:
Peel, M. (1967) *Seeing to the Heart: English and Imagination in the Junior School*. London: Chatto and Windus.

However, both these books should be read with an awareness of the changes in the form and usage of language that have taken place since they were written.

PART V
READING AND WRITING IN THE CLASSROOM

9 Classroom organisation

Everything that I have experienced as a teacher, as a supervisor of students practising in primary schools, as an external examiner of university, polytechnic and college students on teaching practice, and as a frequent observer of teachers in primary schools, indicates the need for teachers to regard themselves as the teachers of individuals within small groups, and as the organisers, not the teachers, of classes of children. Whether it be teaching children to read, to write, to do physical exercise, to understand mathematics, to participate in science and art and craft experiments or environmental study, or to appreciate – that is, fully appreciate – a story read aloud to them, the small group of five children, plus or minus two, is the optimum size that allows the teacher to give intensive instruction and to interact with the children in any meaningful and child-specific way. Only in the small group will the child's strengths and weaknesses, his understanding or lack of it, reveal themselves and thereby enable the teacher to give effective help.

It is in the context of interaction within a group that the children are released from inhibitions; if treated on an individual basis, the child becomes wary of exposure and tends to hide deficiencies wherever possible; he suffers a feeling of isolation as a learner who appears in his own eyes to be the sole person with difficulties within the class. Interaction within the group, between children and between teacher and children, tends to free the child from fear of failure or to reduce that fear, to show that child that other children have difficulties and that to have difficulty is not abnormal amongst his peers. It encourages the child to bring his difficulty out into the open and, with the cooperation of others, resolve it rather than hide it. Group cohesion and interaction foster confidence, and it is confidence to explore difficulties and seek solutions that is basic to learning and subsequent progress.

For this to happen, the group must be small enough to provide intimacy and adequate practice in interaction. Groups will vary in size according to the purpose in hand. Children must be able to find plenty of opportunity to participate within the group, and this would not be possible with a class-sized group. Class discussion, for example, is a mockery. How can twenty or thirty children discuss something? All they can do is listen to others discussing, whilst waiting for their turn of a few moments' active involvement in the discussion, and the chances of that coming at the most opportune moment for what any child wants to say are remote indeed! Yet we have all sat listlessly through 'discussions' and boring meetings – boring that is, because we are not doing much of the talking. Why expect differently of children? They, like us, will feel involved and will become mentally engaged only if they are making substantial contributions to the discussion. Infant educators have for long realised this and they have consequently worked on a small-group basis: three or four children comparing volume at the water or sand tray by measuring cup- and jugfuls whilst vocalising what is being done, commenting upon it and drawing verbal comparisons; two or three children with the teacher trying to sort out a number exercise, or read a text and decide what an unfamiliar word could be, and in doing so identifying a difficulty common to several children that can be tackled and possibly resolved with guidance and support from the teacher; a child struggling to build a tower of blocks whilst a small group with the teacher discusses his chances of success and anticipate in expectant language the crash that will inevitably occur.

Junior school teachers, on the other hand, have in general terms been tardy in their approach to group work. Perhaps they have been put off group work by the frequently futile time wasting that masquerades under the guise of group discussions on inservice courses for teachers! Whatever the cause, it is undoubtedly ineffective for children to be taught en masse, so it is up to junior schools to organise small-group *interaction* and not to be satisfied merely with children sitting in groups whilst working individually, frequently at a level in common with all the other children in the class. Such an arrangement is a deceit and simply tries to mask the fact that a heterogenous group is being treated as a homogenous entity, in which there is no interaction between learners; there is only interaction by the learner in isolation with his problem. Surely there is little point in children sitting facing each other if they are not going to interact with one another, learn from discussion, compare their standards with those of their peers, and in the best sense of the word, copy from those more competent than themselves at a particular task (for many of the skills that we acquire in life are learned through copying or emulating hopefully the best in others!). And to achieve maximum benefit from interactive group work, the teacher must ensure that the children have something to interact about. In other words, motivation and guidance must be provided in the form of stimuli, procedural outlines, or steps to follow, as well as allowing interactions to arise spontaneously from the work! Work sheets rather than work cards should be the norm because they provide more space in which to include suggestions for interactive behaviour. However, many work sheets that are concerned with writing merely suggest a topic and provide a list of items to be covered. This method simply regards the writer in isolation. What is needed instead is something which suggests that the writer finds out relevant information from his peers within the group and, in doing so, is thereby forced into some discussion. This will lead to the interaction in thought and in speech which provides a sound basis for writing. If this is followed by a requirement that the writing should be read and commented upon by those peers, then there will be further interaction around a specific text.

Frequently, the argument is heard that small-group teaching can only be arranged where class numbers are small. This is an inexact statement. It should really be stated that, of course, small-group teaching is easier to plan and organise and execute if the number of children in the class is smaller rather than larger. However, it was when confronted with a very large class of 52 mixed ability ten year old children that I felt the greatest need to operate on a small-group basis. How else could I have attempted to meet the needs of children with intelligence quotients between 70 and 80 and those of children at the other end of the intelligence scale with quotients of one hundred and thirty and above? The composition of the groups that I established was not invariable. It depended upon the nature of the work and the objectives I had in mind for it. For some work children of low ability went with others of low ability, but for other work slow learners were joined by the more able children; the criteria for the choice of group composition was the mixture most likely to meet successfully the objectives of the activity or exercise. For example, where the central purpose is the development of spoken language, or where spoken language is an important element in the activity, there is much to be gained from a mixed ability grouping. The more able children are challenged to clarify the issues whilst the less able or the less fluent children can only benefit from hearing ideas expressed fluently. Frequently a highly sequential subject like mathematics poses problems for mixed ability grouping; it is not always acceptable to use the argument that children should all be on the same mathematical topic but working at different levels on that topic. This seems to be a recipe both for holding back the more able and catering inadequately for the slow learners. However, there are many problems that can be resolved mathematically through logical thought, and it is problems such as those that can frequently be put before a mixed ability group and resolved through teacher-guided discussion. What the teacher has to avoid is, on the one hand, the dilution of the work to a level where all can cope with it and, on the other hand, rigidly unchanging ability groups. The former is academically unsatisfactory whilst the latter is socially divisive as well as academically wasteful in some types of work.

This approach to the organisation of a class to meet specific objectives requires several things from teachers. They must be clear about the objectives in any learning or practice activity. For example, reading and writing are usually individual activities, whereas preparation for reading and writing is not necessarily an individual activity. Frequently, preparation is better done as a group activity where help and guidance in that preparation come from the teacher and from other children. Thinking about describing an event can often be done more thoroughly through discussion; the understanding of a text is more readily accomplished if the reader's knowledge about some aspect dealt with by text is reactivated through discussion. Similarly the improvement of a piece of writing or the acquisition of a clearer understanding of a text is frequently accomplished more competently through discussion of what has been written or read and followed by further individual reading. Thus the objectives in each manifestation of an activity vary and, consequently, demand differing forms of organisation. In the above instances those forms begin as a group activity, move to an individual activity, then return to group activity and, finally, end in individual activity.

This need for varying forms of organisation demands clarity of forethought by the teacher and a flexible approach to the organisation of activities. The teacher of the future must give far more thought to objectives and to the most effective ways of achieving them. She must plan the amount of time she thinks she will need to allocate to each group, she must ensure that only one group needs her undivided attention in the first instance, and she must programme her progression to other groups as she thinks necessary. This should be clearly stated in the student's lesson notes, giving a clear outline of her progression and the part she will play in the classroom during a specified period of time. She will have planned the work so that some groups need more attention than others; some will be practising what has been previously learned and will not require the same amount and degree of attention as those who are acquiring new knowledge or new skills. Furthermore, the teacher must be prepared to deviate from her plans in order to meet unforeseen problems, and she must be confident enough to change the organisation of the class or the activity of an individual or a group at a moment's notice. Flexibility, spontaneity based on substantial forethought, and ingenuity are essential qualities of a primary school teacher.

However, teaching is not just about preparation and presentation; it is also concerned with follow-up work by teacher and children and with the reinforcement of learning. We cannot assume that children learn on the instant. A few things are learned very quickly, but many things have to be 'worked at'; there has to be application on the part of the learner; he has to imbibe what he learns, process it and incorporate it into his store of knowledge or repertoire of skills so that he understands it and can use it at will. Many teachers seem to forget how hard they had to work to acquire the necessary learning to attain academic success, to say nothing of the effort they had to put into their school practices! It is important that children in primary schools learn that effort and hard work are frequently necessary. One of the disturbing aspects of the 'creative and uninhibited writing' craze that swept through our schools was the tendency to regard writing, and especially 'poetry', as easy and something that could be accomplished by the child unaided after listening to a few bars of music or being told to recall without any prompting some supposedly exciting event. Any adult faced with writing an examination essay or an article surely knows that there is more to it than just writing; and those adults have many of the skills required for writing already developed and readily available for use, whereas children are less adequately equipped for the task! The craft of writing and the interpretation of texts, like so many other aspects of the primary school curriculum, are things that have to be learned, and they can only be learned through application on the part of the child and through sensitive but persistent help from the teacher.

Hence the need for application and conscious effort on the part of the learner is something of which the children must be aware throughout their primary schooling. They must not be left with the idea that learning and ability to do things just happen, and it is within the small group that they can be made aware of this without being left with the notion that they alone find learning difficult.

In order to ensure that adequate and appropriate reinforcement takes place, the teacher must keep full and meaningful records of each child's strengths and weaknesses in all aspects of intellectual, social and physical development. Mark lists are insufficient, because they seldom indicate precisely the strengths and weaknesses upon which it is necessary for teachers to base their plans for subsequent lessons. Weaknesses must be remedied and strengths must be fostered, and teachers should not deceive themselves that they can remember all the weaknesses and strengths of every child in the class. These must be recorded and referred to in the planning of subsequent work for the children.

Some students will be apprehensive about setting up the type of organisation that is being advocated. They may even be advised by some of the backwoodsmen who can still be found in some schools 'to stick to class teaching and not jump in at the deep end'. The answer is that we cannot base teacher training on easy options. We must be concerned with effective options, and class teaching is not an effective basis for the organisation of teaching. However, we can accept a gradual progression towards the ideal form of organisation.

A student entering a class organised as a homogenous unit may wish to begin very simply by having three roughly chosen groups: one to be taught something and the other two to practice skills already acquired to some degree, such as reading, writing or the solution of mathematical problems that have been introduced previously. These three groups can be rotated, so that each has a turn at the three activities. To these can be added other activities as the student gains confidence and with growing confidence, attention can be given to the composition and size of the groups. Ability and mixed ability groups will be used according to the type of work and the objectives for a particular activity. Eventually the student will want to consider the establishment of designated areas within and without the classroom in which work will be laid out and to which the children can move at will. The advantages of this are: the work is always available for children to move to at will; mixed ability groups can operate as well as ability groups; the ambience created in the area will be conducive to work on the provisions of the area; time need not be a constraining factor so that various paces of working amongst the children can be catered for; and the teacher can easily detect at a glance what is being done in the area and whether it is the form of behaviour appropriate to the type of work that is required in that area. Reading and writing require a fair degree of silence, except when discussion and consultations within the group are required; craft requires behaviour that varies from high individual concentration through discussion of technique and effort to excited response to achievement; problem solving of any kind – in scientific experimentation, in mathematics, in project work and in the interpretation of texts – frequently requires children to discuss with others possible solutions. Almost every activity in the primary school curriculum requires more than one form of behaviour. When they are checking individually what they have written, children may need to read silently. Nevertheless, they may derive benefit from reading aloud what they have written in order to check that it 'sounds right'. Thus the school must provide quiet corners where children can work quietly, if need be, whilst at the same time ensuring that at appropriate times children will be interacting with one another – helping each other, discussing problems, practising their powers of persuasion and generally learning to learn in a social setting, just as later in life they will usually be expected to work in a social setting.

We are not training citizens to do as they are told but encouraging them to act responsibly, to assess what needs to be done to accomplish any task, and then to have the confidence to set about its accomplishment in the most effective manner commensurate with concern and consideration for any others involved in the process. Children in the primary school can be prepared for such behaviour through the above mentioned organisational arrangements. They must not be rigidly controlled at all times; they must feel free to initiate learning themselves and they must acquire a flexible approach to learning. The primary school provides for flexibility, but the teacher must ensure its implementation. That is why group and area formations have been advocated. The former provides for flexibility of methodology whilst the latter – area based working, with children learning to circulate and arrange their own sequence of work within a stipulated programme – provides flexibility of timing to suit the moods and needs of children.

Finally, because learning and teaching are both complex activities, it is essential that students of teaching should acquire early in their practice a clear conceptual framework within which to operate. This framework should not be so detailed as to defy easy recall and easy adaptation to differing, changing and often intricate situations. The two aspects – learning and teaching – are covered in this book by two models which the writer has found effective to use and easy to convey to others. The first model was specifically applied by Whitehead (1955) to learning. It consists of a cycle of romance, precision and generalisation and has been closely associated in this book with writing, but it underlies also learning to read, to spell and the other aspects of communication. This model or cyclic process can be adopted in parallel with the teaching model, which in itself is simple – viz., Stage One: preparation, introduction and motivation; Stage Two: specific teaching, guidance and the introduction to new or renewed learning; Stage Three: provision for the use and practice of new material and for the reinforcement of learning. In the case of reinforcement or renewed learning, ie learning which was not adequately accomplished on a previous occasion, further preparation and re-motivation may be necessary. This teaching model ensures that the cyclic process of learning is unimpeded.

These models are necessary because they act as a reminder of the main thrusts that are incorporated in teaching and in learning, and by their cohesive nature in combining disparate activities, they enable the teacher to orchestrate her own actions and the activities of the various group and individual activities under her control. It is this ability to orchestrate all the elements of learning and teaching to meet the requirements of specific situations that Brophy and Evertson (1976) found to be the distinguishing mark of an effective teacher.

Further Reading
Barnes, D. (1976) *From Communication to Curriculum.* Harmondsworth : Penguin.
Bennett, N. (1986) Interaction and achievement in classroom groups. In N. Bennett and C. Desforges, Recent Advances in Classroom Research. *British Journal of Educational Psychology*, Monograph Series No. 2. Edinburgh: Scottish Academic Press.
The latter reference describes the research that has been done into the small-group type of classroom organisation, and it indicates the urgent need for more meaningful research into ways of achieving optimum results from a small-group interactive method of organising for teaching and learning.

The small-group interactive-activity approach, together with a more general discussion of the models for learning and teaching proposed in this book, are to be found in:
Education, Science and Arts Committee (1986) *Achievement in Primary Schools.* Appendix 50: The organisation of learning in primary schools (G.R. Roberts). London : HMSO.

PART VI
APPENDIXES AND
BIBLIOGRAPHY

Appendix 1: Summary of an integrated speaking, reading and writing programme for the early stages of reading and writing based upon purposeful activities

Phase one: play, talking and stories, all to be regarded as specific bases for mental and language development.

Phase two: group oral composition and 'reading', using *Breakthrough* type activities based on the child's play and experience. Early scribbling and 'writing' to be encouraged, with the teacher transcribing for undirected comparison with the original. Incidental help with letter formation with the objective of calling attention to the existence of letters rather than specifically coaching the children in handwriting skills.

Phase three: recall of known stories, contained in nursery rhymes, folk stories and jingles, accompanied by 'reading' those rhymes and stories as a group. Continuing writing-like activities – scribbling, tracing, overwriting, copying and 'writing' stories. Again with the teacher leading the 'reading' and transcribing the 'writing'.

Phase four: oral composition and 'reading' with some actual selection of words and reading. Overwriting of compositions, copying and beginning to write individual compositions and report personal activities. The teacher's role will be less dominant, assuming a more supportive and suggestive role as the children assume the initiative.

(Accompanying each of these phases will be an increasing awareness of written language patterns including clause, phrase and word study of varying degrees, all encompassing speech, reading and writing.)

Phase five: reading specially selected materials, including stories written by the teacher and by the children, work sheets, information sheets, booklets and labels, books from reading schemes and/or individually published books – Young Puffin, Puffins and other literature of quality. Group discussions, involving very small numbers of children, centred on reading, writing and other activities in order to emphasize the reality of all those experiences.

Phase six: wide reading of works of literary merit, the use of reading for information and learning and writing as a means of communication for oneself and with others.

(Continuing language study throughout phases five and six.)

Appendix 2: Pumfrey's coding of reading errors

Sentence to be read	Error category	Method of recording error	Example
Which is the way to the house on the hill?	Substitution	Underline the word misread and write in word substituted	Which is the way to the 'home' house on the hill?
	No response	If the child waits to be prompted or asks for a word, underline with a dashed line	Which is the way to the house on the hill?
	Addition	Use caret mark and write down word or part-word added	Which is the way 'go to' to ∠the house on the hill?
	Omission*	Where words are omitted, circle them	Which is the way to the ⦅house⦆on the hill?
	Self-correction	Where errors are self-corrected, record by using initial 'S. C.' over the words	Which is the way S. C. to the house on the hill?
	Repetition	Record word/s repeated by putting 'R' over appropriate section	Which is the way to the R house on the hill?

Mispronunciations	Indicate where stress is placed	
Ignores punctuation	Circle punctuation ignored	Which is the way to the house on the hill?...
Reversals	This is a form of substitution, but may be of diagnostic significance if part of a regular pattern	Which is the way to the 'no' house on the hill?

* Child does not wait for help

Table 2:   Coding for recording error types

Taken from Pumfrey, P. D. (1976) *Reading: Tests and Assessment Techniques*. London: Hodder and
    Stoughton.

It will be noted that *r* is not sounded and, therefore, not depicted, when it appears at the end of a word or when it is followed by another consonant: *far* = /fa:/ and *farm* = /fa:m/. However, the *r* is pronounced and depicted when it appears at the end of a word which is immediately followed by a vowel: *far* away = /far əwei/.

In some of the examples that are given above, variations in regional accents will mean that the reader will have to make slight adjustments if the letters are to portray his sounds accurately. In this sense the IPA code is not absolutely foolproof.

Appendix 4: Nursery rhymes as a basis for word and language study

Note: the repetition of sounds, basic letter formations and the rhyming linkings; the cohesion and the organisation that give form to the stanzas, and the richness of language patterns that bring vitality to the stories; and the homophones – *where* and *there* alongside *chair* – by which children can come to terms with two spelling patterns representing the same sound.

LITTLE BO-PEEP

Little Bo-peep has lost her sheep,
And can't tell where to find them;
Leave them alone, and they'll come home,
And bring their tails behind them.

Little Bo-peep fell fast asleep,
And dreamt she heard them bleating;
But when she awoke, she found it a joke,
For they were still all fleeting.

Then up she took her little crook,
Determined for to find them;
She found them indeed, but it made her heart bleed,
For they'd left their tails behind them.

It happened one day, as Bo-peep did stray
Into a meadow hard by,
There she espied their tails side by side,
All hung on a tree to dry.

She heaved a sigh, and wiped her eye,
And over the hillocks went rambling,
And tried what she could, as a shepherdess should,
To tack again each to its lambkin.

Cohesion
⬭ references to sheep
▢ references to Little Bo-peep

THREE BLIND MICE

Three blind mice, see how they run!
They all ran after the farmer's wife,
Who cut off their tails with a carving knife,
Did you ever see such a thing in your life
As three blind mice.

PUSSY CAT

'Pussy cat, pussy cat,
Where have you been?'
'I've been up to London
To see the Queen.'

'Pussy cat, pussy cat
What did you there?'
'I frightened a little mouse
Under the chair.'

Appendix 5: A simple story frame or schema

Categories and types of causal relations occurring in a simple story taken from Stein and Trabasso (1972):

1 SETTING	Introduction of the protagonist; contains information about the social, physical, or temporal context in which the story events occur.
Allow Episode:	
2 INITIATING EVENT	An action, an internal event, or a physical event that serves to initiate the storyline or cause the protagonist to respond emotionally and to formulate a goal.
Cause	
3 INTERNAL RESPONSE	An emotional reaction and a goal, often incorporating the thoughts of the protagonist that cause him to initiate action.
Cause	
4 ATTEMPT	An overt action or series of actions, carried out in the service of attaining a goal.
Cause or Enable	

5 CONSEQUENCE   An event, action, or endstate, marking the attainment or nonattainment of the protagonist's goal.

Cause

6 REACTION   An internal response expressing the protagonist's feelings about the outcome of his actions or the occurrence of broader, general consequences resulting from the goal attainment of the protagonist.

Example of a well formed story:

Setting
1 Once there was a big grey fish named Albert.
2 He lived in a big icy pond near the edge of a forest.

Initiating event
3 One day, Albert was swimming around the pond.
4 Then he spotted a big juicy worm on the top of the water.

Internal response
5 Albert knew how delicious worms tasted.
6 He wanted to eat that one for his dinner.

Attempt
7 So he swam very close to the worm.
8 Then he bit into him.

Consequence
9 Suddenly, Albert was pulled through the water into a boat.
10 He had been caught by a fisherman.

Reaction
11 Albert felt very sad.
12 He wished he had been more careful.

Taken from Stein and Trabasso (1982).

Bibliography

APPLEBEE, A.N. (1978) *The Child's Concept of Story*. Chicago: Chicago University Press

ARNOLD, H. (1982) *Listening to Children Reading*. London: Hodder and Stoughton

ARNOLD, H. (1984) *Making Sense of It: Graded Passages for Miscue Analysis*. London: Hodder and Stoughton

AUSUBEL, D.P. (1968) *Educational Psychology: A Cognitive View*. New York: Holt, Rinehart and Winston

BADDELEY, A.D., ELLIS, N.C., MILES, T.R. AND LEWIS, V.J. (1982) Developmental and acquired dyslexia: A comparison. *Cognition, II*, 185–99

BARNES, D. (1976) *From Communication to Curriculum*. Harmondsworth: Penguin

BEARD, R. (1984) *Children's Writing in the Primary School*. London: Hodder and Stoughton

BEARD, R. (1987) *Developing Reading 3–13*. London: Hodder and Stoughton

BECK, I., McKEOWN, M.C., MCCASLIN, E.S. AND BURKES, A.M. (1979) *Instructional Dimensions That May Affect Reading Comprehension: Example from Two Commercial Reading Programs* (LRDC Publication 1979/20) Pittsburgh: Learning Research and Development Center

BENNETT, J. (1985) *Learning to Read with Picture Books*. Stroud: Thimble Press

BENNETT, N. (1986) Interaction and achievement in classroom groups. In N. Bennett and C. Desforges, *Recent Advances in Classroom Research*. British Journal of Educational Psychology, Monograph Series No. 2. Edinburgh: Scottish Academic Press

BENTON, M. and FOX, G. (1985) *Teaching Literature; Nine to Fourteen*. Oxford: Oxford University Press

BEREITER, C. and SCARDAMALIA, M. (1985) Children's difficulties in learning to compose. In G. Wells and J. Nicholls (eds) *Language and Learning: An Interactional Perspective*. London: Falmer Press

BERNSTEIN, B. (1970) A critique of the concept of 'Compensatory Education'. In D. Rubinstein and C. Stoneman (eds) *Education for Democracy*. Harmondsworth: Penguin

BETTELHEIM, B. (1976) *The Uses of Enchantment*. London: Thames and Hudson

BIEMILLER, A.J. (1970) The development of the use of graphic and contextual information as children learn to read. *Reading Research Quarterly, 6,* 75–96

BISSEX, G.L. (1980) *GNYS AT WRK: A Child Learns to Read and Write.* Cambridge. Mass.: Harvard University Press.

BOLT, S. and GARD, R. (1970) *Teaching Fiction in School.* London: Hutchinson Educational

BRIERLEY, J. (1987) *Give Me a Child Until He is Seven; Brain Studies and Early Childhood Education.* London: Falmer Press

BRITTON, J. (1983) Writing and the story world. In B.M. Kroll and G. Wells (eds) *Explorations in the Development of Writing.* New York: John Wiley

BRITTON, J., BURGESS, T., MARTIN, N., McLEOD, A., and ROSEN, H. (1975) *The Development of Writing Abilities (11–18).* London: Macmillan.

BROPHY, J.E. and EVERTSON, C.M. (1976) *Learning from Teaching.* Boston: Allyn and Bacon

BROWNJOHN, S. (1980) *Does it Have to Rhyme?* London: Hodder and Stoughton

BROWNJOHN, S. (1982) *What Rhymes with 'Secret'?* London: Hodder and Stoughton

BRUNER, J.S. (1957) On perceptual readiness. *Psychological Review, 64,* 123–52

BRUNER, J.S. (1960) *The Process of Education.* Cambridge, Mass.: Harvard University Press

BRUNER, J.S. (1975) The ontogenesis of speech acts. *Journal of Child Language, 2,* 1–19

BRUNER, J.S. (1980) *Under Five in Britain.* London: Grant McIntyre

BRUNER, J.S. and HASTE, H. (1987) *Making Sense.* London: Methuen

BRYANT, P. (1986) Phonological skills and learning to read and write. In B. R. Foorman and A. W. Siegel (eds) *Acquisition of Reading Skills.* Hillsdale, N. J.: Lawrence Erlbaum

BRYANT, P. and BRADLEY, L. (1985) *Children's Reading Problems.* Oxford: Blackwell

BURKE, E. (1976) The development of reading strategies among primary school children. Doctoral thesis, University of Manchester

CALTHROP, K. and EDE, J. (1984) *Not 'Daffodils' Again: Teaching Poetry 9–13.* London: Longman

CAMPBELL, R. (1981) An approach to analysing teacher verbal moves in hearing children read. *Journal of Research in Reading, 4*

CAMUS, A. (1948) *The Plague.* London: Hamish Hamilton

CASHDAN, A. (1969) Backward readers – research on auditory–visual integration. In K. Gardner (ed.) *Reading Skills: Theory and Practice.* London: Ward Lock Educational

CASS, J. (1967) *Literature and the Young Child.* London: Longman

CAZDEN, C.B., CORDEIRO, P. and GIACOBBE, M.E. (1985) Spontaneous and scientific concepts: young children's learning of punctuation. In G. Wells and J. Nicholls (eds) *Language and Learning: an Interactional Perspective*. London: Falmer Press

CENTRAL ADVISORY COUNCIL FOR EDUCATION (ENGLAND) (1967) *Children and their Primary Schools*. London: HMSO

CHOMSKY, C. (1970) Reading, writing and phonology. *Harvard Educational Review*, 40(2), 287–309

CHOMSKY, C. (1976) After decoding: what? *Language Arts*, 53(3)

CHOMSKY, C. (1979) Approaching reading through invented spelling. In L.B. Resnick and P.A. Weaver (eds) *Theory and Practice of Early Reading*, Volume 2. Hillsdale, N. J: Lawrence Erlbaum

CLARK, M.M. (1976) *Young Fluent Readers*. London: Heinemann

CLARK, M.M. (ed.) (1985) *New Directions in the Study of Reading*. London: Falmer Press

CLAY, M.M. (1969) Reading errors and self-correction behaviour. *British Journal of Education Psychology*, 39, 47–56

CLAY, M.M. (1975) *What Did I Write?* Auckland: Heinemann

CLAY, M. (1980) Early writing and reading: reciprocal gains. In M.M. Clark and T. Glynn (eds) *Reading and Writing for the Child with Difficulties*. Birmingham: Faculty of Education.

CLAY, M.M. (1982) *The Early Detection of Reading Difficulties: A Diagnostic Survey with Recovery Procedures*. Tadworth, Surrey: Heinemann

CLAY, M.M. (1983) Getting a theory of writing. In B.M. Kroll and G. Wells (eds) *Explorations in the Development of Writing*. Chichester, N.J.: John Wiley

CLEGG, A.G. (1964) *The Excitement of Writing*. London: Chatto and Windus

COHEN, A. and L. (1988) *Early Education: the Pre-School Years*. London: Chapman

COLTHEART, M. (ed.) (1987) *The Psychology of Reading*. Attention and Performance XII. London: Lawrence Erlbaum

CORBETT, P. and MOSES, B. (1986) *Catapults and Kingfishers: Teaching Poetry in Primary Schools*. Oxford: Oxford University Press

CURTIS, A.M. (1986) *A Curriculum for the Pre-School Child: Learning to Learn*. Windsor: NFER/Nelson

DALE, N. (1988) *On the Teaching of English Reading*. London: Dent

DAVIES, F., GREENE, T. and LUNZER, E. (1980) *Reading for Learning in Science*. A discussion paper from the Schools Council Project, Reading for Learning in the Secondary School. University of Nottingham

DAVIES, J.A. (1980) A developmental study of children's reading miscues. Unpublished M.Ed. thesis, University of Manchester

DAVIS, F.B. (1972) Psychometric research on comprehension in reading. *Reading Research Quarterly*, 7, 628–78

DEPARTMENT OF EDUCATION AND SCIENCE (1975) *Language for Life* (The Bullock Report) London: HMSO

DEPARTMENT OF EDUCATION AND SCIENCE (1988) *Report of the*

Committee of Inquiry into the Teaching of English Language. (The Kingman Report) London: HMSO

DEPARTMENT OF EDUCATION AND SCIENCE (1988) *English for Ages 5 to 11.* Proposal of the Secretary of State for Education and Science and the Secretary of State for Wales (The Cox Report). London: HMSO

DONALDSON, M. (1978) *Children's Minds.* London: Fontana

DONALDSON, M. and REID, J. (1985) Language skills and reading: A developmental perspective. In M.M. Clark (ed.) *New Directions in the Study of Reading.* London: Falmer Press

DOWNING, J., AYERS, D. and SCHAEFER, B. (1983) *Linguistic Awareness in Reading Readiness* (LARR) Test. Windsor: NFER–NELSON

DOWNING, J. and THACKRAY, D.V. (1971) *Reading Readiness.* London: University of London Press

DUCKWORTH, E. (1979) Either we're too early and they can't learn it or we're too late and they know it already: the dilemma of 'applying Piaget'. *Harv. Educ. Rev., 49,* 297–312

EDUCATION, SCIENCE AND ARTS COMMITTEE (1986) *Achievement in Primary Schools.* Appendix 50: The organisation of learning in primary schools (G.R. Roberts) London: HMSO

EGOFF, S. et al. (eds) (1969) *Only Connect: Readings in Children's Literature.* Toronto: Oxford University Press

EHRI, L.C. and ROBERTS, K.T. (1979) Do beginners learn printed words better in context or in isolation? *Child Development, 50,* 675–85

EHRI, L.C. and WILCE, L.S. (1980) Do beginners learn to read function words better in sentences or in lists? *Reading Research Quarterly, 16,* 452–76

ELDER, R.D. (1966) A comparison of the oral reading of groups of Scottish and American children. Unpublished doctoral dissertation. Department of Education, University of Michigan

EPSTEIN, J. (1969) 'Good bunnies always obey': books for American children. In S. Egoff, G.T. Stubbs, and L.F. Ashley (eds) *Only Connect: Readings in Children's Literature.* Toronto: Oxford University Press

FERNALD, G.M. (1943) *Remedial Techniques in Basic School Subjects.* New York: McGraw-Hill

FERREIRO, E. (1978a) *The Relationship Between Oral and Written Language: The Children's View Point.* New York: Ford Foundation

FERREIRO, E. (1978b) What is written in a written sentence: a developmental answer. *Journal of Education, 160,* (4), 25–39

FISHER, M. (1964) *Intent upon Reading.* London: Brockhampton Press.

FOX, G., HAMMOND, G., JONES, T., SMITH, F. and STERCK, K. (1976) *Writers, Critics, and Children.* London: Heinemann Educational

FRANCIS, H. (1975) *Language in Childhood: Form and Function in Language Learning.* London: Paul Elek

FRANCIS, H. (1982) *Learning to Read: Literate Behaviour and Orthographic*

Knowledge. London: Allen and Unwin
FRIES, C.C. (1964) *Linguistics and Reading.* New York: Holt, Rinehart and Winston
FRITH, U. (ed.) (1980) *Cognitive Processes in Spelling.* London: Academic Press
FRY, D. (1985) *Children Talk About Books: Seeing Themselves as Readers.* Milton Keynes: Open University Press
GAHAGAN, D.M. and G.A. (1970) *Talk Reform.* London: Routledge and Kegan Paul
GALTON, M., SIMON, B. and CROLL, P. (1980) *Inside the Primary Classroom.* London: Routledge and Kegan Paul
GATES, A.I. (1927) *The Improvement of Reading.* New York: Macmillan
GATES, A.I., PEARDON, C.G. and SATORIOUS, I. (1931) Studies of children's interests in reading. *Elementary School Journal, 31,* 656–70
GATTEGNO, C. (1969) *Reading with Words in Colour: A Scientific Study of the Problems of Reading.* Reading, Berks : Educational Explorers
GIBSON, E.J. and LEVIN, H. (1975) *The Psychology of Reading.* Cambridge, Mass.: MIT Press
GIBSON, E.J., SHURCLIFF, A. and YONAS, A. (1970) Utilization of spelling patterns by deaf and hearing subjects. In H. Levin and J.P. Williams (eds) (1970) *Basic Studies on Reading.* New York: Basic Books.
GLENN, C.G. and STEIN, N.L. (1980) *Syntactic Structures and Real World Themes in Stories Generated by Children.* Urbana: University of Illinois
GODDARD, N.L. (1958) *Reading in the Modern Infants School.* London: University of London Press
GOELMAN, H., OBERG, A. and SMITH, F. (eds) (1984) *Awakening to Literacy.* London: Heinemann Educational
GOLLASCH, F.V. (ed.) (1982) *Language and Literacy: the Selected Writings of Kenneth S. Goodman,* Volumes 1 and 2. London: Routledge and Kegan Paul
GOODACRE, E. (1971) *Children and Learning to Read.* London: Routledge and Kegan Paul
GOODACRE, E. (1979) *Hearing Children Read.* Reading: University Centre for Reading
GOODMAN, K.S. (1969) Analysis of oral reading miscues: applied psycholinguistics. *Reading Research Quarterly, 5,* 9–30
GOODMAN, Y.M. and BURKE, C.L. (1972) *Reading Miscue Inventory.* New York: Macmillan
GOODNOW, J. (1977) *Children's Drawing.* Glasgow: Fontana/Open Books
GRAVES, D.H. (1979) What children show us about revision, *Language Arts, 56* (3), 312–19
GRAVES, D.H. (1979) The growth and development of first grade writers. Paper at Canadian Council of Teachers of English in Ottowa, Canada
GRAVES, D.H. (1983) *Writing: Teachers and Children at Work.* London: Heinemann Educational Books

HALLATT, A., THOMPSON, R. and WIGGLESWORTH, C. (1970) *Worlds in Words*. Edinburgh: Holmes McDougall

HALLIDAY, M.A.K. (1969) Relevant models of language. *Educational Review, 22(1)*, 26–37 and in M. A. K. Halliday (1973) *Explorations in the Functions of Language*

HALLIDAY, M.A.K. (1973) *Explorations in the Functions of Language*. London: Edward Arnold

HARLOW, H.F. (1949) The formation of learning sets. *Psychological Review, 56*, 51–6

HARTOG, P.J. and LANGDON, A.H. (1907) *The Writing of English*. Oxford: Oxford University Press

HEEKS, P. (1981) *Choosing and Using Books in the First School*. London: Macmillan

HENDERSON, L. (1982) *Orthography and Word Recognition in Reading*. London: Academic Press

HENDERSON, L. (1987) Word recognition: a tutorial review. In M. Coltheart (ed.) *The Psychology of Reading*. London: Lawrence Erlbaum

HERRIOT, P. (1971) *Language and Teaching*. London: Methuen

HESKETH, P. (1966) Writing a poem. In T. Blackburn, *Presenting Poetry: A Handbook for Teachers*. London: Methuen

HEWITT, G. (1980) A preliminary study of pupils' reading difficulties. *Educational Review, 32*, 231–44

HOEY, M.P. (1979) *Signalling in Discourse*. Birmingham: English Language Research, University of Birmingham

HUCK, C.S., HEPLER, S. and HICKMAN, J. (1987) *Children's Literature in the Elementary School*. Fourth Edition. New York: Holt, Rinehart and Winston

HUEY, E.B. (1908) *The Psychology and Pedagogy of Reading*. Cambridge, Mass.: MIT

HUGHES, J.M. (1970) *Aids to Reading*. London: Evans

HUGHES, J.M. (1972) *Phonics and the Teaching of Reading*. London: Evans

HUGHES, T. (1967) *Poetry in the Making*. London: Faber

HULME, C. (1981) *Reading Retardation and Multi-Sensory Teaching*. London: Routledge and Kegan Paul

INGRAM, T.T.S. (1971) Specific learning difficulties in childhood: a medical point of view. *British Journal of Educational Psychology, 41(1)*, 6–13

JANSEN, M. (1985) Language and concepts: play or work? – seriousness or fun? – basics or creativity? In M.M. Clark, *New Directions in the Study of Reading*. London: Falmer

KARMILOFF-SMITH, A. (1978) The interplay between syntax, semantics and phonology in language processes. In R.N. Campbell, and P.T. Smith (eds) *Recent Advances in the Psychology of Language*. New York: Plenum Press

KATZ, L.G. (1977) *Talks with Teachers*. Washington, D.C.: National Association for the Education of Young Children

KLEIN, G. (1985) *Reading into Racism*. London: Routledge and Kegan Paul

KOHL, H.R. (1977) *Writing, Maths and Games in the Open Classroom*. London: Methuen

KRESS, G. (1982) *Learning to Write*. London: Routledge and Kegan Paul

KROLL, B.M. (1981) Developmental relationships between speaking and writing. In B.M. Kroll and R.J. Vann (eds) *Exploring Speaking–Writing Relationships: Connections and Contrasts*. Urbana, Illinois: NCTE

KROLL, B.M. and WELLS, C.G. (eds) (1983) *Explorations in the Development of Writing: Theory, Research and Practice*. Chichester, N. J.: John Wiley

LANE, S.M. and KEMP, M. (1974) *A Language Development Programme for Primary Schools, Books 1–4*. London: Blackie

LANGDON, M. (1961) *Let the Children Write*. London: Longman

LOBBAN, G. (1975) Sex-roles in reading schemes. *Educational Review*, 27(3), 202–10

LUNDSTEEN, S.W. (1976) *Children Learn to Communicate: Language Arts Through Creative Problem Solving*. Englewood Cliffs, N.J.: Prentice-Hall

LUNZER, E.A. and GARDNER, K. (1979) *The Effective Use of Reading*. London: Heinemann Educational for the Schools Council

McCALL, P. and PALMER, S. (1986) *Presenting Poetry*. Edinburgh: Oliver and Boyd

McINNES, J.A. (1973) Language pre-requisites for reading. In M.M. Clark and A. Milne (eds) *Reading and Related Skills*. London: Ward Lock

MACKAY, D., THOMPSON, B. and SCHAUB, P. (1970) *Breakthrough to Literacy; The Theory and Practice of Teaching Initial Reading and Writing*. London: Longman

MACKAY, D., THOMPSON, B. and SCHAUB, P. (1978) *Breakthrough to Literacy; Teacher's Manual*. London: Longman

McKENZIE, M. (1986) *Journeys in Literacy*. Huddersfield: Schofield and Sims

MACNAMARA, J. (1972) Cognitive basis of language learning in infants. *Psychological Review*, 79, 1–13

McTEAR, M. (1985) *Children's Conversation*. Oxford: Blackwell

MANDLER, J.M. and JOHNSON, N.S. (1977) Remembrance of things passed: story structure and recall. *Cognitive Psychology*, 9, 111–51

MARCHBANKS, G. and LEVIN, H. (1965) Cues by which children recognize words. *Journal of Educational Psychology*, 56, 57–61

MARSHALL, S. (1970) *Expression*, Books 1 to 6. London: Rupert Hart-Davis

MARSHALL, S. (1974) *Creative Writing*. London: Macmillan

MARTIN, N.C. (1966) Children Writing Poetry. In T. Blackburn, *Presenting Poetry: A Handbook for English Teachers*. London: Methuen

MATTINGLY, I.G. (1979) Reading, the linguistic process, and linguistic awareness. In J.F. Kavanagh and I.G. Mattingly. *Language by Ear and*

by Eye. Cambridge Mass.: MIT Press
MAXWELL, J. (1977) *Reading Progress from 8 to 15.* Slough: NFER Publishing Co.
MEEK, M. (1987) *Learning to Read.* London: Bodley Head
MEEK, M. (1988) *How Texts Teach What Readers Learn.* Stroud: Thimble Press
MEEK, M., WARLOW, A. and BARTON, G. (eds) (1977) *The Cool Web: The Pattern of Children's Reading.* London: Bodley Head
MERRITT, J. (1970) The intermediate skills. In K. Gardner (ed.) *Reading Skills: Theory and Practice.* London: Ward Lock Educational
MILES, T.R. (1971) More on dyslexia. *British Journal of Educational Psychology, 41*(1), 1–5
MILLER, G.A. (1956) The magical number seven, plus or minus two: some limits on our capacity for processing information. *Psychological Review, 63,* 81–97
MOON, B. and C. (1986) *Individualised Reading* (18th edition). University of Reading: Reading and Language Information Centre
MOORE, M. (1985) Talk as a productive beginning. In B. Wade (ed.) *Talking To Some Purpose.* Educational Review, Occasional Publication. University of Birmingham: Faculty of Education
MOOREHEAD, A. (1959) *No Room in the Ark.* London: Reprint Society
MORRIS, C. (1984) *Advanced Paper Aircraft Construction* Mark I and Mark II. London: Cornstalk Publishing
MOSELEY, D. (1975) *Special Provision for Reading.* Slough: NFER
NAIDOO, S. (1971) Specific developmental dyslexia. *British Journal of Educational Psychology, 41*(1), 19–22
NATIONAL CURRICULUM COUNCIL (1989) *English 5–11 in the National Curriculum.* York: National Curriculum Council
NEISSER, U. (1967) *Cognitive Psychology.* New York: Appleton-Century-Crofts
NELSON, Katherine (1974) Concept, word and sentence: interrelations in acquisition and development. *Psychological Review, 81*(4), 267–85
NEWMAN, J. (1984) *The Craft of Children's Writing.* Toronto: Scholastic Book Services
NEWSON, J. and E. (1968) *Four Years Old in an Urban Community.* London: Allen and Unwin
NOLD, E.W. (1981) Revising. In C.H. Fredericksen and J. Dominic (eds) *Writing: The Nature, Development and Teaching of Written Communication, Volume 2, Process Development and Communication.* Hillsdale, N.J.: Lawrence Erlbaum
OLSON, D.R. (1977) From utterance to text: the basis of language in speech and writing. *Harvard Educational Review, 47,* 257–81
OSGOOD, C.E. (1957) Motivational dynamics of language behaviour. In M. R. Jones (ed.) *Nebraska Symposium on Motivation.* Lincoln: University of Nebraska Press

PATTERSON, K. and COLTHEART, V. (1987) Phonological processes in reading: a tutorial review. In M. Coltheart (ed.) *The Psychology of Reading*. London: Lawrence Erlbaum

PAVLIDIS, G.T. and MILES, T.R. (eds) (1981) *Dyslexia Research and Its Application to Education*. London: John Wiley

PEEL, M. (1967) *Seeing to the Heart: English and Imagination in the Junior School*. London: Chatto and Windus

PERERA, K. (1984) *Children's Writing and Reading: Analysing Classroom Language*. Oxford: Blackwell

PETERS, M.L. (1967) *Spelling: Caught or Taught?* London. Routledge and Kegan Paul

PHILLIPS, T. (1985) Beyond lip-service; discourse development after the age of nine. In G. Wells and J. Nicholls, *Language and Learning: An International Perspective*. London: Falmer Press

PIAGET, J. (1953) *The Origins of Intelligence in the Child*. London: Routledge and Kegan Paul

PIAGET, J. (1955) *The Child's Construction of Reality*. London: Routledge and Kegan Paul

PIAGET, J. (1960) *Language and Thought of the Child*. London: Routledge and Kegan Paul

PLAISTED, L.L. (1909) *The Early Education of Children*. Oxford: Clarendon Press

PUMFREY, P.D. (1976) *Reading: Tests and Assessment Techniques*. London: Hodder and Stoughton

READ, C. (1971) Pre-school children's knowledge of English phonology. *Harvard Educational Review, 41*, 1–34

REASON, R. and BOOTE, R. (1986) *Learning Difficulties in Reading and Writing: A Teacher's Manual*. Windsor: NFER/Nelson

REED, G.F. (1969) Skill. In E.A. Lunzer and J.F. Morris (eds) *Development in Human Learning*. London: Staples

REID, J. (1966) Learning to think about reading. *Educational Research, 9,*(1), 56–62

REID, J.F. (1970) Sentence structure in reading primers. *Research in Education, 3*, 23–37

REID, J.F. (ed.) (1972) *Reading: Problems and Practices*. London: Ward Lock Educational

REID, J.F. and DONALDSON, H. (1977) *Reading: Problems and Practices*. (Second edition). London: Ward Lock Educational

REID, J.F. and LOW, J. (1973) *The Written Word*. Edinburgh: Holmes McDougall

ROBERTS, G.R. (1960) A study of motivation in remedial reading. *British Journal of Educational Psychology, 30*, 176–9

ROBERTS, G.R. (1961) An active approach to remedial reading. *Forward Trends*, Guild of Teachers of Backward Children

ROBERTS, G.R. (1965) Writing continuous prose, *Times Educational Supplement*, 30th April

ROBERTS, G.R. (1969) *Reading in Primary Schools*. London: Routledge and Kegan Paul

ROBERTS, G.R. (1970) Reading: an initial course. In Select Committee on Education and Science, *Teacher Training* (Minutes of Evidence) London: HMSO

ROBERTS, G.R. (1972) *English in Primary Schools*. London: Routledge and Kegan Paul

ROBERTS, G.R. (1982) Research and development in reading, 1970–1980. In L. Cohen, L. Manion and J. Thomas (eds) *Educational Research and Development in Great Britain*. London: NFER/Nelson

ROBERTS, G.R. (1986) The organisation of learning in primary schools. Memorandum 50. In Education, Science and Arts Committee (House of Commons), *Achievement in Primary Schools*. London: HMSO

ROBERTS, T. (1975) Skills of analysis and synthesis in the early stages of reading. *British Journal of Educational Psychology*, 45, 3–9

ROBERTS, T. (1978) The language of children's books. *Education 3–13 6* (1), 37–9

ROBERTS, T. (1979) Auditory blending in the early stages of reading. *Educational Research*, 22 (1), 49–53

ROMAINE, S. (1984) *The Language of Children and Adolescents*. Oxford: Blackwell

ROSEN, C. and H. (1973) *The Language of Primary School Children*. Harmondsworth: Penguin

RUDDELL, R.B. (1965) The effect of oral and written patterns of language structure on reading comprehension. *The Reading Teacher*, 18, 270–5

SANSOM, C. (1965) *Speech in the Primary School*. London: Black

SCHONELL, F.J. (1945, 1975) *The Psychology and Teaching of Reading*. (1975) Edinburgh: Oliver and Boyd

SCOLLON, R. and SCOLLON, S.B.K. (1981) *Narrative, Literacy, and Face in Interethnic Communication*. Norwood, N.J.: Ablex

SHAUGHNESSY, M.P. (1977) *Errors and Expectations: A Guide for the Teacher of Basic Writing*. New York: Oxford University Press

SIGNAL Published by The Thimble Press, Stroud, Gloucestershire. Ed. Chambers and Namley

SIMON, B. (1985) Towards a revitalized pedagogy. In C. Richards with B. Lofthouse (eds) *The Study of Primary Education: A Source Book* Volume 3. London: Falmer Press

SMITH, F. (1971) *Understanding Reading*. New York: Holt, Rinehart and Winston

SMITH, F. (1982) *Writing and the Writer*. New York: Holt, Rinehart and Winston

SMITH, F. (1985) *Reading* (second edition). Cambridge: Cambridge University Press

SOUTHGATE BOOTH, V. (1985) *Star Series* (40 titles). London: Macmillan

SOUTHGATE BOOTH, V., ARNOLD, H. and JOHNSON, S. (1981)

Extending Beginning Reading. London: Heinemann Educational for the Schools Council

SOUTHGATE, V. and LEWIS, C.Y. (1973) How important is the infant reading scheme? *Reading*, 7(2), 4–13

STAUFFER, R. G. (1970) *The Language-Experience Approach to the Teaching of Reading*. New York: Harper and Row

STEIN, N.L. and GLENN, C.G. (1979) An analysis of story comprehension in elementary school children. In R.O. Freedle (ed.) *Advances in Discourse Processes, Volume 2, New Directions in Discourse Processing*. Norwood, N.J.: Ablex

STEIN, N.L. and TRABASSO, T. (1982) What's in a story: an approach to comprehension and instruction. In R. Glaser (ed.) *Advances in Instructional Psychology*, Volume 2. Hillsdale, N.J.: Lawrence Erlbaum

STOTT, D.H. (1962) *Programmed Reading Kit*. Edinburgh: Holmes McDougall

STRENG, A.H., KRETSCHMER, R.R. and KRETSCHMER, L.W. (1978) *Language, Learning and Deafness*. New York: Grune and Stratton

STRICKLAND, R. (1962) The language of elementary school children: its relationship to the language of reading textbooks and the quality of reading of selected children. *Bulletin of the School of Education*, 38(4). Bloomington: University of Indiana

STUART-HAMILTON, I. (1986) The role of phonemic awareness in the reading style of beginning readers *British Journal of Educational Psychology*, 56, 271–85

STUBBS, M. (1980) *Language and Literacy: the Sociolinguistics of Reading and Writing*. London: Routledge and Kegan Paul

STYLES, M. and TRIGGS, P. (eds) (1988) *Poetry 0–16: A Books For Keeps Guide*. London: Books For Keeps

SULZBY, E. (1987) Children's development of prosodic distinctions in telling and dictation modes. In A. Matsuhashi, *Writing in Real Time: Modelling Production Processes*. Norwood, N.J.: Ablex

TEALE, W.H. and SULZBY, E. (eds) (1986) *Emergent Literacy: Writing and Reading*. Norwood, N.J.: Ablex

THACKRAY, D.V. (1971) *Readiness for Reading with i.t.a and t.o.* London: Chapman

TODD, J. (1982) *Learning to Spell*. Oxford: Blackwell

TORBE, M. (1985) *Teaching Spelling*. London: Ward Lock Educational

TOUGH, J. (1976) *Listening to Children Talking: A Guide to the Appraisal of Children's Use of Language*. London: Ward Lock Educational

TOUGH, J. (1977) *The Development of Meaning*. London: University of London

TOUGH, J. (1977) *Talking and Learning: A Guide to Fostering Communication Skills in Nursery and Infant Schools*. London: Ward Lock Educational

TOWNSEND, J.R. (1987) *Written for Children* (3rd Edition). Harmondsworth: Penguin

TRUDGILL, P. (1975) *Accent, Dialect and the School.* London: Edward Arnold

TUCKER, N. (1981) *The Child and the Book: a Psychological and Literary Exploration.* Cambridge: Cambridge University Press

UNDERWOOD, G. and J. (1986) Cognitive processes in reading and spelling. In A. Cashdan (ed.) *Literacy: Teaching and Learning Language Skills.* Oxford: Blackwell

VERNON, M.D. (1957) *Backwardness in Reading.* Cambridge: Cambridge University Press

VERNON, M.D. (1971) *Reading and Its Difficulties.* Cambridge: Cambridge University Press

VYGOTSKY, L.S. (1962) *Thought and Language.* Cambridge, Mass.: and London: Staples

VYGOTSKY, L.S. (1978) *Mind in Society: the Development of Higher Psychological Processes.* Cambridge, Mass: Harvard University.

WADE, B. (ed.) (1985) *Talking to Some Purpose.* Educational Review, Occasional Publication Number Twelve. University of Birmingham: Faculty of Education

WALKER, C. (1975) *Teaching Pre-Reading Skills.* London: Ward Lock Educational

WATERLAND, L. (1985) *Read With Me: An Apprenticeship Approach to Reading.* Stroud: Thimble Press

WEBER, R.M. (1970) First graders' use of grammatical context in reading. In H. Levin and J.P. Williams (eds) *Basic Studies on Reading.* New York: Basic Books

WELLS, C.G. (1985) *Language Development in the Pre-School Years.* Cambridge: Cambridge University Press

WELLS, C.G. (1987) *The Meaning Makers: Children Learning Language and Using Language to Learn.* London: Hodder and Stoughton

WHITEHEAD, A.N. (1955) *The Aims of Education.* London: Benn

YOUNG, P. and TYRE, C. (1983) *Dyslexia or Illiteracy.* Milton Keynes: Open University Press

ZIPES, J. (1979) *Breaking the Magic Spell.* London: Heinemann

ZIPES, J. (1983a) *Fairy Tales and the Art of Subversion.* London: Heinemann

ZIPES, J. (1983b) *The Trials and Tribulations of Little Red Riding Hood.* London: Heinemann

Index